No Foreign Bones in China

THE UNIVERSITY OF ALBERTA PRESS

PETER STURSBERG

*Memoirs of Imperialism
and Its Ending*

No Foreign Bones
in China

Published by
The University of Alberta Press
Ring House 2
Edmonton, Alberta T6G 2E1

NATIONAL LIBRARY OF CANADA CATALOGUING IN PUBLICATION DATA

Stursberg, Peter, 1915–
    No foreign bones in China

    Includes bibliographical references and index.
    ISBN 0-88864-387-X

    1. Stursberg, Peter, 1915– —Family. 2. China—History—19th century—Biography.
3. China—History—20th century—Biography. I. Title.
DS755.3.S78 2002   951.035'092'2   C2002-910294-4

Proofreading by Christine Lyseng Savage.
Printed and bound in Canada by Friesens, Altona, Manitoba.
∞ Printed on acid-free paper.

The University of Alberta Press acknowledges the financial support of the Government of
Canada through the Book Publishing Industry Development Program for its publishing
activities. The Press also gratefully acknowledges the support received for its program from
the Canada Council for the Arts.

To my Japanese grandmother

Contents

PREFACE

THE BEGINNING OF A NEW MILLENNIUM is a time for looking back and a time for looking ahead. A time for looking back to the nineteenth century and my grandfather, Captain Samuel Lewis Shaw, the merchant seaman, the captain of the King of Burma's yacht, whose second wife was my Japanese grandmother, and to my German grandfather, Johann Peter Stursberg. A time for looking back on the days of Empire and the subjugation of China. A time for looking ahead: in the last chapter of the book, I return to China and the places I knew, and see the extraordinary changes that have occurred, how China has risen from being a virtual colony to the status of a great power that is casting its shadow on the twenty-first century.

Much of this book is based on the recollections of my mother, father, and other relatives. Aside from the brief biography on his elaborate tombstone and the obituary in the weekly issue of the Foochow *Daily Echo* of June 27, 1908, my grandfather, Captain Samuel Lewis Shaw, left no real memoirs, or at least none that survived. There was the account that his son, Frederick William (Willie), gave his daughter, Mary Kuck Wannamaker, as well as the memories of my mother and father, which I recorded when they visited Ottawa in December 1972.

However, the best account of Grandfather was in the remarkable two-hour-long interview of his eldest daughter, Julia, my Aunty J, by Wendy Barnes, which was broadcast by Radio Hong Kong on November 23, 1971. Julia was ninety years old at the time of the broadcast but as a practitioner of oral history I have found that older persons often have very good memories. This was borne out during the course of the interview when Aunty J talked about the girls at her school in Shanghai and Wendy Barnes wondered whether one of them wasn't the mother of so-and-so. Julia corrected the interviewer and said, No, that was another girl, and gave her name.

As for my Japanese grandmother, I went to Japan to seek out information about her. It was difficult to find, and I had to put together bits and pieces from interviews and letters. On the other hand, there was a lot of reference material on the rest of the family's experience in colonial China: the official records of my father's service in the Chinese Customs and Post Office, the memoirs he sought to write but that were little more than haphazard diary notes, the letters he wrote when he was engaged to my mother, letters to his father during the Great War, and most of all, the letters he wrote to my mother when he returned to China on his own in 1925. The latter amounted to a daily diary; he made carbon copies, some of which were difficult to read, and had them bound in fifteen binders. There were also the recollections of missionary friends, and my own memories of our life and times, particularly in Kaifeng.

It was through the Chinese Maritime Customs (the Post Office began as a branch of the Customs) that the British effectively controlled China. The best account of this control is in S.Y. Teng's book *The Taiping Rebellion and the Western Powers*. The chaos caused by this great uprising, the bloodiest civil war in history, led to the foreign, really British, takeover of the Customs "at the cost of Chinese sovereignty."

According to Teng, Sir Robert Hart, the first Inspector General, had almost autocratic powers: "It was said his will was law and against his decision there was no appeal." The Chinese were excluded from all higher positions. With further research, I learned that the archives of the

British-run Customs have been preserved by the Communists; they consist of more than fifty thousand volumes of administrative records, almost all in English.

Then there was my German grandfather. There is an active *Stammesverband* (association) Stursberg in Germany, from whom I received a genealogical account of the Stursbergs. However, it was my cousin, Mabel, who dug up so much information for me and answered my numerous questions. She was still living in Forest Gate, not far from the Congregational Church where Grandfather was a deacon.

Finally, I was with Chester Ronning when he visited China as the guest of Premier Chou En-lai in 1971. It was at the time of the opening to the West, the lifting of the so-called Bamboo Curtain, and aside from making a number of broadcasts to Canada, I made the first reports from "inside Communist China" for the American news media. Since then, I have been back several times.

In 1981, my wife and I went there to attend Aunty J's hundredth birthday party, but also to look up the places that meant so much to me: the Commissioner's house in Kaifeng, the house in Foochow where my mother and father met, and the church where they were married. In 1986, I returned to complete my book *The Golden Hope*, about the Canadian Protestant missionaries. At that time I visited towns where the missionaries had been and found it difficult to pick out their houses, schools, and hospitals, since they seemed to have melded into the Chinese street scene.

In 1998, I travelled up the Yangtse as my father had done long years before, and saw the great changes that had been made in the past decade. In Shanghai they have left the Bund as a sort of Imperialist relic but moved the centre of the city across the Huangpu River to Pudong where there is a forest of skyscrapers, one of which, the Jinmao Building, is eighty-eight storeys high. Our guide boasted that Shanghai would outdo Hong Kong and have the tallest building in the world. In Beijing, the Jing Guang Centre has an office tower fifty-three storeys high. And so the last chapter of this book is based on my observations.

While this book was originally seen as millennial project by the University of Alberta Press, Leslie Vermeer, the managing editor, had to contend with organizational difficulties which caused delays. However, her persistence paid off, and these memoirs owe a lot to her diligence. Leslie proved to be one of the best and most constructive editors I've ever had, and it was a pleasure working with her. I want to thank Col. Bob Gross for his help in finding me a publisher, and my friend, Gen. Bill Milroy, for his interest and assistance. I'm grateful to Clifford H. Phillips (Lei Houtian) for checking my Chinese spelling. Also, I would like to express my gratitude to Betty Jane Corson, my former agent, for her early encouragement, and to my wife, Jessamy, for her grammatical aid and support.

PETER STURSBERG
West Vancouver
November 2001

The Cast

Lillian Stursberg Dunn *My Aunt Lillie*
Walter Arthur Stursberg *My father*

OTHERS
Sir Robert Hart *Empire builder and founder of Chinese Maritime Customs*
Theophile Piry and H. Picard Destilant *Director Generals, Chinese Post Office*
Pastor Hendon Harris and Florence Harris *American missionaries (Southern Baptist); parents of my friends* Miriam *and* Hendon Harris, Jr.
Bishop William C. White *Anglican missionary and collector of Chinese art, Royal Ontario Museum*
Norman Bethune *Canadian doctor; hero of Communist China*
Tzu Hsi *Dowager Empress*
Pu Yi *Last Emperor of China*
Yuan Shih-kai *First President of China; wanted to be emperor*
Feng Yu Hsiang *"Christian General," warlord*
Sun Yat-sen *Revolutionary leader and President of China*
Chiang Kai-shek *Nationalist leader and last President of China*
Mao Tse-tung *Communist leader and Chairman, People's Republic of China*
Chou En-lai *Premier, People's Republic of China*

Chinese Language Note

CHINESE IS A DIFFICULT LANGUAGE, as all foreigners who seek to learn it as adults discover. Even the romanization or alphabetic transliteration of the characters, which was meant to help us, has its problems since there are two different spellings, the Wade Giles system and the modern Pin Yin method. I have used the former throughout this book because it was the one known to my father and other relatives and to "old China hands." It was in the textbooks they used to learn the language and in newspaper reports and common daily communications.

The Wade Giles system was developed by a couple of Victorian linguists and sinologists, Sir Thomas Wade and Professor Herbert Giles, when China was virtually a colony. It was remarkable that this imperial transliteration of the Chinese characters should have lasted so long; it was only replaced by the People's Republic in the 1960s with Pin Yin, which is in some ways closer to pronunciation (Pin Yin means "spelling sounds"). The Wade Giles system has its own peculiar conventions, such as a hard P and a K that has the sound of a J. Thus, "Peking" should be pronounced "Beijing," which is the way the capital of China is spelled in Pin Yin.

While Pin Yin is closer to the way that Mandarin (or Putonghua, as it is called, meaning "common language") is spoken, it uses the letters X, Q, and C in ways that baffle Westerners. What is one to make of "Xian" or "Qing" or "Ci," for instance? X stands for a "shh" sound, Q for a "chh" sound and C for "tzu" in the old spelling. Thus Xi'an is Sian (a former capital), Qing is Ching (dynasty), and Ci Xi is Tzu Hsi (the name of the Dowager Empress). However, Pin Yin was devised not for the benefit of foreigners but as a teaching aid for the ordinary Chinese people; it is the instrument by which the Communists are making Mandarin the common language for the whole of China. The characters represent words and are virtually the same in Japanese or Korean, although the languages are very different. The only way to spread Mandarin is by romanization, and Pin Yin has been very successful.

Although I have used the Wade Giles system for Chinese names, wherever possible, I have included the Pin Yin spelling in parentheses.

THERE ARE ALSO other notes at the back of the book that speak to explain certain aspects of the text, as this note on the Chinese language does, without interrupting the flow of the story.

INTRODUCTION

MY MATERNAL GRANDFATHER, Captain Samuel Lewis Shaw, who was of Irish descent, was born in 1821. It was the year Napoleon died, six years after the Battle of Waterloo, and two years after the birth of Queen Victoria, whose name was given to the age in which he lived. He married twice, and his second wife was my Japanese grandmother, known as Ellen O'Sea, although we never really knew her surname. Captain Shaw was sixty-five years old when my mother was born, the fifth of the eight children of his second marriage. My paternal grandfather, Johann Peter Stursberg, was born in Garschagen in the Rhineland in 1840 but left Germany for England as a young man. He also married twice, and his second marriage was considered by some of his relatives to be morally reprehensible and almost split up the family. My father was the youngest of the nine children whom John Peter Stursberg (as he now called himself) had by his first wife, a West Country English lady named Emily Eliza Hague.

The Victorian age was a time of tumultuous change, of aggressive nationalism, and, above all, of imperialism. The Industrial Revolution, which had its roots in England, swept the old order of individual crafts-men and artisans from their bucolic surroundings into the agglomeration of mills and factories in the crowded cities. London spread like a dark brown sludge over the green countryside of southern England and, with a population of some two million in the early years of the nineteenth century, was said to be the biggest city anywhere. At any rate, London was cer-tainly the financial capital of the world, and while the Industrial Revolution had produced the most appalling social conditions, it made the British rich, powerful, and ready to embark on fresh imperial ventures.

It was trade that created the Empire on which the sun never set. My grandfather Shaw spent most of his long life directly or indirectly "trad-ing in the Far East," as his elaborate tombstone proudly recorded. He followed the British tradition of going to sea at the age of thirteen. He was in China before the First Opium War (1841–42), and it was the Opium Wars, the second of which occurred in 1858, that opened the country, by means of the so-called treaty ports, to trade and commerce with the European powers, and eventually turned this ancient but decay-ing empire into a virtual colony.

At about the same time as the British were establishing their hege-mony over China, they were consolidating their hold on India by taking over the government from the surrogate East India Company after the 1857 uprising known as the Indian Mutiny. While India might have been considered the jewel in the crown, China, although not formally part of the Empire, was the greatest prize. Certainly, the Christian churches regarded it as such: they mounted the largest campaign ever, sending thou-sands of missionaries, more than ten thousand at one time, to spread the Gospel among the Chinese, convert them, and bring this most populous country into Christendom. It was to be the last Crusade.

The British had a head start in overseas expansion and imperialism, but there were others in the running for colonies—the French, the Dutch, the Spanish, and the Portuguese. Soon little was left in Asia and, for that matter, in Africa that was not in European hands. However, the Germans and Italians were so late in uniting as nations that they got little of the spoils of empire. The Prussians were determined to make amends for this, and my grandfather Stursberg was caught up in the harsh military campaign to forge a German Empire. In 1860, the annual levy for the army was greatly increased by King William I (who was to become Emperor William 1), and Grandfather, who was twenty years old, fled to London.

In 1854, more than a decade after the First Opium War, a flotilla of American warships under Commodore Perry forced Japan to open its ports to trade. This marked the beginning of convulsive changes in Japanese society, the destruction of the feudal order and the military rule of the shoguns and the samurai. There was savage fighting, assassinations, and atrocities on both sides until the imperial forces were finally victorious in the Meiji Restoration of 1868. My Japanese grandmother was born in 1857, three years after Commodore Perry's demarche, and she grew up amidst the awful tumult and slaughter of a civil war.

My father came to China in 1906 as a young man of nineteen to join the British-run Chinese Maritime Customs. The Chinese Customs was the most important imperial service since it collected much of the country's revenue and controlled its credit; in this way the British were able to exert their hegemony over China. Customs also took care of harbours and pilotage, and charted the rivers and coastline; it formed a branch to look after the mail, which eventually became the Chinese Post Office. Shortly after joining the Chinese Customs, my father got himself transferred to the relatively new postal service.

The Western imperialist mandate in China continued with only minor upheavals such as the 1900 Boxer Rebellion, which was brutally suppressed, and the 1911 republican revolution. It was not until the outbreak of the First World War that the façade of European supremacy in Asia began to crack. Here were the great imperial powers, the rulers of the world, tearing each other apart in internecine conflict. Anti-German feeling in Britain was so malignant that many members of the Stursberg family changed their names. My grandfather did not. The illusion of European supremacy was dealt its final death blow in the Second World War with the defeat of the imperial powers in Asia by the Japanese.

My father left China and quit his job as commissioner in the interior city of Chengtu, Szechwan (Sichuan) Province, during the great 1927 exodus when thousands of Westerners, mostly missionaries, fled from the rioting and depredation caused by the Nationalists' so-called Northern

Expedition. The Post Office and the Chinese Maritime Customs persisted, with the British having less and less control, until 1949, when the Communists swept all foreigners and foreign influence out of China, including their graves.

OUTWARD BOUND

I

for CATHAY, 1834

My only recollection of my maternal grandfather, Samuel Lewis Shaw, who died several years before I was born, is of his grave with its magnificent Victorian tombstone. I never saw the grave but there was a large, framed picture of it taken by S. Kimura, a commercial photographer in Foochow, which my mother had on her dressing table. It showed a white marble angel with head bowed and hands clasped above a well-proportioned plinth; nearby were a palm tree and a lesser grave, and in the background the high wall enclosing the small British cemetery and separating it from the rest of China. On the front of the marble base beneath the angel's grieving gaze was an epitaph:

In affectionate remembrance of SAMUEL LEWIS SHAW born at Hampstead, England, 13 October 1821, called away at Foochow 8 June 1908, 87 years of age. Erected by his sorrowing widow and children: "Thy will be done." A loving husband and a devoted father: "His children arise up and call him blessed."

✦ My grandfather's grave
in the British Cemetery
in Foochow

On the back, under the angel's outspread wings, was a brief biography:

Third son of Lees Shaw and Caroline Chippendall. Grandson of
Robert Shaw of Bushey Park, Dublin and Terenure, Ireland. Nephew
of Sir Frederick Shaw, Recorder of Dublin. Left home to visit the
East 1834. Arrived Macao 1836. Selected the sea as his profession,
trading in the Far East. First command 1839. Commanded the King
of Burmah's yacht. Last command SS *Dumbarton* 1867. Never an
accident. From 1868 Marine Surveyor at Pagoda Anchorage.

In 1821, when Grandfather was born, Hampstead was a village on the
outskirts of the crowded and spreading "infernal wen," as historian Francis
Sheppard called London of that period. Hampstead was a country place

to which the city's well-to-do merchants and business people went for summer holidays. Among these vacationers were the Ruskins: John Ruskin's father was a prosperous wine merchant who had a terraced house in Saint Pancras but every summer from the early 1820s moved his family to lodgings in Hampstead. His famous son had fond memories of his childhood in the bucolic surroundings where the view, he wrote, before the railroads came, was "entirely lovely: westward at evening, almost sublime, over softly wreathing distances of domestic wood." Besides being an art historian, painter, and social reformer, John Ruskin was also the great prophet of the British Empire, who spoke of its "destiny now possible to us, the highest ever set before a nation"—the Empire that Samuel Lewis Shaw would help to build and in whose embrace spend his long life.

The best surviving records of my grandfather were photographs, including one taken by my father at a picnic in the last year of Grandfather's life. The photo shows him seated in a wicker sedan chair resting on a field outside Foochow, looking directly and confidently at my father bent over his stand camera. He was large, beneficent, the patriarch, in his Homburg hat with his white beard spread over his dark suit—and in the background, the chair coolies on their haunches, staring wide-eyed at the strange goings-on. There were other, earlier photographs of him and his family, which were probably taken by Mr. Kimura, the Japanese commercial photographer in Foochow, but they were all of his later years. The only picture of him as a younger man was a painting by his cousin, Sylvia Shaw, who was a considerable portrait artist in London. I can see in the shaded blue eyes of this handsome man, with his reddish brown hair and beard, the dauntless sea captain, the intrepid trader in the Far East.

Little of his writing remains. His eldest son by his second marriage, George Lewis Shaw, known to us as Uncle G, had his father's papers. He had been investigating the family roots and had even gone to Ireland to look up the Shaw forebears in Fermoy and Dublin. However, Uncle G died suddenly in Foochow during the war (on November 30, 1943), and all his records, all the information he had accumulated, all his personal and business files, not only in Foochow but in Antung, Manchuria, where he had an office, for he was a wealthy merchant and ship owner, disappeared in the tumult of the Japanese advance into South China during World War Two.

It is apparent that the Shaws, or the branch of the clan to which Grandfather belonged, were part of the Anglo-Irish or Scots-Irish establishment. His grandfather, Robert (listed as Robert Shaw of Terenure Manor 1750–1796 in one family tree), made a fortune as a merchant in Dublin and, according to one account, was the founder of the Royal Bank of Ireland. Robert's eldest son, also named Robert, was created a baronet and was M.P. representing Dublin at Westminster for more than twenty years, from 1804 to 1826. The third baronet, Sir Frederick, the Recorder of Dublin, was actually Samuel Lewis' cousin, not his uncle; among his other distinguished relatives were an earl, a brace of knights, a Queen's Counsel, the commander of the Dublin militia, and the Chief of the Fire Brigade, which was apparently an important honourary position. The Shaw family could trace its lineage to William White, a captain of Ponsonby's Horse, who so distinguished himself in the battle of the Boyne that he received a grant of some of the forfeited lands in Kilkenny, and to Oliver Cromwell himself, the conqueror of Ireland and Lord Protector of England, through his daughter, Elizabeth. Grandfather was proud of his forebears and would let the snobbish colonial society know that he came from an illustrious family, which was the very heart of the Protestant Ascendancy in Ireland.

The patriarch, Robert Shaw of Terenure Manor, had an older brother, William, who was the great-grandfather of George Bernard Shaw. It is doubtful if Samuel Lewis knew about his celebrated cousin, who was much younger; and if he had known he would not have mentioned him to his imperialist colleagues, as GBS was contemptuous of the family that Samuel Lewis held so dear. The famous author jeered at "a forlorn set of Protestant merchants in a Catholic country, led by a petty plutocracy of stockbrokers, doctors and land agents, and camouflaged by that section of the landed gentry who ... play at being court and aristocracy."

Grandfather's eldest son, George, had no such inhibitions and entertained Bernard Shaw when he visited China on his world tour in the 1930s. Uncle G arranged for Bernard Shaw to go to a Chinese opera. While the great playwright, who had started off as a music critic, seemed to be intrigued by the gongs and the high-pitched pipes of the orchestra and the shrill voices of the actors in their extraordinary traditional make-up and costumes, he was fascinated by the way that attendants during the intermission flung hot towels to members of the audience. He remarked on this to his host.

Lees Shaw, Samuel Lewis' father, left Ireland and the family's high standing in Dublin for England. The trouble was that Robert Shaw had married twice and had five sons and two daughters by his first wife and two sons and two daughters by his second wife—eleven children altogether. It was a big estate but not big enough, and Lees was the youngest son. Perhaps he fell on hard times or the civil service job that he was purported to have had was not munificent enough for his large and growing family; at any rate, insolvency was the reason that Grandfather, while born in Hampstead, spent his childhood in Fermoy, County Cork, Ireland, at the home of his Uncle George and Aunt Maria. Families were more closely knit in those days and it was quite a common practice for them to share children under certain circumstances. Lees had ten children. Samuel Lewis was the third child, while George and Maria, who were well off, had none; furthermore, Maria was his mother's sister.

Fermoy was an ideal place for a boy to grow up. It was a small market town on the Blackwater River; all around were farms and glens and woods, and the river itself was renowned as a salmon and trout stream. His uncle and aunt, who had a large, comfortable house, doted on him as a childless couple would. However, he was raised not as an "only child" but as a "first-born," since his father sent another of his children to the Fermoy household, a daughter, Julia Maria, named after Aunt Maria. This sibling did not provide much companionship on his hikes around the Irish countryside as Julia Maria was the seventh child and at least six years younger. However, he remembered her as his little sister whom he loved and protected and the only link with rest of his brothers and sisters whom he never really knew since they were so far apart. The journey from London to Fermoy by stagecoach and sailing ship would have taken several days, if not a week, and would have been very costly. Aside from his little sister, he was on his own and his singular upbringing made him self-reliant and independent.

As a schoolboy in Fermoy, young Samuel Lewis would have learned of the British defeat of Napoleon—after all, the Battles of Waterloo and Trafalgar had been only a few years before and were still vivid memories, especially Waterloo. He might even have spoken to the veterans of that last great victory, as there was a large army camp at nearby Kilworth. The portrait of Nelson hung in Uncle George's house as in so many houses, and would be draped in black on the anniversary of Trafalgar and the admiral's death. Samuel Lewis was an adventurous, intelligent lad, and there was so much to explore: besides Kilworth, the seaport and naval base of Queenstown was not far away. It was an exciting time in which to grow up and there were so many he met with stories to tell about the places they had been and the sights they had seen. Thus, he learned about the Far East, especially Cathay, so glamorous, so mysterious, and he was told of the great prospects there for a young fellow like him who didn't mind voyaging far from home.

Samuel Lewis' uncle was a director of the East India Company, "The Governor and Company of Merchants of London trading into the East

Indies," which was more than a company as it had its own armed forces and had taken over and ruled large parts of Asia. Indeed, it was a surrogate for the Crown, much like "The Governor and Company of Adventurers of England Trading into Hudson's Bay." The East India Company was granted its charter by Queen Elizabeth on December 31, 1600, while the Hudson's Bay Company was incorporated by Charles II in 1670. However, the East India Company did not have a monopoly like the Hudson's Bay Company, as East India Companies were established by many trading nations such as France, Holland, and Spain, which meant there was fierce competition and even the odd armed clash.

So, when the captain of an East Indiaman visited his uncle and aunt in Fermoy, and asked young Samuel Lewis if he would like to go to sea, he jumped at the chance. He was only thirteen years old, but he was a big, strapping boy who looked older than his age. And thirteen was not an unusually early age to go to sea or to start work in the those days. In the 1800s, boys of fourteen, thirteen, even twelve, from good families, were packed off to join the Royal Navy. (Nelson was only twelve when he joined HMS *Raisonnable*.) People grew up more quickly then. Life was shorter: the average life expectancy at that time was around thirty-four or thirty-five years, and only reached forty-five by the turn of the century.

His aunt, like any mother, did not want him to go, but his uncle, who was overwhelmed by the boy's eagerness, agreed. However, according to his eldest daughter, Julia Maria, who was named after the little sister he left behind, his uncle told the captain of the East Indiaman "to bring him back on his return trip," which would have been in two to three years' time. Young Samuel Lewis, without knowing it, was joining an army of his contemporaries, of his age or older, in leaving home for the Far East and the opportunities that imperialism presented there. They were the brightest and best, these youthful adventurers, the "hearts of oak" who created the greatest Empire the world had ever known.

Take up the White Man's burden—
Send forth the best ye breed—
Go bind your sons to exile
To serve your captives' need;

To wait in heavy harness,
On fluttered folk and wild—
Your new caught sullen peoples,
Half-devil and half-child.

—RUDYARD KIPLING

As a young fellow from a good family, Grandfather would have begun as an apprentice or cadet, the equivalent of a midshipman in the navy, and his first job was that of a cabin boy. The British East Indiamen were run like the Royal Navy's ships. However, the merchant vessels had superior crews who were recruited and well paid and were exempt from the Navy's press gangs; they were even allowed a certain amount of private trading so that they shared to some extent in the take. The black-bordered "In Memoriam" column in the Foochow *Daily Echo* of June 27, 1908 suggested, while not being certain, that Grandfather set sail for the Orient in the *King William*. There were a couple of *King Williams* in the East India Company's fleet; and if he were on one of them, it must have been a new ship honouring William IV who came to the throne in 1830, some four years before Grandfather left home in 1834.

The East Indiamen were heavily built, three-masted square riggers. They were the largest and finest ships of their time and were regarded as "Lords of the Ocean." Highly gilded and decorated with carvings, they were "furnished internally for comfort and luxury." The cabins had bunks and even wash basins and a commode, although they carried few passengers. The East Indiamen were essentially freighters. Those in the China trade were the largest, around twelve hundred tons, with a crew of some two hundred. They were armed with thirty to fifty guns (eighteen-pounders) on two decks, and the larger vessels were often mistaken for line-of-battle ships. However, while they were out-classed by real warships, they could fend off smaller frigates and their armory was a protection against piracy, which was rife at the time. The eighteen-pounder guns restricted the amount of cargo, and by the mid-nineteenth century, when hostilities between the British, French, and Dutch had died down, most of the guns were removed and the gun ports caulked. But that was some time after Grandfather had set sail.

The harsh rules of seafaring prevailed on the *King William*, and the young Samuel Lewis was subject to floggings during the long voyage to China. Lord Fisher, called "the greatest British sailor since Nelson," the father of the *Dreadnought* and first sea lord in the First World War, became a midshipman at the age of thirteen in 1854. "The day I joined as a little boy," Fisher recalled, "I saw eight men flogged—and I fainted at the sight." The food aboard ship was bad, Fisher said, maggoty biscuits and foul water. Although the crew of the *King William* were voluntary and thus had to be given greater consideration, it is unlikely that the food, or at least the hardtack, would have been much better: storage was difficult on these sailing ships.

Despite these conditions, Grandfather was happy to have been accepted in the ship's company of the East Indiamen and, as his tombstone recorded, chose seafaring as his life's work; he opted to stay in the Far East and not return home. He often spoke of that first voyage, but the only story that his eldest daughter, Julia (our Aunty J), recalled was of a mishap which might have proved painful. One day, he was bringing tea to the mate who was taking a nap in his cabin. The officer was apparently having a nightmare and let out a yell in his sleep, which so startled the apprentice that he dropped the teapot. Whether he was flogged for this Julia was unsure, but she said he certainly got roundly cursed and shouted at by the aroused mate.

It so happened that my grandfather set sail at the beginning of what was really the "second phase" of the British Empire. The first phase, as James Morris comments in his *Pax Britannica* trilogy, was "the older mercantile empire of America, India (the trading ports) and the sugar colonies"; it ended with the defeat of the imperial forces in America and the independence of the United States. "The American revolution," according to Morris, "helped to sour the notion of Empire." Yet by the time Victoria became Queen, a new and greater Empire was underway, until much of the world—a third of the world—was under British rule. It was to be an empire, as the imperialist orators never failed to say, "on which the sun never set."

The 1830s were a time of supreme confidence for the British. They had not only triumphed militarily but also industrially. Napoleon, whom they had captured and incarcerated, had referred to them contemptuously as a "nation of shopkeepers" and ignored the fact that many of the shops were machine shops. The Industrial Revolution had occurred first in England, and despite the wrenching changes that it wrought—the blight it spread, the "dark satanic mills," and the inhuman labour conditions, with women and little children working twelve-hour days in mines and factories—it made the country wealthy and the dominant power in Europe. On Queen Victoria's accession in 1837, London had some two million people and was the largest city in the world, or so it was claimed; at any rate, London was the unchallenged financial capital of the world.

Beside their great material achievements, the British, as they embarked on the course of empire at the beginning of the nineteenth century, had a feeling of righteousness and moral superiority. Slavery had been abolished throughout British dominions and possessions in 1834, while the slave trade itself had been made illegal in 1807. The abolitionists such as William Wilberforce were mostly evangelical Christians, and they wanted more than the end of slavery: they wanted to spread the Gospel throughout the world and saw the expansion of empire as a means of reaching the heathens and idolators and "saving them from eternal damnation." The London Missionary Society was set up in 1794, and foreign missionary work became popular and fashionable. The churches preferred to send missionaries to Asia and Africa rather than to the slums of London or the mill towns of the Midlands.

As the East Indiaman sailed slowly and majestically down the West Coast of Africa, the teenaged Samuel Lewis Shaw would have noticed his ship exchanging signals with a number of British warships. For some forty years, from the time of the abolition of the slave trade in 1807, the Royal Navy's main task was the interception of the slave ships, the great majority of which were British. The new apprentice would learn from his shipmates that there was a bounty of five pounds for each liberated slave. The captive would be taken to the main port of the British territory of Sierra Leone, which was aptly named Freetown, and there released. A bounty of half that sum was paid for each dead slave, and if Samuel Lewis had wondered why, he would have been told that slave traders, in order to escape arrest, would kill the slaves by pushing them overboard.

However, even before the abolition of the slave trade, the mortality rate on the slave ships was twenty percent; after, due to atrocities committed in trying to avoid capture, it rose to fifty percent. Yet enforcement by the Royal Navy did lead to a considerable reduction in the slave trade and the freeing of tens of thousands of slaves.

The slave traders faced transportation for life (to Australia) if caught, but so much money was involved that they were willing to take that risk. The prosperity of many prominent British families, including that of William Ewart Gladstone, who was several times prime minister, was based on the slave trade. Despite the generous bounties, the Royal Navy found the anti-slave patrols along the so-called Slave Coast, which stretched from Senegal to the Cameroons, a frustrating and dirty job in the equatorial heat. I worked on a cattle boat in the 1930s and recall that the stalls were not cleaned during the entire length of the voyage; and in many ways, the slaves had worse conditions than these Augean stables. The stench of the slave ships was appalling, and some of the crew of the *King William* could remember the nauseous odour, although they were miles away.

By the time the *King William* had sailed around West Africa and left behind the Royal Navy's anti-slave patrols, weeks if not months had passed. It took the fastest ships at that time five months to reach India and much longer to get to China and Japan. "Arrived Macau 1836," according to Grandfather's tombstone, which would have put him at sea for more than a year. The East Indiaman stopped at many ports in its long voyage down the coast of Africa, among them probably Freetown in Sierra Leone and the island of St. Helena. There was revictualing and some trading to be done, and the apprentice and his mates would be delighted at the chance of going ashore, a welcome break from the endless time spent on the open sea, sometimes driving forward with the whip of the sails and the whole ship shuddering under the force of a fair trade wind, other times becalmed and rolling aimlessly, or awash in an angry sea with the masts bending and cracking before a storm. St. Helena was a memorable visit. Napoleon had been dead for a little more than a decade, and the seamen could say they had seen his unmarked grave: "Here lies..." and no name. It was not till 1840 that Napoleon's remains were brought back to Paris and given a hero's interment in the Invalides.

A sailing ship could spend days in port. On most voyages, there was no rush, no tight schedule to keep—an exception was the race back to England with the first China tea. The longest time the *King William* spent in port was at Cape Town, as it was the main way station on the route to India. It must have been a thrilling sight for the young Samuel Lewis, the fine houses and public buildings and churches, the gardens and broad oak-lined avenues, at the foot of magnificent Table Mountain. This was a civilized community which an Englishman or an Irishman could call his own, and Cape Town looked more like places back home than the primitive African ports, with their rickety docks and mud huts around the menacing slave castles, at which the ship had stopped on the way down.

In his obituary, Captain Shaw was described as "a connecting link with the 1830 days." This was a signal distinction. It meant that he was a precursor of imperialism, that he had been in China even before the Opium Wars and the opening of the first five treaty ports, of which Foochow was one. Before setting out for China, the *King William* spent some time in Indian ports. There were cargoes for the Company, the machinery and spare parts, the casks of wine and brandy, the firearms and ammunition, and other materials that the Company's officials had ordered more than a year before. The East Indiaman also took on goods to be used for trading with the Chinese, the main purpose of this long voyage.

The *King William* could have stopped at Hong Kong, which was just a fishing village in a natural deep-water harbour then, before proceeding to Macau. It would be a day's sail across the wide estuary of the Pearl River, a journey that now takes an hour on the hydro-jets that ferry gamblers to the casinos of the former Portuguese colony. Although Macau was an important trading post, the real clearing house for trade with China was Canton, and while no mention of it is made on Captain Shaw's tombstone or in his obituary, there is no doubt that his first voyage took him on the East Indiaman quest for Chinese silk and tea. In fact, Canton was probably the ship's last port of call before returning home.

By all accounts of the times (and one of the best is Jason Goodwin's book *A Time for Tea*), the arrival at Whampao, thirteen miles downstream from Canton, was a colourful and exciting event. That was as far as the large merchant ships could go, and fifty or more would be anchored in a long line, a huge trading armada towering over the flat reaches of paddy, pennants flying from their tall masts, the national flags of Holland and France, Portugal and Spain, Britain, the United States, and other countries fluttering from their sterns. The *King William* would have broken out the company's own ensign, a striped flag with the Union Jack in the fly; and when the ship had reached its anchorage, the band on board would have struck up "God Save the King."

Even before that happened, all manner of sampans would have attached themselves to the East Indiaman as it glided toward the mooring: wash boats to do laundry, boats filled with live chickens, ducks, and other foodstuffs, flower boats (really floating brothels). A great clamour of pidgin English arose as the occupants cried out for custom. "You wantee washee, washee," they would yell; "You savvee me, I makee mendee..." "Ah, you, chiefee, maitee, you wantee chow chow!" The finest sight on the river, according to Jason Goodwin, was the "Mandarin Boats": they were painted ultramarine and white, with red ports and white oars flashing in the sun, and at the stern a billowing white ensign bearing red characters. These boats carried custom officials as well as soldiers, and patrolled the creeks on the lookout for smugglers.

It must have been fascinating for young Samuel Lewis and yet, at the same time, frightening, for daily and sometimes more often, a boat decked out with black pennants and rowing to a funeral drum beat would carry an unfortunate shipmate to a last resting place in the European cemetery ashore. A cortège would form as boats from other ships would join as a gesture of respect. In the subtropical heat, sailors frequently bathed or fell in the polluted waters of the Pearl River; they would then succumb to what was called variously "poisonous vapours" or "river fever."

Along the riverbank were the factories, as the foreign business houses were known. There were thirteen of them, belonging to Dutch, French, Spanish, Danish, British, and other national trading companies, built close together and separated only by alleys. The East India Company Factory had the atmosphere of a gentleman's club. No women, foreign or native, were allowed in its premises; this was not a company rule but on the orders of the Chinese government, which was against any foreigners taking up residence and expected the factor and his officials to spend the winter months in Macau or anywhere else but in China. A gravel path led to the pillared verandah, and on the first floor was a billiard room, a library, and a great dining hall with chandeliers and candelabra, where thirty guests, company and ships' officers, and supercargoes (as the businessmen and traders were called) could eat off silver plate with a silk-gowned Chinese servant behind each chair. The history of the East India Company notes that the captains of the East Indiamen were men of high social standing; they were "chosen from merchants of stature who could deal with Emperors and princes." The Factory's upper floors had the offices and comfortable quarters for visitors, as well as for the Factor and his staff, which included a chaplain, two surgeons, and a score of clerks and inspectors. In the rear were warehouses or godowns.

Although there was trade in silk, it was tea that the merchant ships were after, and the stately East Indiamen were derisively referred to as "tea wagons." The *King William* had picked up bolts of cotton and other textiles in India but, by all accounts, there was precious little in the way of Indian cloth or Western goods that the Chinese wanted. Chiming watches and clocks and musical boxes (known in pidgin as "sing-songs") were in demand but also in short supply; otherwise, payment had to be made in silver.

However, there was opium, which was produced in Bengal and a number of other Indian states. It is most unlikely that the ship in which my grandfather sailed to China in the mid 1830s had chests of opium in the holds. While the East India Company had a monopoly of the opium trade with China, it was careful to keep its own ships clean in order to prevent the Chinese officials, to whom the foreign traders were beholden, from taking any action that would hinder the shipment of tea. Instead, smaller coastal ships, sloops and brigs, known as "country ships," were used to transport opium. Such a subterfuge did not hide the East India Company's involvement in the drug business, for opium bore the Company's stamp and was sold at Company auctions in Calcutta.

The opium trade had to be carried on surreptitiously, and while the tea trade was carried on formally and legitimately, the opium trade soon came to equal it in value. As might be expected, this pushing of illegal drugs did not raise the status of the foreign traders in the view of the

Chinese officials, the Mandarins, who looked down on them as "barbarians" and called them "foreign devils." The Chinese scorn of foreigners or Westerners, the "ta pi-tzu" (long or big noses), continues to this day; the epithet "yang-kwei" (foreign devils), if not worse, is still to be heard in modern China. However, at the beginning of the nineteenth century, when the British were at the height of their power and self-esteem, they found it particularly galling to be treated in such a cavalier manner. They resented the fact that they could not negotiate with the Mandarins; their proposals, their complaints went unheard. The desire for a dialogue was one-sided, and thus there was none.

British diplomats refused to grovel, to kowtow, before the Chinese emperor who regarded them as the representatives of a vassal state, and thus there were no normal diplomatic relations. The evidence of this was to be seen in the East India Company Factory where a full-length portrait of George IV hung in the great dining hall. It had been left behind by Lord Amherst, who had tried to present it to Emperor Chia-ching but was unceremoniously and disdainfully sent away without even an audience. It was a clash of civilizations, a new and aggressive industrial civilization against an ancient universal civilization which held that the centre of the world was the centre stone of the Altar of Heaven in Peking.

Despite orders from on high to stamp out the opium trade, it continued to flourish, and part of the blame for this was the Chinese themselves, the corruption and venality of the local officials who facilitated the landing of the contraband goods. Finally, Lin Tse-hsu, the Imperial Commissioner, acted. He was newly appointed by Emperor Tao-kuang, who had commanded him to put an immediate end to traffic in illegal drugs. The Imperial Commissioner used soldiers and the gendarmerie to force the British to surrender their large opium stocks in the warehouse of the East India Company Factory and had them burned. Such effrontery infuriated the British traders and was the spark that led eventually to the First Opium War.

All of this occurred some time after my grandfather's arrival in China. Commissioner Lin's action was in 1839, and the First Opium War and the humiliation of the Celestial Empire did not occur until a couple of years later. The youthful Samuel Lewis Shaw was supposed to return home with his ship—in fact, the captain of the *King William* had been "instructed to bring him back." However, something happened to obviate his return. His daughter, Julia, assumed that the ship was sold and the crew remustered. It is more likely that he talked his way into staying abroad.

The ship had been his school as it was for so many boys who were apprentices on the East Indiamen and midshipmen in the navy. Class distinctions were such in those days that the officers and apprentices were educated and most of the crew illiterate; and while Grandfather as a boy towered over almost everyone else aboard, the officers were on the average taller than the ordinary seamen. Samuel Lewis learned to "hand, reef, and steer," the writing, reading, arithmetic of sailing. He was shown the best way of handling ropes and hawsers, the intricacies of knotting and splicing, and the use of blocks and tackles and all the complexities of the rigging and the sails—the main sail, the fore and aft sails, the flying jib, and the spanker; he took courses in navigation. Big for his age, Samuel Lewis might have been an awkward cabin boy, but he was a bright lad and was soon "keeping watch" under the attentive eye of a senior officer.

An adventurous young Irishman of his social standing would be in demand at Canton, Macao, or elsewhere in the East Indies and could easily get another job. He might well have been offered a position during the long wait of three months or more for the tea shipments, and an even longer wait for a large order of silk. At any rate, the next that was heard of Samuel Lewis was up the China coast, presumably on a trading ship. "He was in the River Min as far as Quantoa in 1838," according to the obituary in the Foochow newspaper. The Min is the river that, wide and muddy, slides through Foochow, the river on whose banks my grandfather was to spend the last forty years of his life.

2

CAPTAIN *of the*
KING *of* BURMA'S YACHT

THIRTY YEARS PASSED from the time Samuel Lewis Shaw was reported to have been on the Min River to when he returned to become marine surveyor at its mouth, Pagoda Anchorage, the deep water port of Foochow. During most of this time, he seems to have been engaged in coastal shipping and trading in the East Indies which, in those days, not only included India but stretched as far as the Malay Straits and Indonesia, known then as the Dutch East Indies. By 1838, when the Foochow newspaper said that he was on the Min River, he must have graduated from the rank of apprentice to that of officer or mate. While one learned on the job in the sailing ships of yore, one had to take an examination to become an officer, and Samuel Lewis probably got his papers at an East India Company station in Calcutta or Penang. His tombstone records "First command 1839," which would have made him just eighteen years old, but his son, Frederick William (named after Samuel's youngest brother), said he was nineteen when "he was made captain of coasters trading out of India to Java, Malay Straits, etc."

A tall, good-looking young Irishman, my grandfather was often seen in Singapore, even then a great entrepôt. He could hardly have been missed, as he was six feet, four inches tall, according to his daughter, Julia, and weighed more than fourteen stone or two hundred pounds. He would have made a commanding figure among the British seamen, whose average height, according to vital statistics of the times, was around five feet, five inches, and he would have appeared a giant to the even smaller Asians, the Chinese and Lascar crews of the sloops and brigs that were the coastal trading vessels.

As a young man, he made his home and headquarters in Penang, a Malaysian port that was originally developed by the East India Company. When the island of Penang was ceded to the Company by the Sultan of Kedah in 1785, it was almost uninhabited. Thus Penang, built on a promontory close to the mainland where there was a great natural harbour, was the quintessential colonial town. The native quarters, the go-downs, the markets, the ship chandlers, and the offices were down by the docks, while the airy bungalows of the Company's officials (graded according to rank) and the pillared mansions of the taipans were on the cooler high ground. So were a couple of churches and a hospital (the native hospital was below), but the centre of this very British community was the club. Since the East India Company's men brought their Indian servants with them and the immigrant Chinese were quick to provide shops and services, the first native inhabitants of Penang were Indians and Chinese, and to this day the Malays are in the minority.

It was in Penang in 1842 that Captain Shaw became a Freemason. His son had confirmation of his membership from the Grand Masonic Lodge in London. The Masonic Order provided Samuel with fellowship and fraternity, and with a sense of solidarity that he had missed since going to sea. The membership in Penang was made up of Company officials and traders and sailors like himself. Furthermore, while he was not particularly religious, Freemasonry, with its Protestant emphasis and anti-Catholic bias, appealed to him, coming from a leading Protestant family in Ireland. At any rate, the brotherhood meant a great deal to Captain Shaw. He rose through the various degrees to become a Master Mason, and he sent his eldest son and daughter, George and Julia, to a boarding school run by English Freemasons in Shanghai. And it was at his expressed wish that he was given a Masonic funeral and the emblem of Freemasonry was engraved on one side of the base of his elaborate tombstone.

It was also in Penang that the young Samuel Lewis Shaw met an English girl, Anna Charlotte Nail, the daughter of the colony's doctor. In 1843, they were married. It was a sign of what a dashing figure the young captain must have been that he could have taken her as his wife in his twenty-second year, since there were so few white women of a marriageable age in the colonies. A photograph purported to be of her in her middle age showed a strong, determined-looking woman in one of those black Victorian dresses with a high bodice, long sleeves, and full, floor-length skirt; she was seated by a small table and had on a white cap with streamers. However, little is known of the first Mrs. Shaw.

Grandfather had three children by his first marriage: two daughters and a son, named after him, who was known as Lewis; Lewis was born in 1851. Nothing is known about the daughters, Caroline Cecilia and Annie, and a search of consular and other records of the times did not uncover any listing of their births, marriages, or deaths. Since my mother did not know of their existence, and they would have been her half-sisters, it is possible they died in early childhood. However, Samuel Lewis Shaw II was well known to my mother and most of us in the second family.

While there were signs that his father rather neglected him, perhaps because of being away frequently, Samuel Lewis Shaw II seems to have had a happy childhood in Penang. (Like any man who made his living on the sea, Captain Shaw was absent from his family for long stretches at a time.) However, like so many other British children in the colonies, at the age of six or seven Lewis was sent to Europe for his schooling. (Some missionary children in China were sent home at this early age and only saw their parents every five years when they were on furlough.) According to family records, Lewis was educated in England and France. That he ended up in France was due to the fact that a cousin of his father's, John Chippendall, had become an equerry to Napoleon III in Paris, which in itself was an extraordinary story. Aunty Julia's account of the story is like the classic fairy tale of the beggar who turns out to be a prince. Perhaps it is indeed a fairy tale because I could find no historic confirmation of this story, but here it is.

This cousin (Grandfather's mother was a Chippendall) was the part owner of a small hotel on the outskirts of London. One day, he saw a man trudging along the road outside "looking very lean and tired and hungry," so he asked him to come in and have a good meal. The man said he had no money, but Chippindal said he would take care of it. Unbeknown to him, the vagrant was Charles Louis Napoleon Bonaparte, who was at the time down and out as a refugee in England. Some years later, Chippindal's kindness was repaid when the man he had befriended, newly proclaimed Emperor Napoleon III, made him a member of his court! At any rate, John Chippendall invited young Lewis, after he had finished school in England, to join him in his palatial quarters in Paris, and, according to Julia, her half-brother not only learned French but exercised the Emperor's horses.

However, Lewis never forgot the warm, comfortable life of his early years in the Orient, the freedom he had, the servants with whose children he used to play. He returned as soon as he could to the Far East and eventually settled in Bangkok. He took up trade, as his father had done, and made a lot of money in mining and in the export business, mainly in teak. In 1887, he married a widow, Rosina Blackmore Hawkin. He must have met her in Bangkok because she had been married before to Henry Augustus Sax Morton, who was really an Imperialist mercenary. On his son's birth certificate, Sax Morton was listed as "captain in the Siamese Army." While Siam was regarded as an independent country, much of its commerce and military affairs were in the hands of the British. In fact, Siam was on the same level of independence as China, for a treaty that granted extra-territorial rights to the British was signed by the Siamese in 1855.

Samuel Lewis Shaw II had two children, Percy Archibald Shaw and Delphine, who would have been my half-cousins although they were about the same age as my mother. Shortly after the war, I met Delphine at a tea party in Belgravia; it might have been at her brother's house, although I don't remember meeting him. She was an older but pretty woman with fluffy white hair. She was on a visit to London from her home in the Bahamas. I learned later that Delphine was married to a Canadian-born engineer, A.E. Worswick, who had made a fortune building electric power plants and railways in South Africa and Latin America and was one of the wealthiest men in the colony. They had a fine waterfront mansion in Nassau and were friends of the Duke and Duchess of Windsor when the Duke was governor of the Bahamas.

On his return to the Orient, Lewis did not see much of his father, my grandfather; their paths did not often cross in their journeys to the far reaches of the Empire. Lewis became a successful businessman but there was no report of his ever visiting Foochow. When he left the Orient for good, he did not come to say goodbye. Perhaps he did not approve of his father taking a Japanese woman as his second wife. At any rate, they were not very close, although Captain Shaw seemed to be proud of him and his accomplishments. Of all his children, the obituary in the Foochow newspaper mentioned only the "son of the first marriage [who] is now retired and living in London."

It must have been in 1860 or the early 1860s that my grandfather became captain of the King of Burma's yacht. The tombstone mentions this appointment but gives no date, while the obituary records that he held this command for five years. Since he returned to England and Ireland, for the first and last time, when he was in his mid forties and was marine surveyor at Pagoda Anchorage, Foochow, from 1868, it is reasonable to assume that he went to Burma in 1860 or 1861 at the latest. This would have been about the time that his son, Lewis, had completed his education and returned to the Orient. There was no mention of Captain Shaw's wife accompanying him to Burma. He would not have left her, even if they did not get along—that sort of thing was not done at that time in the colonies or elsewhere. The only indication that their marriage was not a happy one is the fact that Captain Shaw never spoke of her and no one remembered his making even a passing reference to her. She must have died. A search of the records turned up nothing on the fate of Anna Charlotte Nail Shaw. However, there was a report that she had had a nervous breakdown in the mid to late 1850s and was put in a "mental home" in Penang or Java where she died of malaria.

At about the time Grandfather was taken on as captain of the King of Burma's yacht, Mrs. Anna Leonowens was hired as a governess for the royal family in Siam. Such appointments represented an "Opening to the West," as the Oriental courts felt the pressure of expansionist forces of British and French imperialism close upon them. The British had already encroached a couple of times on Burma, taking over a few strategic islands, hacking off the provinces of Assam and Arakan and attaching them to the Indian Empire, while at the same time imposing reparations and thus making their expedition self-supporting.

The so-called Second Burma War occurred in 1852 and was the result of carping complaints from British traders of their mistreatment by the native authorities and from American missionaries who regarded the Burmese as "liars, thieves, idolators, and heathens." A British fleet arrived and, after the pretext of being fired on, bombarded and soon captured Rangoon. This time the province of Pegu was annexed, including Rangoon, but the Raj (the East India Company at that time) did not want the burden of further colonial administration and so left Mandalay and the landlocked bulk of the country to the Burmese Court.

The Second Burma War was a catastrophe that led to the downfall of the Burmese King. The royal house, with its scores of wives and hordes of children, was typical of Oriental despotism and, due to inevitable disputes and schisms within the extended family, inherently unstable. The humiliating defeat soured already-bitter relations and led to cabals and fratricidal strife. Prince Mindon, the half-brother of the King, was a moderate who had not been involved in the war. The collapse of the Burmese forces provided him with the opportunity and, according to Oliver B. Pollak, "Mindon secured his hold on the throne in the traditional manner, via royal, official, and territorial marriage alliances." As a prince he had at least six wives; immediately following his rebellion "he took at least eight more wives." By the 1860s, when Grandfather became captain of his yacht, King Mindon had some forty wives and more than one hundred children.

While Mrs. Leonowens recorded her experiences at the Siamese Court in the many letters that she wrote (forming the basis of the musical *The King and I* and Margaret Landon's book *Anna and the King of Siam*),

Captain Samuel Lewis Shaw left no letters about his relations with the King of Burma—or at least none that survived. There might have been some written records in the keep of his eldest son, George, our Uncle G, but he died in Foochow in 1943 and what papers he may have had were lost in the chaos of the Japanese invasion in the Second World War. What was my grandfather's life like as an officer of this Oriental court? We can only surmise but we have accounts of the times by travellers and missionaries to draw on and also the somewhat frenetic history of Burma in the 1860s.

King Mindon was determined to transform the Burmese state from a typical Oriental despotism, complete with eunuchs and slavery, into a viable nineteenth-century nation. He introduced a limited program of what he called "defensive Westernization"; he tried to modernize the court and attempted to eliminate corruption. For the first part of his reign, he was known as "Good King Mindon." He sought to improve transportation and communications, and as a result, Pollak says Mindon became interested in the latest Western technology, the steamboat. The King ordered several of these new "self-propelled" vessels; they were "most expensive" and "plunged Mindon into interminable wrangles" ending in litigation, as the steamers, which were built by the British, often did not meet specifications.

It is unlikely that one of these modern steamboats was the yacht that Captain Shaw commanded. They were more like tugs and were used to draw barges filled with rice and other agricultural products up and down the Irawaddy. The yacht might have been one of the ceremonial oar-powered craft, the "golden boats of Burma," which were said to be such a fascinating sight, but my grandfather would not be needed to run such a vessel, which would be better in the hands of a Burmese. The probability is that the yacht was a sloop the King had obtained from the British, or perhaps that the British had given him in order to keep a watch on him (a likely scenario considering the politics of the times). If so, it was a gift Mindon could not refuse. Captain Shaw had years of experience being master of a sloop, as this was the type of vessel used in coastal trading; moreover, he was used to dealing with the Orientals and would therefore be a knowledgeable supervisor.

As captain (and as a pseudo-agent), Captain Shaw would probably have made his headquarters, at least off the yacht, in Rangoon and not in the royal capital of Amarapura, near Mandalay, where conditions were rather primitive and could be demeaning for a foreigner who would be expected to follow Oriental customs. He would have made regular trips up the Irawaddy to attend on the King.

Rangoon had been in the hands of the British for a decade and had some of the colonial comforts that Captain Shaw had known in Penang, including the inevitable club. Although Rangoon had the wondrous, golden magnificence of the Shwe-Dagon pagoda and other Buddhist temples, and resounded to the tinkling of temple bells, it was a dingy, dirty place in those days. The British had not done much for the native quarters, and major conflagrations during the 1850s burned down rickety bamboo houses. The creeks that criss-crossed the town were foul-smelling open sewers. Colourful crowds thronged the narrow streets; about this, one visitor wrote, "saffron-robed priests with shaven heads, naked children smoking cigars, and sad-faced lepers begging for alms."

My grandfather must have been in regular contact with the King, but how did he get his orders? It is unlikely that he went to court, as the kowtow was expected—in fact demanded. Captain Shaw was a domineering presence, if only because of his towering height, and would have been appalled if he had been expected to go barefoot, down on his hands and knees, and knock his head on the ground like a cringing supplicant. He would have refused, but he did not have to as his imperialist masters in the British Raj forbade such "barbarous conduct." He might have sent a subordinate, but it is more likely that he met the King away from the court or on the yacht.

Mindon would have liked to do away with the kowtow. He was trying to modernize his country and had sent his ministers to Europe and his children to be educated in England and France. He had welcomed the appointment of a British resident, but when London insisted that the resident be received at court "in accordance with international usage," the King expressed his regrets. He was courtesy itself, but he said that he could not change his court customs. The resident was withdrawn and Mindon's personal relations with the British ceased.

✦ *This painting of Captain Shaw was done in London when he returned to Britain in 1866; he would have been forty-three years old.*

It was in 1866, after his commission as commander of the King of Burma's yacht, that Grandfather returned to Britain. It was the first time he had set foot on his native land in more than thirty years. But why did he leave this prestigious post when he did? Captain Shaw told his son, Frederick William, he got bored with the job: "He was tired of doing nothing and getting big pay." King Mindon was probably not using the vessel. His Western outlook had waned, and he likely never liked looking up to Captain Shaw as he must have had to do whenever he spoke to him—from a royal perspective, it must have been degrading. So he was probably glad to inform Captain Shaw that he was getting rid of the British boat as soon as the captain's five-year commission was up. At about this time, Grandfather received a letter from his uncle George, the uncle who had brought him up, urging him to return as he was ill and wanted to see him before he died.

Captain Shaw must have seemed a glamorous figure, the merchant sailor from the East Indies, the former captain of the King of Burma's yacht, just arrived from the Orient, and he cut a mean swath in a London all agog over the Empire. He was a widower in his mid forties, handsome and wealthy, in the prime of life. "He lived in great style," his daughter, my mother, recalled. "He had a carriage and I remember I had the buttons off the uniform of his coachman." According to my mother, he met "Lady Annesley [a relative], who treated him royally." Both my parents agreed that Captain Shaw had lots of money and, as my father said, "like a sailor, he threw it around." However, all was not partying and good times. He did keep his commitment, and Frederick William asserted that Shaw visited his Uncle George and stayed with him until he passed away. He also went to see his father, Lees Shaw. According to Aunty Julia, Lees told him, "Lewis, if we had met in heaven, we would not have known each other."

How did Grandfather make all the money that he was flinging around in this rake's progress? It must have been in the twenty or so years when he was in coastal shipping and trading in the Far East, before he became captain of the King of Burma's yacht. His son, Frederick William, spoke of "cases of silver under his bunk." It is possible that during at least part of the time from 1840, when he had his master's certificate, to 1860 he was engaged in the opium trade. The East India Company sold opium at public auctions in Calcutta to private firms or agents who arranged for its transportation in coastal ships. These ships had Chinese or Lascar crews and British commanders, and as Captain A.R. Williamson reports, "quick promotion and profit attracted many high-spirited young men from the junior ranks of the East Indiamen and the Navy." The government of India, which for most of this period was the East India Company, actually licensed these coastal ships; it was concerned about its monopoly of the opium trade with China, and the licenses, according to Williamson, had an express stipulation that the documents would be invalid if the ship carried any opium other than that purchased through government sales in India.

A comparison can be made between the nineteenth-century opium trade with China and twentieth-century bootlegging of liquor to the

United States. Although the Canadian government was not involved in bootlegging *per se*, the liquor was manufactured by government-licensed companies and shipped by various nefarious means to the United States; it was only then that gangsters took over its distribution. A friend of mine, Ray McNess, was a wireless operator on a packer chartered by distillers in Vancouver. The packer cruised along the twelve-mile limit, out of reach of the American coast guard cutters. It could be rough and unpleasant work but mostly boring, McNess said, just drifting along in the open Pacific. They were in touch with the gangsters by wireless, and when he let them know the coastal waters were clear, that the coast guard cutter that had been trailing them had gone, the gangsters arrived in fast motorboats and cases of liquor were off-loaded and taken ashore. In a similar way, the British-run coastal ships would deliver opium to remote islands or hidden coves along the China coast. It was the so-called Canton agents who, as Williamson says, looked after the criminal side of the enterprise, the "bribery [of officials] and the clandestine arrangement for disposal of the drugs."

The missionaries deplored the opium trade. They railed against it in sermons and in fundraising tracts. Dr. Virgil Hart, a pioneer evangelist in China, called it "a deep, dark damnable blot" upon the name of Britain. Like other Methodists, Dr. Hart considered cigarettes and alcohol almost as evil as opium, and would have agreed with another missionary who compared "the sin of the American tobacco companies ... selling the accursed cigarettes" with that of "Christian England selling opium to this heathen land." Yet it was the Opium War of 1841–42 that opened up the country to the missionaries; this fact posed a real dilemma for them, for there was no hiding the deep, dark, damnable truth.

As for the opium traders, they were not in the least conscience-stricken as the missionaries were. In many ways, they were the upwardly mobile of those engaged in commerce in the Far East, after adventure and profit. After all, opium and opiates, such as laudanum, were in common use by the British in the nineteenth century. They were mostly taken as medicine; indeed, according to one historian, opium, which came in pills, was the "Victorian's aspirin." Opium was a common household remedy and was in fact used in the treatment of colds, influenza, and almost every illness. Cough lozenges were based on opiates, and children's cordials like Godfrey's Cordial and Dolby's Carmanative were laced with laudanum. It was also cheap: pills or twenty to twenty-five drops of laudanum could be bought for a penny. In fact, the medicinal use of opium continued until the middle of the twentieth century. Dill water, which was given to infants as a sedative or an antidote for colic, had laudanum as its main ingredient. The bulk of the opium came from Turkey, largely because it was closer than India. By 1859, the amount of opium landed in London and other British ports increased to more than sixty tons (127,000 kilograms) a year.

Opium was also consumed for pleasure. Coffee houses, like Garraway's Coffee House by the Royal Exchange in London, carried "a diverse selection of opium," and businessmen and the well-to-do could have opiates with their coffee. It was not only the upper classes who indulged. The poorly paid British working people also consumed opium because it was cheaper than ale or spirits. There were, as might be expected, harmful consequences; many children became addicted, and some died of overdoses. However, there did not seem to be much opposition to the drug, and the Society for Suppression of the Opium Trade was not founded until 1874.

Samuel Taylor Coleridge and Thomas de Quincy were the best known of the authors who used opium, largely because they wrote about it (Coleridge's poem "Kubla Khan" was supposed to be the product of an opium-induced vision). But Byron, Shelley and Keats, Francis Thompson, Wilkie Collins, Sir Walter Scott, Dickens, and most other nineteenth-century British writers took opium as medicine, as analgesic, or for enjoyment. Coleridge felt guilty about his dependence on the drug, which he could not break, and later wrote tracts warning about "the insidious effect" of opium.

Thus, young merchant seamen like my grandfather had no moral compunctions about shipping opium to China. Like my bootlegging friend, they simply had a well-paid, if dreadfully dull, job. Those involved in the opium trade with China never thought about the deleterious effect the drug might have; they often had, in any case, a low opinion of the Chinese. From their lofty imperial heights, they looked down on the natives as lesser breeds. American sinologist Harold Isaacs calls the period between the Opium Wars and the beginning of the twentieth century "the age of contempt for China."

We do not know when Captain Shaw left Britain once again to return to the Far East. His son said he spent a couple of years in the old country visiting friends and relatives; my mother thought he was certainly there for more than a year. And nobody knows why he left and why he returned to the Orient. He was an attractive figure, a handsome, suntanned captain from the distant Indies, and there must have been romances. Among the letters to Captain Shaw that my mother kept were several from a cousin, Sydney Garrett, the niece of Lady Annesley, who seemed to be in love with him. In one of them she wrote,

> You are such an unreasonable creature! I don't know how to scold you sufficiently for saying when you were "out of sight out of mind." I am afraid it has been only too much the other way, as many of the things I have in daily use recall you to my mind.

Sydney was apparently living with her aunt, Lady Annesley, at Castlewellan in the Mountains of Mourne, Ireland. Captain Shaw's youngest brother, Frederick Arrowsmith, was the steward or manager of the Annesley Estate, and Grandfather was pleased to get to know him. It would have been the first time that he had ever met his "little brother," and they had long walks and talks around the estate where he must have been a frequent visitor. He liked Fred, this new-found brother, and was so taken with Fred's wife, Mary Ellen Claire Shaw, that he named his second wife, my Japanese grandmother, Ellen after her; he also gave her names, Mary Ellen, to his second daughter of his second marriage, my mother.

In a letter, Sydney wrote that she had discovered "another peculiarity of sailors, namely impatience!" and said, "I am sure I was not long in answering your letter." She added, "Aunt Annesley will be shocked at all the letters going to you." In another, she berated Shaw for not writing to his son, Samuel Lewis Shaw ii: "I had a long letter from your son yesterday he tells me you have not written once to him since you left ... very naughty of you. Write now to him [that is] Please do!!" There was also a dispute whether a relative had disgraced the family. Captain Shaw felt she had not, but Sydney disagreed and wrote, "The very fact of a girl marrying without the consent of her parents, not to mention the deceit Clara was guilty of is a disgrace to any family—but that is no reason why they should not forgive for we are told to forgive till seventy times seven."

Most of Sydney's letters were written in a bold, flowing hand on fine notepaper embossed with the Annesley coat of arms. In one, she wanted her letters destroyed: "Please burn my letters when you have read them, or before, if you like! It might be the best thing to do with them." She addressed Captain Shaw as "My dear Lewis" and always signed herself with a flourish, "Yrs. Affecately [sic], Sydney Garrett." Letters were sent to Capt. S.L. Shaw at different addresses in Highgate, London; the last was dated September 2, 1867 which shows he did not leave for the Orient till late in 1867.

Judging from these letters, Captain Shaw seemed to be fond of Sydney and perhaps intended to marry her. But something happened. Did they quarrel? Did he find Sydney too bold, too assertive, too censorious about his neglect of his son, perhaps, too much like his first wife? Then there was the mystery about his first wife, Anna Charlotte Nail Shaw, particularly about her death. Evidently, he had no proof of her death, no death certificate; without one, he would have difficulty marrying again in Britain. Also, there was the phenomenon that affected many men who had spent years in the Far East, which was that they came to look on the most alluring of Oriental women as a standard by which beauty was to be judged. One of Sydney's letters contains a curious note in which she refers to a book of photos Shaw had given her; according to her everyone was "quite astonished at the beauty of the Chinese ladies."

His relatives expected him to retire to Ireland or one of the shires, as so many who had made their fortune in the Far East had done, and there was every indication he wanted to do so. In this connection, I remember staying at Plassey House, the home of an old China Hand and friend of my father's. A handsome Palladian mansion on the banks of the Shannon, Plassey House was one of the stately homes built for Lord Clive, the conqueror of India. There were many more such estates that had their origin in the wealth of the Empire. Captain Shaw had been spending lavishly, but there was no sign he had run out of money. However, after the first rhapsody of returning to Britain and especially to Ireland, perhaps he found life there, in the dull dampness of a cold climate, stiff and formal— so different from the easygoing, uninhibited life he had known in the sunshine of the Indies.

At any rate, my grandfather returned to the Far East at the end of 1867. There are letters from this period from his mother and his youngest sister, Mary Ann; the latter's was dated February 19, 1868 and addressed to Capt. S.L. Shaw, Resident Marine Surveyor, Pagoda Anchorage, Foochow, China. Both of them expressed sorrow and disappointment at his returning to the Far East, and Mary Ann asked, "If you have not often thought of us all—we often look at your picture which hangs over the mantelpiece." She wondered whether they would ever see him again. A letter from Lady Annesley, with a note from Sydney, said they were think- ing of him at Christmas (1868) and said they had "asked God to grant you health of soul and body thro' this New Year and such measure of worldly prosperity as He knows to be best for you."

For a time, Grandfather was said to be sailing from Hong Kong to Shanghai, on the China coast run that was owned by one of the great hongs (foreign mercantile establishments), Gibb Livingstone and Company. However, there is some question whether he did not do this before going to Britain. The obituary in the Foochow Daily Echo spoke of his com- manding the sloop *Kitty*, convoying junks on the China coast, and acting for a time as a coast pilot for the Pacific and Orient Line. Then it says, "He went home in 66, returning the next year and either in 67 or 68 he settled down as marine surveyor at Pagoda Anchorage." However, his tombstone speaks of his "Last Command ss *Dumbarton* 1867," so there must have been a short period between the time he left London and set- tled in Foochow that he was back to sailing. He was probably based in Shanghai, as I have a letter addressed to him "care of J. Sharp Esqre, Gibb Livingston and Co., Shanghai," from Castlewellan; the letter bears no date but was probably written in early 1868. His last command, it should be noted, was a steamship.

It was through his old employer and patron, Gibb Livingstone and Company, that he got this shore job at Pagoda Anchorage, the deep-water port of Foochow. He knew Hugh Bold Gibb, whom the obituary describes as "a great friend to him." As marine surveyor, Captain Shaw represented German Lloyds, French Veritas, and other insurance companies in certifying that the ships were seaworthy and loaded properly with cargo, mainly tea. It was, according to my father, "a sort of superannuation or retirement for him in Foochow." Was this compensation for the work he had done in the opium trade? Gibb Livingstone, like Jardine Matheson and most of the other great hongs, had his beginnings as a Canton agent in the opium trade. With the passage of time, many of these foreign China corporations, including Gibb Livingstone, have disappeared. However, Jardine Matheson, acknowledged to be the first and foremost in the illegal drug business, survives; but it had left Hong Kong for Singapore some time before its return to China in 1997.

3

MARINE SURVEYOR

at PAGODA ANCHORAGE

WHEN MY GRANDFATHER CAME TO FOOCHOW to take up his post as marine surveyor, he found the Chinese city to be much like Penang or Manila, Singapore or Djkarta, Calcutta or Rangoon. There were the spacious European (mainly British) houses with their wide verandahs on the high ground of Nantai Island, the churches (including the small Anglican church where my mother and father would later be married), the smart new club on the highest ground overlooking the muddy Min River, crowded with junks and sampans, and the massive clutter of the Chinese city. It would not have surprised Captain Shaw to find such familiar colonial surroundings: he had become used to empire, whether British, Dutch, French, Spanish, or Portuguese, taking over every part of Asia—at least every part he had visited. Before moving to Foochow, Grandfather had visited Chinese ports and sailed in Chinese waters, but this was the first time that he had ever lived in China, and he was to live there for the next forty years.

It could be said that Foochow was as much a part of the British Empire as Hong Kong, but in a different way. Hong Kong was ceded in

1841 by means of the Treaty of Nanking, which ended the First Opium War; the wretched Manchu Court was forced to give the British extra-territorial rights and what amounted to suzerainty in five other ports: Canton (Guangzhou), Amoy (Xiamen), Ningpo, Shanghai, and Foochow (Fuzhou). Further treaties opened up or turned over more ports, even those like inland Hankow (Wuhan) and Ichang and Chungking (Chongqing) high up the Yangtse River, until the only city of any importance left to the Chinese was Peking. Even in the capital there was a foreign enclave, the Legation Quarter, and large occupation forces. In the early 1860s, some years before Captain Shaw moved to Foochow, the British took over the Chinese Maritime Customs Service and thus got control of the main government revenues and credit. For all practical purposes, China was part of the Empire; the Manchu Court was left nominally in charge, which was a nice arrangement as it relieved the British of the burden of administering this huge country.

Captain Shaw probably never gave it a thought, for as a trader he was interested only in commerce and was not concerned with the different political structures in parts of the Empire. Some parts, in fact, most of them, were colonies where British officials ran the government of the territories down to the smallest district. Others were protectorates in which the chiefs, kings, sultans, nawabs, and maharajahs were ostensibly the rulers, if under the strict surveillance and guidance of British residents; these included most of the princely states of India. As for India, it was more than a colony: it was an empire, the Indian Empire, within the British Empire.

There were also the self-governing dominions made up of former white British colonies. Canada came into being in 1867 with confederation, but Australia, New Zealand, and South Africa achieved dominion status much later. In fact, the last convicts to be shipped to any part of Australia went in 1867, the date of the British North America Act and Canadian confederation. The British penal system of "transportation" had come to an end. Various attempts were made to unite the Australian colonies in a federation, and as a result, the Commonwealth of Australia was proclaimed in 1901. Six years later, New Zealand was given dominion status within the British Empire. South Africa was created by an Act of the British Parliament in 1909. Newfoundland was an ambiguous case. It was granted "responsible government" in 1855, but lost its status as a dominion in 1933 and reverted to that of a crown colony because it was virtually bankrupt.

Next were the mandates of former enemy territories of the First World War which became known as "trusteeships" after the Second World War, in which British rule was indirect but effective and sometimes iron-handed. Finally, there was the part of the political structure of the British Empire with which Captain Shaw was familiar: subjugation by means of treaties. This imperial mode applied not only to China but to Siam, which was long regarded as being independent; a treaty granting extra-territorial rights to the British was signed in 1855. While the French and the Americans acquired concessions in Siam, the British were really in charge, and thus much more of the map could be painted red. With the addition of China and Siam, the British Empire could be said to cover almost half the world instead of a third.

As marine surveyor, Captain Shaw was stationed some twelve miles downstream from Foochow at Mowi, which the British called Pagoda Anchorage after the Sung Dynasty pagoda high on a hill that served as a landmark. The large ocean-going sailing ships had to anchor there because further up the river was too shallow. There was no way of com-muting in those days; the road, if there was a road, would have been a dusty trail, used by farm animals and carts. When my wife and I visited Foochow in 1981, it took us only half an hour to drive to Pagoda Anchorage, but in my grandfather's day, the only way to get there was by sampan. It would have been quicker going downstream to the deep-water harbour where the clipper ships lay, perhaps an hour and a half to two hours, depending on the oarsmen, but obviously much longer going upstream on the journey to the city.

About the only conveyance in Foochow for foreigners or Mandarins was the sedan chair. There were few wheeled vehicles, certainly no shoals of bicycles, no trucks or cars, as there were when I visited there. The main bridge across the Min River, the Bridge of Ten Thousand Ages, was nar-row, and the picture my father took of it when he first visited Foochow in 1907 showed a couple of sedan chairs and pedestrians as the only traffic.

The sedan chair came in various models, from the work-a-day wicker seat to a plush-lined palanquin. The importance of its occupant could be told by the number of coolies: if there were four in fine livery bearing the chair and shouting to clear the way, the chair bore a taipan or a high official; if only three, a missionary or an ordinary "foreign devil."

So Captain Shaw had to move to Pagoda Anchorage and give up the good colonial life of Foochow with its various amusements such as the race meetings. In his trilogy *Pax Britannica* James Morris notes that the race course (and there was one in almost every town in the British Empire) was the equivalent of the amphitheatre in the Roman Empire, "with much the same meaning." It did not go as far as providing the hoi polloi with bread and circuses, but it did give them a diversion and amusement, although this was somewhat restricted in smaller locales.

The race course in Foochow could not be compared with the great arenas in Hong Kong, Shanghai, or Singapore. It was a bare ground on the outskirts of the city that had been railed off; within the perimeter of the semicircular track was a football field. The British ran the meetings and owned the horses, or ponies in the case of the Foochow races; they let the native Chinese take part only as spectators. A pigtailed crowd turned out in large numbers for this contest (compare with the Roman Circus), and my father took a photo of a Chinese crowd watching with what seemed to be close attention the antics of the European jockeys. There was no opportunity for them to put any money on the horses, as there was in Shanghai, and this would have been a disappointment as the Chinese are inveterate gamblers. A selling sweepstake, held in the Foochow Club, from which the Chinese were excluded, was the only form of organized betting.

I have a 1906 race card that belonged to my mother. On it she lists the winners and makes some comments on the meeting, especially on her brother's entry. Her brother, Frederick William, who was known as Willie, had a pony named Camarade, which was ridden by a German friend from Shanghai. Some of the entries were ridden by their owners, others by amateur jockeys. My mother's race card indicates Willie was not very successful at that meeting. During the three days of the meeting, the owners' wives put up little decorated bowers near the stables where

✦ *Pagoda Anchorage: the Shaw house beside the Pagoda,*
where my mother was born in 1885

they would dispense refreshments to the racing enthusiasts, British or European, but not to the Chinese spectators. The races were a great social occasion, probably the greatest in the colony's social calendar, and there were race "tiffins" (the Anglo-Indian word for lunches which was in common use in China), and the meeting wound up with a ball at the Foochow Club.

Captain Shaw probably lived in rented quarters when he was first at Pagoda Anchorage, and while they were few in numbers, some foreigners did have houses there. Later he bought a house that had been built by ship chandlers E. Lee and Company, at the very base of Luojing, the ancient seven-storey pagoda—in fact, the garden wall was just eight feet from the eleventh-century edifice. It was a fairly large building, in Indian colonial style, with pillared verandahs overlooking the wide stretch of the Min River where a score of sailing ships would be anchored in the spring. The house changed hands a couple of times, and, according to his daughter Julia, Captain Shaw bought it from the British consulate, who had moved to more spacious quarters in town. The consulate had constructed half a dozen prison cells (mainly for drunken British sailors) behind the main building, and in Captain Shaw's time they were used as quarters for the Chinese servants. My mother, Mary, was born in the house beside the pagoda, and so were her two sisters and five brothers (George, Uncle G, was the eldest, and then came Julia, Henry, Willie, Mary, Robert, Ceci, and Leo), all the children of Captain Shaw's second marriage.

Captain Shaw was in his forty-eighth year when he took up the appointment of marine surveyor at Pagoda Anchorage. While he seemed fit enough, and a portrait done of him while he was in London shows neither grey hair nor wrinkles, forty-eight or fifty was judged to be really old in those days, old enough for a "superannuation job." Although he seemed to have a strong constitution, his obituary said that "fifty or sixty years ago [when he would have been in his twenties or thirties] he could not get his life insured as he was considered a bad risk." What illness did he have? Probably consumption, a common ailment of the nineteenth century.

Captain Shaw had lived in Penang and been the captain of the King of Burma's yacht, but he never learned any native language. His means of communication with his Chinese or Lascar crews was pidgin English, and in this, he was no different from many of his fellow traders and empire builders, all those who were not engaged in actually running the colonies or its police or armed forces. There were thousands of foreigners, British, French, Americans, mostly merchants and businessmen, who lived and died in Shanghai without speaking Chinese.

Pidgin, which by all accounts was a Chinese corruption of the word "business," was the *lingua franca* not only of Cathay but of the East Indies, the Middle East, and the Far East. It was similar to basic English but without any rules of syntax or grammar, with usually about five hundred words of English, often mispronounced, and some thirty or so common words of the vernacular. Yet this bastard jargon (it originated in the business or trade between the Chinese and English in the eighteenth century) has added some words to the great lexicon of the English language, such as "cash" (a corruption of Portuguese), "chow" (food), "chop-chop" (hurry up), and "savvy" (understand). Then, there was "chin chin" which meant talk or discuss and was the equivalent of "jaw jaw" of Churchillian fame (instead of "war war"). It was used also as a greeting, as is evident in a letter of felicitation to my mother on her marriage which ends with "Give my best Chin Chin to your mother and sisters."

Although he never learned another language, Captain Shaw must have picked up some Chinese, if only by osmosis, in the forty years that he lived in Foochow; however, his daughter Julia said that he only knew two words, "both of them bad." That would bear out his view that Chinese was a "filthy" language; he would not allow his children to learn or speak it. My grandfather's contempt for native languages was shared by most of those who laboured east of Suez for the greater glory of the British Empire. It was an expression of the racial superiority they felt and that came naturally to them as members of the Raj. Even those colonial officials and police officers who had to acquire some knowledge of the vernacular in the course of their duties looked down on the native tongues as a sordid means of communication. This arrogant attitude of the British toward all native languages (the feeling that they were incomprehensible, second-rate and split up into so many different dialects) and their refusal to learn them had the effect of spreading English throughout the vast extent of the Empire and thus turning it into a world language.

Years before the Opium War of 1841, British traders had realized that they could cut costs by shipping tea from Foochow rather than from Canton. (Grandfather's obituary said he was on the Min River in 1838; his ship was probably on a reconnoitering voyage.) The tea from the gardens on the hills around Wuyi took only three days to come down the river to Foochow, whereas the same tea had to be carried by mule train overland to the factories at Canton, a journey of some six weeks, which added greatly to the cost. That is why the merchants insisted that the Treaty of Nanking include Foochow among the five "treaty" ports opened to foreign commerce.

For several post-Treaty years, the Mandarins in Foochow, who despised the *ta-pitzu* and their crass, money-grubbing ways, were able to keep the port closed to the tea trade, but eventually, inevitably, they were overwhelmed by the tidal wave of the market. By the time my grandfather became marine surveyor, Foochow had become the greatest tea port on the China coast, and in the whole world, and was to remain as such until the 1880s, when steam, and Indian tea, lost its pre-eminence.

The ships had changed. The big, heavy East Indiamen, the erstwhile Lords of the Ocean and the tea wagons of yesteryear, had been replaced by the sleek, beautiful clipper ships. Clipper ships were three-masted square riggers like the old East Indiamen, but they carried much more sail, a vast expanse of canvas, and had much lower, streamlined hulls with lengthy bowsprits. This made them the fastest large sailing ships ever built, and they could, with a good wind, knife through the water at eighteen knots. Indeed, they could on occasion go faster than the newfangled steamers. American marine historian A.B.C. Whipple recounts that on July 25, 1889 the famous clipper ship *Cutty Sark* passed the new mail steamer *Britannia* at a "speed reckoned to be about seventeen knots," and beat her into Sydney Harbor.

Premiums and prizes were offered in London for the delivery of the first crop of the season. As a result, there was an annual race, and the clipper ships were built for this race—or, to be precise, the first clipper ships were built for the China tea trade. The greatest race, which has gone down in history and become the stuff of legend, was between the *Ariel* and the *Taeping* in the spring of 1866. The *Ariel* was the favourite that year, and although she got away first, the *Taeping* overhauled her and beat her to the London docks; after ninety-nine days of sailing, only about a mile—or about ten minutes—separated them at the finish, an incredibly narrow margin after a 15,000-mile passage from China.

The arrival of the first tea clippers at the East India docks of London was an exciting annual event. There was feverish commercial activity, according to Jason Goodwin: sample chests were snatched off the ships and, as soon as the tasting was done, the brokers in Mincing Lane began bidding. By the following morning the new tea was on sale in the city of London and the boroughs of the home counties. The British felt that the freshest tea was the best, and that the taste of tea deteriorated with time. The Chinese did not agree; they liked their tea aged a little, like vintage wines. While the clipper ships carried "the first and finest pluckings of the spring," Goodwin compares all the "razzmatazz and hype" in the sale of the new tea in England as the way "Beaujolais Nouveau sells nowadays." It was, he says, "a talking point which had a cachet for snobs." Just as with

French wines, there were all kinds of Chinese teas, each with a particular taste and each with its ardent supporters. Among the most popular for the British market in the 1860s and 1870s were oolong, named after the Oolong River that meets the Min in the middle of Foochow, and jasmine, which, as its name implies, was a tea scented with the jasmine flower.

The job of marine surveyor was no sinecure. Once the loading began, it went on at a feverish pace around the clock for several days, with no rest on Sundays and no loafing. (Any Chinese coolie seen to dawdle was liable to be hit with a bamboo cane by the *tou-mu*, the head man.) And Grandfather had to see that it was properly done, not just on one ship but on the whole fleet of a dozen or more clipper ships. Most were being loaded at the same time, which meant that he had to work day and night boarding ships and seeing that the tea chests were tightly stowed. This was Captain Shaw's responsibility, and no ship could leave without a certificate from him. Just as his tombstone boasted "Never an Accident (at sea)," so there seemed to be no complaints from the insurance companies for whom he worked: never a claim.

"Loading a clipper was a fine art," notes Whipple. Tea was such a light cargo that, on the average, a couple of hundred tons of ballast (scrap metal and beach pebbles) had to be carried to keep the ships on an even keel. Both the ballast and the cargo had to be tightly packed to prevent them from shifting at sea. (At the beginning of the great tea race, the *Ariel* was down at the bow due to shoddy loading. This cut her speed, and desperate but successful efforts were made to shift the weight to the stern.) Planking was laid over the ballast, and the tea chests were packed in. The poorer-quality teas were placed in the bottom layers, with the better teas on top, away from any bilge water. The chests were hammered into place so that, as Whipple says, "not a hair's breadth of space remained between them." A tarpaulin was stretched over the top layer and the hatches closed and sealed.

The clipper ships reached Foochow in the spring, around the middle of April. Many of them had come from Hong Kong or Shanghai where they had been delivering the merchandise and supplies they had taken on in London for their China agents. They arrived early because they could not be sure how long the haggling over the price for the new crop of tea would take—the average wait at the Pagoda Anchorage was some forty days before the tea reached them and they began their long race home, usually at the end of May or the beginning of June. It was hard bargaining: the Chinese could hold out for weeks in fixing an acceptable price because they knew Foochow had the advantage in the tea trade over Shanghai and the other ports. The foreign buyers were anxious to keep costs down, but they also had to negotiate for cargo space on the clipper ships, whose fees were set according to their speed. The fastest could demand a premium, and the agent who had spent a lot in lining up a race favourite would be anxious to close his deal first.

At last, and for some reason it usually happened at night, a price was accepted. Then the rush was on to get the tea to the clipper ships. The tea chests were weighed and labelled, and sampans or lighters, known as "chops," drove down the twelve miles of river from Foochow to Pagoda Anchorage and the great assembly of clipper ships, the oarsmen rowing furiously. There was a hubbub of shouting and yelling as the chop captains cried out for the ship for which their cargo was destined. It was extraordinary that in all this tumult the tea chests were delivered to the right ships, and soon the clippers were surrounded by sampans and lighters and the precious cargo was being hauled aboard. In a couple of days, the tea chests were properly stowed in the holds and the great race could begin, but my grandfather saw to it that, under an agreement with the captains, no ship could leave until all had received their certificates.

This feverish activity and the wild competitive rush only occurred before the clipper ships took off for the open sea. Before that were weeks of waiting when nothing happened, and the officers and crews had a difficult time keeping occupied. There was shore leave, which sometimes resulted in disturbances in the native quarters of Foochow. The British sailors could not be arrested or imprisoned by the Chinese authorities, even if they got involved in a fight and killed someone. The Treaty of Nanking, and the other treaties that had opened the ports such as Foochow, had conferred extraterritorial rights upon the signatories, and crew men could only be tried in a British court, which meant arrest by the British police and incarceration in the consulate's prison cells. But they were not jailed for long before being turned over to the captains of their ships. The miscreant would be roundly and loudly cursed as the captain expressed his outrage, but aside from that, he would not likely receive any further punishment as his services were needed in the coming race home. (If the reverse occurred and a Chinese knifed one of the clipper's crew, let alone killed him, the British would see that he was summarily convicted and beheaded.)

For the captains and the senior officers, the weeks of waiting were a time for socializing. Captain Shaw, as the resident marine surveyor, was expected to entertain, and he did, as best he could, in the limited facilities at the Pagoda Anchorage. However, the most lavish receptions and dinners were given by the taipans in Foochow, the local representatives of the great hongs that served as agents of the clipper ships in the tea trade. My father, who was in Foochow a generation later in 1907, recalled that they dressed for dinner and for parties: it was white tie and tails. He remarked on the way that the Chinese servants polished the dinner table until it shone and decorated it with great vases of flowers and other ornaments including "wonderful patterns of colored sand." But by then, the great days of the tea trade were over and social life in the treaty port had declined.

Most of the servants of the Empire—the administrators, officers, traders—were from the middle classes; some were of more humble origin, but in colonial China and the other colonies they lived like lords and ladies—like the landed gentry in their stately homes whom they had left behind in England. They had the superior attitudes of the aristocracy, as well as the confidence, the arrogance, that came from their status as members of the ruling race. Somerset Maugham visited Foochow in 1920, a full half-century after Grandfather was the resident marine surveyor, and wrote:

There was about the party a splendour which has vanished from the dinner tables of England. The mahogany groaned with silver. In the middle of the snowy damask cloth was a centre piece of yellow silk ... and on this was a massive epergne. Tall silver vases in which were large chrysanthemums made it possible to catch only glimpses of the persons opposite you, and tall silver candlesticks reared their proud heads two by two down the length of the table. Each course was served with its appropriate wine, sherry with the soup and hock with the fish; and there were two entrees, a white entree and a brown entree, which the careful hostess of the [1890s] felt were essential to a properly arranged dinner.

Somerset Maugham also commented on the immense size of the houses:

The merchant princes of that day [1870s] built magnificently. Money was made easily then and life was luxurious. It was not hard to make a fortune and a man, almost before he reached middle age, could return to England and live the rest of his days no less splendidly in a fine house in Surrey ... members [of the foreign community] entertained each other lavishly. They gave pompous dinner parties, they danced together, and they played whist ...

But the author agreed that the great days of the tea trade were over; as he put it, "this agreeable life was a thing of the past. The port [of Foochow] lived on its export of tea, and the change of taste from Chinese to Ceylon had ruined it. For thirty years, the port had lain a-dying."

It was steam that brought about the end of the clipper ships and the tea trade. For more than two hundred years, sailing ships (the East Indiamen before the clipper ships) had delivered tea to England only once a year, usually in September. The wholesalers were thus able to keep control over its distribution and maintain a steady price, which allowed the agents in China to assess costs and the quantities needed. However, the steamships could deliver tea all the year round, not only from China but from India and Ceylon, and the Suez Canal, which was opened in 1870, meant a shorter passage. The price of tea collapsed, which was fine for the British consumers but bad for the China tea trade.

The great year for Foochow was 1879. As Goodwin says, that was the year

China exported more tea than ever before, but in the following year, for the first time, exports of tea from the British Empire (mainly

India and Ceylon) overtook those of China. Queen Victoria helped by giving her title to "Her Majesty's Blend", a mixture of Indian and Ceylon teas. Within twenty years (by the turn of the century) the tea industry in Fuzhou [Foochow] was suffocating.

While the tea trade, and the loading of the clipper ships, was the most notable and important job for the resident marine surveyor in Foochow, there was other work. Even when at the height of the trade, not all the merchant ships at Pagoda Anchorage were after tea; there was other merchandise, such as export china and lacquerware for which Foochow was famous, as well as silk. Somerset Maugham was too gloomy when he remarked that "the port had lain a-dying." There was still plenty of business and a full roster of foreign consulates when my father came to Foochow in 1907. However, it was true that the British consul had two vice-consuls to help him in his work in the great days of the tea trade; by the beginning of the twentieth century, he was on his own.

As marine surveyor, Captain Shaw was not only concerned with the loading of the cargo but also with the seaworthiness of the vessels. His daughter Julia said he had a long steel hammer with a sharp point and small cross bar on which his two fingers could rest as he gripped it. He carried the hammer aboard ship and "used to beat it into [the side] of the ship to see whether the wood was rotten or not." The tea trade sputtered out at the turn of the century, but Foochow or Pagoda Anchorage still remained a busy port. However, by then Grandfather was in his late seventies, too old to clamber up the side of ships, and had retired.

Among the last clipper ships Captain Shaw boarded were the *Cutty Sark* and the *Thermopylae*. They were great contenders in the 1870s but they never had as thrilling or as famous a race as the *Taeping* and the *Ariel*, and it seemed that the *Thermopylae* always won. However, a decade or so later, when they were both involved in the Australian wool trade, the *Cutty Sark* set a record of seventy-three days for the run from Australia around Cape Horn to England. Both of these great clipper ships sailed into the twentieth century. After a long and varied career, serving for years as a Portuguese freighter and lastly as a British training ship, the *Cutty Sark* has been put in a specially built dry dock on the Thames and restored to her pristine glory. My wife and I made the journey to Greenwich and saw her in all her splendour, her tall masts dominating the river and the townscape. Earlier, Montague Dawson had painted the *Thermopylae* being towed by a steam tug for her last voyage to a Viking funeral in the open sea; the title of the picture is *Thermopylae Leaving Foochow 1907*, the year before my grandfather died.

4

My Japanese

GRANDMOTHER

ALTHOUGH NO RECORD COULD BE FOUND of her death, it is probable that Anna Charlotte Nail Shaw died in the late 1850s, which would indicate that my grandfather had been a widower for some twenty years before he married again. Captain Shaw had been the resident marine surveyor at Pagoda Anchorage since 1868 and was married at the British consulate in Foochow (or Foochowfoo, as the district was called then) on December 2, 1879. The marriage certificate lists him as a widower, fifty-eight years of age, and his wife, "Oh Sea (of Japan)," as a spinster, twenty-two years of age. His father's name was put down as "Lees Shaw" with the rank of "gentleman"; her father as "Matson Mullah" and under the notification of rank or profession "none."

A marriage certificate is a private document to be kept in some safe or bureau, and the affidavit that Captain Shaw's second wife, my grandmother, was Japanese became a secret that no one seemed anxious to disclose. It took years for me to find out, and when I raised the matter with my cousin, Basil Summers, he was surprised, even shocked. Basil said he had always assumed that Grandmother was Irish, and this is what

✦ *My Japanese
grandmother, Ellen
O'Sea, before she was
married, ca. 1877*

I also thought—Spanish Irish, which would account for my olive skin
and dark color. Grandfather had called her "Ellen," after the wife of his
brother, Fred, the steward at the Annesley estate in Ireland, and Ellen
O'Sea or Ellen O'Shea certainly sounded Irish.

There was a conspiracy of silence surrounding my grandmother. I cannot remember my mother ever mentioning her mother, and Basil said his
mother never spoke of her, although she often talked about her father, of
whom she was proud. When I began making inquiries about my grandmother, I found an unwillingness to answer my questions, perhaps largely
due to ignorance. During the 1970s I wrote repeatedly to my mother's
older sister, Julia, asking about her recollections; her responses were short
and not very enlightening, and she complained in one letter that I had
asked the same questions more than once (which I did, because she never

answered them). Aunty J had spent most of her long life in Foochow and only reluctantly left China for Macau because of the Cultural Revolution; she died in Macau at the age of 103 in 1984. A letter from a cousin, Sam Shaw, dated August 1977, said that Julia had told him that our grandmother "did not encourage discussion" about her Japanese background.

Sam Shaw lived in Australia, but Sam and his younger brother, Lewis, were my "Japanese" cousins; they were three-quarters Japanese since their father, Uncle G, the wealthy merchant and ship owner in Antung, Manchuria, had married a Japanese lady. One might expect that they would have had a greater propensity for Grandmother, but they knew no more than the rest of us. In a letter from Nagoya, Japan (he lived part of the time in Japan and part of the time in England), Lewis said, "The strange thing is that it took me a long time to realize that she was Japanese." Because Grandmother was known as Ellen O'Sea, Lewis believed, as I did, that she was Irish.

However, Oh-Sea or O'Sea or O'Shea is a girl's first name in Japan, and Lewis was critical of the British consulate for putting down only her first name on the marriage certificate. And letting her sign with her first name! "Surely," he said, "this is irregular." What was this about her father's name being "Matson Mullah?" It did not sound at all Japanese. If it was the consular official's rather indolent and disdainful attempt to anglicize the name that Oh-Sea gave—and she would have done so hesitantly and in the quiet self-effacing manner of Japanese women—what could it have been? Matsudaira, Matsukata, Matsukura, Matsumae, Matsumoto, Matsumura, Matsurato? Lewis opted for Matsumura. However, he was wrong in complaining that no first name was given: the British consul was satisfied that he had the first and last name of the bride's father and had filled out the form properly. "I'm sure," Lewis said, "our grandmother didn't know what was going on." That might have been true, but perhaps she was too shy and timid to correct the consul, and the gruff old sea captain was too embarrassed by the whole procedure.

None of the family seemed to want to delve too deeply into Grandmother's background. When did she come to Foochow? No one seemed to know, although Julia said that Captain Shaw met her through a Japanese business acquaintance. No one seemed to know anything about her family or even her place of birth. Those were the times, as Sam Shaw wrote, "when it was considered socially unacceptable to be the off-spring of mixed marriages" of this sort: native women were usually "kitchen drudges" and anyone of colour who was not a servant, not in the kitchen, was still below the salt and one of the lesser breeds.

"Eurasian" was the kindest name for the offspring of such a mixed marriage—"Anglo-Indian" in India. There was a class connotation about Anglo-Indian as it seemed to apply mainly to the progeny of a Britisher of the lower ranks, a sergeant or an N.C.O., and an Indian woman. During the last years of the Empire, the Anglo-Indians, who were almost all literate, made up the lower middle class in India. They ran the railways and, since they were loyal supporters of the Raj with a pathetic regard for England as "home" which they had never seen, they were recruited for the police. The latter work did not endear them to the populace; in fact, they were spurned by both sides, by both the Indians and the British. The term "Anglo-Indian" did not apply to the descendants of a Nawab or a Rajah or a Sheikh or, for that matter, any Indian and a European woman; they would have Indian names and be regarded as Indians. (Sir Feroze Khan Noon, one of the participants in the 1946 conference on the independence of India in Delhi, had an attractive Viennese wife who was known as "Lady After Noon.")

"Half-caste" and "half-breed" were harsh, pejorative terms, like "mulatto" or "high yellow." Half-breed: I remember my father speaking with revulsion that this name was given to people like my mother. He was an old man in his eighties then and there were tears in his eyes as he recalled a 1914 incident when Mother was cut dead in the Peking Club. She did not know many people at the club and when she saw an English woman, whom she had known well in Foochow, Mother went up to greet her. The woman turned and walked away. I was distressed by my father's tears and his bitter memories, and wondered if he felt this more than Mother, but how was I to know as she never spoke of it.

Apparently, nothing as blatant as this happened in Foochow; otherwise, Mother would not have regarded this woman as a friend. There was no racial discrimination, at least not of this kind—which is an interesting social phenomenon. Captain Shaw, his Japanese wife, and their children of mixed blood were accepted as neighbours and members of the foreign community in Nantai: Mother's brother, Frederick William (Willie), played a prominent part at the race meetings. However, once they left the cocoon of their small community for the capital (my father had been transferred to Peking) where hierarchy and snobbery reigned and where imperialist society's rules were more strictly observed, they could be subject to such racial abuse.

There was a time when my mother and her sisters seemed to glory in their Japanese ancestry. They dressed in kimonos and visited Japan. In fact, Aunty J said, they spent three or four months, between May and November, every year in Japan, but only after 1908, after my grandfather died. In all probability, they wore the kimonos only in Japan. We have pictures of my mother looking beautiful in a kimono and posing under a bower which does not seem to be part of the Shaw garden in Foochow or at Pagoda Anchorage. One visit to Japan was in the summer of 1915, when a group photograph was taken showing my mother and her sisters, Julia and Ceci (Basil's mother), dressed in kimonos standing behind a bench at the end of which Grandmother sat like a matriarch. On the bench and around it were Japanese women and children; in front was a tiny tot, the only one in Western clothes: me, sucking my thumb.

Even three years after her marriage, my mother was still close enough to her mother to go on this family vacation to Japan. She must have known about Grandmother's background, her family, and where she came from, for the Japanese women and children on and around the bench and the youth who was holding me up for the camera must have been relatives—they must have been Grandmother's Japanese family. Yet Mother never said a word about it, never spoke to me of my grandmother. Perhaps the incident in the Peking club slowly burned in her subconscious and she came to realize that, in the higher ranks of colonial society in China and Western society elsewhere, this was not a subject to be raised, and so she put her mother, my grandmother, out of her mind.

Did O'Sea come from Nagasaki? Frederick William said so and cousin Lewis heard that his father, Uncle G, had been in Nagasaki in the 1930s. "Perhaps he was looking for his roots," which would have been a difficult task then and impossible now as the city was destroyed by an atomic bomb in 1945. It is likely that O'Sea came from the southern island of Kyushu, which is the closest part of Japan to China and which has produced most of the Japanese travellers and emigrants; Nagasaki is the main port of Kyushu. However, Julia said the place she remembered best in their visits to Japan was "Myabashi" (probably Myazacki), where the wisteria and laburnums hang down to the ground with enormous flowers, "each blossom the size of an egg." Myazacki is a seaside resort on Kyushu and she spoke of it as if it were her mother's home.

What about O'Sea's parents? When my wife and I visited Macau in 1981 for Aunty J's hundredth birthday, she told me that Grandmother came from a samurai family. Julia was vague about where Grandmother was born, but she said she was brought up in Tokyo. As Grandmother was twenty-two years old when she married in 1879, she would have been born in 1857, three years after Admiral Perry forced open Japan and ten years before the Meiji restoration. It was a time of upheaval and trouble, a break with the closed society of the past and the beginning of the modernization of Japan. Sam Shaw recalled that the destruction of the samurai system had meant that "a lot of feudal retainers had lost their privileges" and would have had to look for new sources of employment and income. However, his brother Lewis was skeptical. "It was unlikely," he wrote, "that a well-born girl would have been allowed to leave Japan at that time." And, he asked, if she were of samurai stock, why did she not say so on the marriage certificate? However, if she was so shy that she did not correct the British consul's spelling of her surname, she would hardly be expected to inform him that her father belonged to the samurai class.

How did Captain Shaw meet O'Sea? It was through her brother, Julia said: the brother was a merchant whose business was in Formosa (now Taiwan). Since there was no direct connection between Japan and Formosa in those days, or even between Shanghai and Formosa, he came to Foochow and got a junk to take him to the island. He did this regularly and got to know Captain Shaw; he even stayed with him in his house by the Sung Dynasty pagoda. On one of his trips, he remarked that Captain Shaw must be lonely without a wife and that he had a pretty younger sister. He would bring her the next time he came. "You marry her," Julia quoted him as saying, and added, "I don't know whether my father laughingly said, Yes or No." But the brother was serious and brought her.

As Aunty J said, my grandfather "had to marry her as she had left Japan for that purpose" and it "would have been a terrible disgrace for her to return to Japan unwed when it was known that that was her reason for going with her brother." There was another reason which Julia never mentioned and that is that she was pregnant. An examination of marriage and birth certificates showed that she had been living with Captain Shaw as his concubine for months before the civil ceremony. Even though he was an adventurer and hard-bitten trader who had gone to sea at the age of thirteen, my grandfather had acquired a moral code through his upbringing and his association with the Masonic Order. He would do the honourable thing and marry his pretty little paramour, although he did leave it rather late: that might have been because she was inarticulate and afraid to tell him until it became all too apparent.

As a businessman, O'Sea's brother had to speak English, and O'Sea must have had a smattering of schoolgirl English; Captain Shaw certainly spoke no Japanese. Ichiro Kawasaki notes that the Japanese are poor linguists: "The average Japanese may study English for years on end but somehow does not succeed in acquiring any fluency in speaking the language." However, from what I was told, my grandmother spoke English well. She could also write in English, and my cousin Lewis got a letter from her while he was at Cambridge University; she had a crabbed hand, he said, which was difficult to read. But when she spoke, Julia said, "you couldn't hear her unless you got very close."

That O'Sea's brother should have arranged this liaison and marriage was not remarkable. Practically all marriages were arranged in Japan and the rest of the Orient at that time, and her brother was acting as head of the family, due probably to the death of her father. Julia saw the brother, her uncle, once when he visited their home at Pagoda Anchorage, and she remembered that he wore Japanese clothes with wide sleeves and "a bowler hat with a flat rather than a round top." He brought dried Japanese persimmons tied with straw and hung them on the hat rack. Julia was very small, "about two feet tall," and her recollection was of looking up and seeing these dried fruit hanging there; she did not know who ate them. At least, this recollection seem to show that the brother did not abandon his sister after successfully arranging her marriage, as some of his compatriots might have done, but visited her in her new home.

During the Meiji restoration, which covered the decade after 1868, there was a rush to acquire the industrial techniques and scientific skills that made the Western powers so dominant. People, mostly men, dressed in Western-style clothing, and the Japanese upper classes set up clubs like those in the colonies. They even indulged in Western ballroom dancing. However, this craze to copy all things Western did not bring about any real change in society and the family, which remained authoritarian and patriarchal. When I visited Japan in 1993 I was struck by how disciplined and orderly the people were. Social historian Ichiro Kawasaki said that the Japanese had a "taste for some kind of regimentation and formal order (such as the mass calisthenics before the day's work), thereby fulfilling the Japanese yearning to 'belong'." The basic strength of Japanese society would be the way that children were brought up: educated, uniformed, and obedient.

The role of a woman was seen as that of a wife and mother, and a newly married woman was expected to serve her husband and his family. Alan Booth, a recent American visitor to Japan who stayed with a Japanese family, noted the way the young wife was ordered about by the husband and even more harshly by the mother-in-law, who treated her as a servant. She made no complaints, the visitor said, and "rushed about smiling uncertainly." Later that night, when everyone had gone to bed, the American heard a clatter in the kitchen where the young wife was washing up and laying the dishes for breakfast. This was by no means an extreme case, and it was probably typical of what happened when my grandmother was a girl. In the feudal family, a daughter was treated as a drudge, and would face the same fate when she married. At that time, marriage was seen not as a union of individuals but of families. A *Nakado*, or go-between, was widely used to arrange suitable marriages, and the Nakado always saw to it that the marriage would be a link between families of similar social status.

Why then did her brother bring his younger sister across the sea to Foochow? With her upbringing, O'Sea would have had to comply, but what was the reason for his action, which must have been extraordinary even then? There is not a hint, not a word of explanation. All that we have is my Aunty J's assertion that it occurred.

Perhaps O'Sea's family had fallen on hard times and could not afford the large dowry that would have been expected for a suitable Japanese marriage. Since her brother acted as head of the family, the father must have died; perhaps he left heavy debts. Some sort of financial disaster must have struck this middle-class family, which had seen that the children had a good education. All of this might have occurred if O'Sea had belonged to a samurai family—and one of her father's possible surnames was Matsurato, a ruling clan under the Tokugawa Shogunate in Kyushu. While Matsamura sounds closer to Matson Mullah, Matsurato might have been what Grandmother said, as she likely would have spoken softly, the way Japanese women deferred to authority.

The fact that she arrived in Foochow to become a concubine, although her brother had promised marriage, must have masked a tragedy. After Commodore Perry brought an end to Japanese isolation and the Americans used the spectre of the Opium Wars in China to force a trade treaty on Japan, the old order began to crumble. There were savage anti-foreign riots. The British bombarded Kagoshima, and a combined Western flotilla silenced the batteries at Shimonoseki, opening the straits and demonstrating the superiority of Western gunners. By the mid 1860s, there was civil war between the Shogunate and the more modern forces of the emperor, and many samurai were killed or beheaded. It is possible that O'Sea's father was executed or committed ritual suicide. His family would have been ruined. The final dissolution of the samurai class was carried out between 1873 and 1876, and it was in 1877 or thereabouts that Grandmother was brought to Pagoda Anchorage.

So O'Sea moved into the old widower's house, the house built so close to the Sung Dynasty pagoda that it seemed almost part of it. She was alone, cut off from relatives, Japan, and all things Japanese. Grandmother must have found the house with its wide verandahs and high ceilings alarmingly large, but there were servants and she ran the household well, much better than it had ever been run before. She was brought up to be a perfect wife. Grandfather must have been pleased (although I doubt if he ever complimented her, because that was not expected). Every year and a half she had a child, eight altogether: five boys and three girls. George, Uncle G, the first-born, went to work at age thirteen, as his father had done, and became a very rich man. So rich that his younger brothers, Henry Lees, Frederick William, and Robert Edward, were in his employ; Robert worked as an engineer on one of George's ships. George was as much of an autocrat as his Victorian father. He sent his youngest brother, Charles Leonard (known as Leo) to Bedford School, a British public school, but when Leo did not become the engineer George wanted him to be, he cut him off without a penny.

By order of Captain Shaw, no Japanese was ever spoken in the house and my grandmother, now known as Ellen, never mentioned her family or her home. She adapted herself to Grandfather, became his alter-ego, and remained such after his death. My cousin Lewis said that she was opposed to his father marrying a Japanese woman, solely on racial grounds. But Grandmother would have done the same if she had been married to a fellow countryman. She was brought up to become part of her husband's family, at all times, even after death, one of his kinsmen.

(Only once did Ellen O'Sea break the rules and speak of Japan and her family in an indirect way. She must have been exasperated with the conduct of her daughter. It was such an unusual outburst that Julia, who could not recall any other remark that her mother had made, remembered it word for word. Aunty J must have been a tomboy as a child, climbing trees and chasing and rampaging around with her brothers in the garden. Her mother admonished her and then said: "If you had gone to Japan when you were a baby, you would be betrothed, at my sister's request, to the baby of the head of my family, and you would be sitting on a pile of silk cushions instead of running around here and fighting with your brothers.")

While she remained loyal to Captain Shaw's credo, Ellen did return to Japan after his death in 1908. The ties of home were always present, but she had suppressed them all those years. It must have been an aching void, but she did not let anyone know how she longed for her country and people. Her duty was to honour, respect, and obey her husband, and this she did. She took her daughters with her on annual trips to Japan; there is no report that her sons ever accompanied her on her visits to Japan.

It must have been a lonely life for Ellen O'Sea at Pagoda Anchorage, but her eldest daughter, Julia, dismissed the thought, saying Ellen was too busy having children and running the large house, the former British consulate, overlooking the deep-water harbour. There were a lot of servants. Each of the infants had an amah. Besides the house servants, there were gardeners—the Shaws grew most of their vegetables—and a night watchman whom the children used to tease. (He had a chair by the verandah where he would snooze and "we would wait till we heard him snoring," Aunty J recounted, "and poke him with a wire or a stick, and he would think it was a mosquito biting him and would jump up.") On his patrols around the house, the watchman carried a large bamboo pole which he would knock on the ground, knock, knock, knock, to show he was on the job. The Chinese living nearby used to listen to the watchman making his rounds and knew by his knocking when it was time to get up.

Perhaps the most important servant was the cook. Julia told Hong Kong Radio about the cook's work in the week before Christmas. The kitchen was on the side of the house and had a big, wood-burning brick stove. The cook would light the fire and let it burn till the wood became charcoal; he would put the flames out with a wet broom, shove a roast in the hot embers, and shut the door. "He knew to take it out in just so many minutes, baste it, and put it in again and so on," recounted Julia. The roast could not have been better done. Julia said that the old cook was master in the kitchen and would not let the youngsters in; in fact, he asked for and got a small gate to keep them out. "He was a very good old man; he was so clean, after lunch every day, he washed the kitchen floor."

The cook, the highest paid servant, was paid seven dollars a month. (This was dollar Mex, the equivalent of half a US dollar.) The tailor, who worked in the house and made all their clothes except for Grandfather's, was an independent operator and got as much as ten dollars a month. For the stylish dresses of the day (needless to say, Grandmother wore English clothes), he used Butterick or Dilineator paper patterns that the family

✦ *The Shaw family in 1890; my mother, Mary, is on her father's knee,*
Julia (my Aunty J) is at left, and George (my Uncle G)
is between his mother and father

ordered from Shanghai. It was beneath the tailor's dignity to do any darn-
ing or mending: that was an amah's work. Firewood and food were cheap:
the cook could get one hundred bundles of wood for a dollar, ninety to
one hundred eggs for a dollar. The milk had to be boiled although it was
fresh from the two cows milked at the garden gate every morning. Other
stores came in bulk—sugar and flour in one-hundred-pound bags, pota-
toes in sacks—from the merchant ships plying the China coast which
would call regularly twice a week at Pagoda Anchorage.

Family life was lived as if they were in the old country, and in this the
Shaws were no different from any of the other British or Europeans in
Foochow, or anywhere else the Empire reached. They made their own
decorations for the Christmas tree, they hung coloured paper chains
across the room, they had stockings for Santa Claus, and Julia even
remembered that the Christmas crackers were "Tom Smith crackers

imported from England." They had regular British meals; they never ate Chinese food, let alone Japanese food. Her brothers and sisters picked up Chinese from the servants' children but never spoke it in the house—at least never in the presence of Grandfather.

However, Aunty J denied that he was very strict. "He wanted us to speak English only," she said, but when asked what words meant or their spelling, the old sea captain would say, "Don't ask me. I had no education. I left home when I was thirteen." Yet Captain Shaw had a very neat, almost copperplate, hand, as his letters show, and was well-read. He might not have been very religious but he accepted the morals and precepts of the Christian church and insisted that his family live by them. Julia recalled, "My father was very careful to see that we said our prayers at night." Among my mother's papers was a yellowing foolscap sheet on which Captain Shaw had written down verses, philosophical musings, or as he put it, "S.L.S. thoughts at sea." There was no date although he signed it as Resident Marine Surveyor, Pagoda Anchorage, Foochow, which meant that it was written after 1868. One verse I felt was exemplary of his thoughts:

For weal or woe in calm or strife
Let "Truth" prevail throughout thy life
What fate imposes man must needs abide
It boots not to resist both wind and tide.

There was an incident Julia recalled as if it had happened yesterday: the French bombardment of Pagoda Anchorage. She was three years old at the time, as the bombardment occurred in 1884. The French had completed their investment of Indo-China the year before with the Treaty of Hue, Vietnam, one of the "unequal treaties" forced on the impotent Manchu court, which effectively ended Chinese suzerainty. The Chinese had signed a convention to restore normal relations, but there was what was described in history as a "misunderstanding" which led to a French defeat on the Tonkin border with China. In retaliation, French warships attacked Foochow, shelled and destroyed, it was said, the newly built arsenal, and bombarded Pagoda Anchorage.

The British consulate had advance warning of this foray because it ordered all foreign residents and their personal servants to the relative safety of the Customs' quarters, a big building on the waterfront. Julia spoke of being in a large room, perhaps the library, when "I saw a cannon ball come through the door and just brush past my brother's [Henry Lees] ear." He was a little fellow, two years old, and he felt the heat of the missile but was not hurt. Her father was having a rest, lying on a bed in a room on the second floor; he "always wore red socks in the summer or winter," Julia said. The next thing she remembered was that he came down the stairs and cried out, "Who put up that flag [the Chinese Customs flag]?" Someone said it was one of the English Customs officers, and Captain Shaw ordered it hauled down. A Chinese boatman, according to Julia, volunteered and when he had taken it down, the bombardment stopped. (Grandfather, with his long experience as a merchant captain in the Far East, had had the odd run-in with rival French traders and knew their temper. They would regard raising the Chinese flag above the Customs building as a provocation.)

In all the confusion, the baby went missing and Ellen O'Sea was desperately looking around, not knowing what had happened to him. The last she could recall was that the amah had taken him; perhaps the amah had taken him outside. So a number of the men went out on the hill behind the Customs building to search for him but found nothing. Ellen O'Sea was weeping and Captain Shaw "was in an awful state; he didn't know what to do." At about six o'clock that evening, the search party went out again. A Customs official, a tide waiter—Julia even remembered his name, F.H. Simpson—heard a baby crying and found the infant in a hole, an abandoned Chinese grave, one of many on the hillside.

What had happened was that the amah had taken the baby in her arms out on the hillside. When the bombardment started, she became so frightened that she ran and, in a panic to get away from the cannonballs, threw the child into the open grave. The amah was never seen again. "It was fortunate," Julia said, "that with all the noise of the bombardment, there were no dogs around; otherwise the baby would have been eaten." There were usually many scavenger dogs roaming the hills around Pagoda Anchorage, the hills that were pockmarked with graves. The infant must have been stunned when he was thrown into the hole: the bombardment started at nine o'clock in the morning, and no sound, no crying was heard till six that evening. The baby, Grandmother's fourth child and third son, Willie, was howling when he was brought in. He was very hungry but otherwise unhurt.

I HAVE A FAMILY PORTRAIT of Grandmother and Grandfather and six of their eight children. It must have been taken around 1890, as my mother, sitting on her father's lap, seems to be about five years old. Robert, the youngest of the children, is leaning against his mother, Ellen O'Sea, who looks tired and somewhat overwhelmed. Next to her, Captain Samuel Lewis Shaw appeared proud and confident; he would have been about seventy yet seemed to be in his prime. A big man with a great grey beard turning white, he is sitting forward, with his eyes on the future. He looks like God—or at least Hollywood's vision of God—and he also behaved like God, as most Victorian fathers were expected to behave.

In this photograph, he does not look as though he had ever had any qualms about marrying a Japanese woman. Yet he had been brought up in the ethos of empire, from the racial superiority of the officers of the East Indiamen, the Royal Navy and the coastal or country ships he had commanded, to the whites-only membership of colonial society and its clubs, and even the Masonic Order. He knew the rules and had lived by them for more than forty years. He must have heard of someone of his own rank who had married or was living with an Indian or Malayan woman and was spoken of contemptuously as having "gone native."

At Weihsien (Weixian), the Japanese internment camp in China for foreigners during the Second World War, there was one Eurasian family. The father had gone out from Britain as a missionary to the interior of China and in middle age had married a Chinese woman who had borne him four children. By the account of his peers, he had "gone native," wearing Chinese clothes, eating Chinese food, and speaking Chinese. At the camp, he and his small family were shunned by his fellow missionaries and lived the same sort of peasant life in one corner of the community they had done before being interned.

It would have made no difference if he had married a Manchu princess, as one Britisher did; he and his family would have been looked down on in the same way. Japanese social historian Ichiro Kawasaki writes that he knew a retired English merchant captain who lived in Yokohama and married a Japanese woman who came from a very respectable Japanese family: "This British friend told me that just because his wife was Japanese he was ostracized by the local British community and was obliged to live a rather solitary life outside his own community."

One can only surmise on why Grandfather broke the rules of colonial society by consorting with an Oriental woman. He had got tired of living alone and taken a mistress; perhaps, he fell in love with her. Most likely, it was his upbringing: he was an honorable man and could do nothing less than marry the girl. Then, he might have felt that he could get away from any opprobrium because he lived in a small outpost. His house, the former British consulate, was on top of a hill beside the Sung Dynasty pagoda, and dominated Pagoda Anchorage. As long as the Shaws lived there, they were treated with the same respect as the families of the British officials and the European merchants in Foochow.

The Shaw children were never allowed outside the gate of their large house: as Julia recalled, "we were never allowed to mix with the natives at all." This was a rule that applied to all British and other European children in most of colonial China, however; the only possible exception might have been Shanghai. (This sort of discrimination, where children of the British rulers were kept confined to their quarters and away from the natives and their children, occurred in most parts of the Empire.) The young Shaws played cowboys and Indians with the servants' children (the servants' children always being the "Indians") and "hide and seek" in the old consulate prison cells that were the servants' quarters. It was a restricted upbringing and, as Julia said, without being allowed out, they had to make their own fun.

COLONIAL LIFE

in CHINA, 1906

5

WHEN MY FATHER, Walter Arthur Stursberg, came to Foochow in February 1907, the Shaws had left the house beside the Sung Dynasty pagoda for a handsome Regency-style villa in the foreign suburb of Nantai. Captain Samuel Lewis Shaw was eighty-five years old and growing weak, and the family felt it would be wise to move into town where there would be much better medical facilities than there were in the small community of Mowi (the Chinese name for Pagoda Anchorage). The only local doctor was a quack, a ship's engineer who had had some medical training. The eldest son, George, my Uncle G, who was in his mid twenties and already a successful businessman, had become de facto head of the family. He bought the house and named it Terenure after his Irish ancestor's estate outside Dublin.

My mother, Mary Ellen Shaw, was delighted at the move into town. When she was not at the convent school in Shanghai but back home at Pagoda Anchorage, she complained that she was lonely, there was nobody there, and nothing to do. It was all right when they were kids, haring around the orange trees in the garden, climbing the pagoda, and playing with the servants' children, but such amusements were not for teenagers who found life cooped up in the house overlooking the anchorage to be achingly dull. As Julia said, dances were "few and very far between." There would be dances at the Customs quarters when the British and foreign gunboats came in. Julia remembered the German gunboats as being "very nice … The captain would send the ship's band to the Customs," she said, "and there would be a dance and the German officers would dance with us."

There was so much more to do in Foochow, so many more parties and dances, and some kind of entertainment every week, such as amateur dramatics, recitals, magic lantern shows, and race meetings. The favourite sport was tennis, and some of the big houses had tennis courts, which were a bit bumpy and not always of standard size. However, what was most fun were picnics to the beautiful countryside around Foochow, to the bamboo forests and the famous Buddhist monastery on Mount Kushan.

George must have been relieved with the move as it provided his sisters with interests and activities that were lacking in the relative isolation of Pagoda Anchorage. For some years, Uncle G had had a very good position with the Gwendoline Mine in Korea, and, like the dutiful family man he was, had been paying for Mary and Ceci's tuition at the Roman Catholic convent of St. Joseph in Shanghai.

He was, therefore, astonished and horrified to learn that my mother had expressed the wish of becoming a nun. In a stern letter dated August 16, 1904 he accused Mary of being wicked and deceitful: "It was very wrong of you to go on writing to me and not telling me, or even hinting to me, that your one desire appears to be to give us all up, all your dear brothers and sisters, and join that Catholic faith which is the ruin of many millions of people." George said that she was not to correspond with the Sisters at the convent.

"I have written to the convent already," he went on, "telling them you will not return and that I would let them know if Ceci is to go back. Remember I feel very strongly on this course of action, and I mean every word I say. I hope, as I have said, that there is a letter of confession on the way from you and that you will promise to be a Protestant as you have been brought up to be one." Apparently, George got this letter of confession and contrition, and that was the end of the matter.

Uncle G had become the main financial support of the Shaw family due to the failure of a bank in India. Grandfather had dealt with this bank since his earliest days in the Far East, and its collapse was a terrible blow. It must have occurred around the turn of the century. Frederick William remembered that "Mother was crying and Papa was very upset when he got the news that the bank in India where he had all of his funds had gone fut, closed its doors, owing lots of money and there was no chance of his getting a cent back." Fortunately, George, although not much more than twenty years old, was on his way to making a great deal of money as a businessman.

My father had come to China in 1906 to join the Chinese Maritime Customs. He was nineteen years old, a good-looking young man of above-average height who had lived at home and had led a quiet, unadventurous life until he succumbed, as many did, to the lure of the Orient and its golden prospects. He had a clerk's job in the British Post Office with limited prospect of advancement, and when his Aunt Polly, his mother's elder sister, took him to tea with friends who had been to China and spoke of the opportunities there, he was all agog. He was given the name of a man in the Chinese Customs, and after writing to him and being assured of employment, decided to take the big gamble. His father put up thirty pounds for a third-class passage on the Nord-deutcher Lloyd liner *Prinz Heinrich*. As the youngest of nine children, he was his mother's favourite and there were tearful farewells when he left Southampton on March 21, 1906.

Arthur Stursberg (he never used his first name) reached Shanghai at the end of April and almost immediately got a job with the Chinese Customs as a uniformed tide waiter. He was assigned to the North Barrier on Soochow Creek, which was in the country outside Shanghai. The work there consisted of checking the cargoes coming down from the interior of China, which could consist of silk cocoons, straw braid, raw cotton, and raw hides, and also the "trains" of barges and passenger boats, hauled by steam tugs, going both up and down river. Sometimes at the end of one of these trains would be a handsome, newly painted, foreign houseboat—a glamorous sight that spoke to him of the good life, so different from his dull and rather menial job as a tide-waiter. On his visits to Shanghai he found that the Customs was divided between an indoor staff and an outdoor staff, and he was on the outdoor staff "where one did not have to possess any outstanding qualifications." The officers were in the indoor staff; the other ranks were in the outdoor staff and wore uniforms and manned the barriers and other stations.

There were only my father and an older man at the North Barrier and when the latter was transferred, he was replaced by a hardy Scot named Campbell who had the ominous habit of taking a daily dip in Soochow Creek. Dad, "nothing loth," followed suit for, as he said, the countryside where they were presented a pleasant picture of cultivated fields on both sides of the waterway, reminding him of the Norfolk Broads—"and who would hesitate about bathing in the Norfolk Broads?" However, Soochow Creek was polluted and served as a sewer for the many Chinese boat people.

Some days later, Arthur collapsed while at work and was rushed to a Shanghai hospital where he was diagnosed as having typhoid fever. He became unconscious and had grinding nightmares, one of which was so vivid that he remembered it to his dying days. He was lying in a deck chair watching two figures in full suits of armour, who had evidently been jousting as one of them lay on the ground, his battered casque beside him. He thought one of the knights must have been his legendary namesake. At any rate, the triumphant knight spoke of various things, including the efficacy of prayer, and his voice trailed off and turned into that of a woman's. My father woke to find a nun on her knees praying for the sick in the ward.

He was lucky to survive, as so many young Europeans of his age, including a fellow he knew, died from typhoid, cholera, typhus, and other endemic diseases soon after they arrived in China. What ever happened to Campbell? Arthur must have wondered about this, but he made no reference to it in his memoirs. When he recovered, and there was a long relaxed period of convalescence in hospital during which he could think about his future, he decided that he did not want to continue in the outdoor Customs staff. After his illness, he was assigned to the Shanghai office where he heard there was a relatively new branch of the Customs service that had charge of postal affairs. He had worked in the London General Post Office—in fact, it was the last job he had before setting sail for China. So he screwed up his courage and wrote to Sir Robert Hart, the Inspector General of the Chinese Customs, the great empire builder and founder of British suzerainty in China, and asked for a transfer to the postal service.

It was a climactic move that set the course of his future life. A week or two after he had applied for a transfer, Dad was thrilled to receive word that he had been appointed Assistant Postal Officer C at Foochow and ordered to proceed there forthwith. This was a fateful decision on the part of the powers-that-be because Arthur could have been sent to one or another of a score or more of postal districts, and an extraordinary one too since it was known that Sir Robert Hart had a high regard for Foochow and spoke of it as "the garden of China."

So why did the Inspector General give this newcomer, this unknown young Englishman with a German name, such a plum posting? The reason might have been that Arthur must have mentioned, in his application, that his last duties with the London Post Office were in its library. The secretariat in Peking, always anxious to cooperate with local authorities, had received a request from Foochow for an English teacher; they must have considered that if this youthful applicant, of whom they had no knowledge, had worked in a library he must be fairly well educated and could serve as an English teacher as well as begin his career with the post office.

At the beginning of February 1907, Dad set sail for Foochow on board one of the steamers that plied the China coast. Although these steamers had Chinese names, they were officered entirely by Europeans, mostly British with Scots usually running the engine rooms, and belonged to companies such as Jardine Matheson, Butterfield and Swire, and Gibb Livingstone; the crews, deckhands, waiters, and stewards, of course, were Chinese. Young Arthur enjoyed the luxury of a two-berth cabin and the fine dining room on the *Hsin-yu*, which was in sharp contrast to the third-class passage from Southampton to Shanghai on the *Prinz Heinrich*. To add to the glamour of this coastal trip, his cabin mate turned out to be a prince, Prince Rospigliosi, a pleasant young Italian with a papal title who was a junior officer in the Customs and, like himself, being transferred to Foochow.

When he arrived, Stursberg was met by two fellow postal workers: an Irishman, James Greenfield, and a German, Friedl Ahrendts. First names were seldom used in those days, and so it was Greenfield or Ahrendts; they soon became good friends. Arthur put up at Brockett's, a small foreign hotel which was no more than a guest house, and he recalled that he had an argument with Brockett about the charges. Brockett wanted to charge him the full rate but he pleaded poverty, saying that the Post Office only allowed him a certain amount, and he got a lower rate. Actually, he was very well off for a twenty-year-old starting a new career; this was because one of the high schools paid him $100 a month for teaching English, and the other $80 a month, and with his postal salary of $120 a month, he was, as he said, "passing rich on $300 per month." (Remember that these were dollars Mex and each worth half an American dollar.)

After work, Father would go around to see Greenfield and Ahrendts who had rooms not far from Brockett's and the main post office. He learned a lot from his friends about life in Foochow as it affected the members of the foreign community, and about postal work and his new boss, Mr. Donovan. He also had his first drink of Scotch and soda, and wondered what his teetotalling parents would think when he reported this in his weekly letter. "I found," he wrote, "that they were both [Ahrendts and Greenfield] ardent believers in the efficacy of whiskey as a prophylactic in a country where the hazard of imbibing unknown water was great." Later he was to find that most foreigners, vide Europeans, were steadfast believers in the prophylaxis theory as far as whiskey was concerned. He might have added that this was the creed of the Empire. (His parents did not seem to be as upset about his falling off the wagon as one of his sisters-in-law, the wife of an older brother, Dr. Otto Stursberg, who was a missionary in India.)

It was through his friends that young Arthur Stursberg met Mary Shaw. Ahrendts was engaged to an Irish governess, Minnie Wright, in the household of a Frenchman, Monsieur Veitch, whose job was recruiting

* *Terenure, the Shaw home in Foochow, ca. 1907; my mother, Mary, is on the steps*

and collecting coolies (indentured Chinese labourers) for shipment abroad. (This business had gone on for a long time—it was such indentured Chinese labourers who helped to build the Canadian Pacific Railway.) The Veitches had an imposing house on a promontory and from it a long flight of steps led down to the Chinese city below. When they first went around, Miss Wright was away in Shanghai acquiring her trousseau, and Julia Shaw was acting as a temporary governess to the Veitches' three small boys. Madame Veitch was away in France. She was a very beautiful woman and, according to local gossip, the French consul in Foochow, who happened to be the poet Paul Claudel, was very keen on her. At any rate, Julia said her younger sister, Mary, had accompanied Minnie on her trousseau-buying mission and would be back soon.

One thing led to another, and the new postal officer of the lowest grade got to know the Shaw family and went to live at Terenure. When he was appointed, he had been told accommodation would be found for him, and after a couple of weeks at Brockett's Hotel, he was given quarters in a Chinese house in the city near the schools where he was teaching English. "I didn't like it very much," he said, as the house had hardly any furniture, was dusty and dirty, and had most primitive toilet facilities. He was, therefore, delighted when the Shaws offered him room and board as a paying guest, and he accepted with alacrity.

The foreign firms in Foochow, like the factories of old, were close together on the waterfront. These were the local branches of the great hongs and other enterprises as well as the Customs headquarters and the Post Office. A street led from these city buildings to Nantai; it was known as "Piccadilly" and was full of Chinese shops. It was "rather noisy and dirty," according to my father, but once "you got through it, you came to a very nice place of small parks" and European houses. There were the mansions of the taipans, and of the Customs' commissioner and the Postal commissioner, and the fine consular residences; but also the more modest homes of lesser officials and merchants and of the missionaries. On the high ground stood the Foochow Club and nearby a Masonic lodge, the small Anglican Church, as well as a larger Presbyterian Church, and the little British cemetery. "Ultimately," Dad said, "you came to Terenure which was on the side of a hill, known as 'One Tree Hill'."

I never knew Terenure in its prime and can only judge it from a photograph that my father took in 1907. There is my mother before she was married in full Edwardian bloom, with a long white dress and bouffant hairdo, standing on the steps leading to the verandah with its high white arches and the shuttered windows of the upper floor, with some of the jalousies open. What struck me were the flowers: they were everywhere, in pots on the steps and along the railings of the verandah, in the border beds, and even in hanging baskets. Terenure's garden was small as gardens went in Nantai but it was a blossomy splendour of flowers and fruit trees with a well at one end.

The house was quite large, and off the entrance hall was a wide staircase. The drawing room had French doors that led on to the verandah and the garden; the dining room was at the back next to the kitchen, which was in an adjoining building that was also the servants' quarters. Captain Shaw and Ellen O'Sea had a bedroom downstairs, while there were four bedrooms and a couple of bathrooms upstairs. Of the children, only Julia, Mary, and Willie were at Terenure. George had his own business in Antung, Manchuria. Henry and Robert were working in Shanghai, and Ceci was at a convent school in the French Concession, while Leo was at an English public school.

While Arthur was pleased with his quarters in this warm, friendly family home, Terenure was quite far from his workplaces, the Post Office and the schools. As a result of spending half his time teaching at the Chinese schools, he got the nickname "Professor." That was the way he was known at the Shaws', and the Professor decided that he had to arrange transportation for himself. He was told that one of the senior postal clerks had a three-man wicker chair for sale, so he bought it and had it converted into a four-man chair. The newly arrived, lowly Assistant Postal Officer C did not realize that the four-man chair was above his rank; he thought it would be more comfortable.

There was no vehicular traffic to speak of in Foochow: the streets in the old walled city were little more than alleyways, and Piccadilly and the streets outside the city walls, where the foreign businesses had their offices, were not much wider. They could accommodate the odd cart, but the most popular form of passenger transport was the mediaeval sedan chair.

Two coolies carried a three-man chair and a third man would relieve one or other of them; when the changes were made, the passenger would be shaken up. But with a four-man chair, two coolies would be in front and two at the back; at a given signal, they would change shoulders, giving a much more restful motion. However, he found that he had to get uniforms for his chair coolies; the livery he chose was in the postal colors of blue and gold. At any rate, Arthur felt like a taipan on his three hundred dollars Mex a month. "It all added up," he said.

So off Arthur went of a morning, his chair coolies loping along. "If they were experienced carriers, there would be a nice swing to the ride," Dad said. "If not, it could be very unpleasant." All his chair coolies did was to take him to the city and bring him back; they had "a pretty lazy time." Passing a friend or an acquaintance while riding in a chair could be very awkward, and thus non-recognition became a standard practice. This was what was known as "sedan chair etiquette." If the person was walking, you would both look the other way. If he or she was in a chair, you would both put your heads down. A greeting meant that you had to stop, get out of the chair, raise your hat, and shake hands; so, to avoid all this folderol, you followed sedan chair etiquette and pretended not to see one another.

The chair coolies would arrive in the early morning, and they would squat and crack sunflower seeds and chat as they waited for the owner. Since Frederick William had a three-man chair there would be two chairs and seven coolies outside the gate of Terenure. Similar numbers of coolies would be outside most of the houses in Nantai as the taipans would have at least a couple of chairs, and even the missionaries had to have one: it was the only means of transportation. The chair coolies were part of the vast retinue of servants in the European suburb of Foochow, but despite their colorful livery, they were far below the cook and the Boy and the amah in the hierarchy of colonial society and did not have quarters in the houses as the indoor servants did. Instead, they trooped to work, together with the gardeners and other outdoor staff, swarms of them, up Piccadilly in the dawn to the high ground where the imperial masters lived, and back down again at nightfall.

Of all the servants at Terenure, the one best remembered was the head Boy or butler, who was known as Peacock because of the way he walked. He was almost the perfect servant: "a good butler, wonderful," according to my mother. He used to decorate the dining-room table, she said, with a beautiful array of flowers from the garden and kept the silverware, the vases and bowls, the flatware, the salt cellars and pepper pots like little pagodas, shining bright. (Chinese silver, with its distinctive embossed patterns of dragons, chrysanthemums, and bamboo, had become as popular with foreigners as the export china of an earlier age.) He folded the serviettes or table napkins in such intricate shapes as roses and birds and temples.

But Peacock had one fault: he would go on drinking bouts and as a result had lost some good jobs. It happened too in Terenure. The Shaws noticed that the level of whiskey and other liquors in the bottles was unaccountably going down. In the end, Willie put the bottles in a cupboard that could be kept locked. Nevertheless, there would be occasions when Peacock would, without any notice, be absent "for days," my mother said, adding, "he used to come back looking terrible but very mild, very quiet." The Shaws put up with this erratic behavior because they knew they could never get a better butler.

An assistant Boy served at the table and tried to fill in for Peacock when he was away on a binge, but there was no replacing him. No one could. He was such a dominant figure and the only servant who could be joshed. One of his duties was to wake up the paying guest. He would knock on the door: "Mr. Berg, time to get up." (It was Captain Shaw who had first called him "Mr. Berg.") There would be a muffled response but no reaction. After a short time, tap, tap, tap: "Mr. Berg, later now." The guest dragged himself out of bed, but by the time he reached the breakfast table he was fully awake and in such a cocksure mood as to try to be funny. "What kind of an egg, Mr. Berg?" "Oh," the young postal official said, "a chicken's egg." Peacock would shake his head and smile sadly.

Captain Shaw did not come to the breakfast table. After he got up in the morning, Julia said, his habit was to have "a large tumbler of A.S. Watson's soda water and a bottle of milk poured together." He would sit slowly drinking this in his bedroom, and in his last years it became his breakfast. Ellen O'Sea probably had her breakfast in the bedroom with Grandfather, as my father made no mention of her being at the breakfast table; in fact, he made no mention of her at all, as if my Japanese grandmother did not exist. It might have been due to young people being so self-centred, then as now, that they paid no attention to the older generation. Furthermore, Ellen O'Sea was so small—Aunty J said that her children towered over her—and so self-effacing that she was not noticed. (Which might have been what she wanted.)

By all accounts, my grandfather was a great storyteller and Julia was told that he was "one of the best whist players on the China Coast." This was because he had a very good memory: he could remember what cards were played, what was turned down, what was in one's hand, and what was left. In his last years, his memory was used in his reminiscences. According to the obituary in the Foochow *Daily Echo*, "He was intensely fond of talking about the good old days." Many of his friends, mostly old sea captains, used to visit him at the Pagoda Anchorage house and at Terenure. They would talk for hours about seafaring as it was when there were no lighthouses on the China coast and "there was nothing to guide them but common sense, second sense, and seamanship." On his eighty-sixth birthday, the writer of the obituary, who turned out to be Brockett, recalled leaving him "at nearly midnight sitting talking to his friends."

However, young Stursberg did not have any memorable conversation with Captain Shaw, at least none that he could recall sixty years later. Perhaps the old man could not relate to this twenty-year-old guest, although, according to my mother, he "thought the world of him." This admiration was not reciprocated. While he was too young and too polite to express any opinion then, my father was to say later that he thought the old man was very selfish and irresponsible in that he made no provision for his daughters. The latter was rather a harsh judgement as Grandfather had lost all his money in the failure of the Indian bank. Dad also doubted if Captain Shaw could have remained a member of the Foochow Club, even if he could have afforded it, because of having married a Japanese. It seemed to me that he was blaming my grandfather for the indignities that his beloved wife, my mother, suffered because of her mixed blood; and this feeling of outrage had remained with him all those years.

Captain Shaw used to sit on the verandah of Terenure, taking the sun. He was in declining health and spent much of his time in bed. He was carefully attended by his faithful wife, Ellen O'Sea. She seemed to know what he wanted before he asked: a pillow, a glass of water, to be helped up or to be moved out of the direct sunlight. Yet the old man was persuaded to go on a picnic, and that was the occasion that my father took the fine photograph of him. Grandfather is seated in a sedan chair that had been set down on a hillside; he has on a hat and is formally dressed as if going to a funeral—but that was the way they dressed to go to a picnic in those days. His white beard reaches down to the middle button of the waist-coat of his dark suit.

Picnicking was a joyous colonial pastime, and at Nantai it was indulged in with great éclat. The Chinese servants knew what to do: they filled hampers with cold collations, chickens and ducks, ham and cheese, and bottles of wine. It was quite a procession that set out from Terenure, what with the sedan chairs and the line of coolies carrying the hampers and cushions and rugs, and leading it all would be Peacock strutting along like a drum major. The ladies were dressed as if going to a garden party with parasols and large Edwardian hats. They rode the sedan chairs while the men, wearing tweedy suits and hats, usually walked. Another photograph of a picnic that my father took shows one gentleman in a dark suit and a bowler hat—one had to keep up appearances in the colonies, and casual clothing was considered the attire of workmen and the lower classes, if not the natives. Ellen, my Japanese grandmother, never went on a picnic—or, at least, she is not in any photographs of picnics that my father took. She likely stayed behind to look after my grandfather and the house. Ellen O'Sea was, above all, the housekeeper, and that was the way that she was regarded by the race-conscious colonial society in Foochow.

There were many places to visit in the beautiful countryside around Foochow. One was the ravine, a dry riverbed full of boulders and set between cool bamboo forests; another was a fairly steep climb to Kushan where there were Buddhist temples and a monastery. The Buddhist monks had set out a table and benches for visiting pilgrims, which were gratefully used by the colonial picnickers.

The most famous picnic was an al fresco tiffin given by the German consul, Herr Siemssen, known jocularly as "the Kaiser," to mark the end of the horse races. As the great tea port, which it no longer was, Foochow attracted a full count of consuls, including a Japanese consul. The race tiffin was held in the mountain resort of Kuliang, where a number of foreigners, including the German consul, had summer homes. It was a stag affair, and most of the male guests set off on foot to climb the steep path interspersed by innumerable flights of rock-hewn steps to the residence where, according to my father, who was one of the guests, there was a breathtaking view of Foochow and the mountains beyond. At the tiffin, as he put it, "a number of toasts were drunk in port wine." My mother's account is more direct: "they guzzled so much wine, they could hardly come down the hill." The mountainside was terraced with paddy fields which were dry at this time. "So on the way down," my father recalled, "the most agile of us took a more direct route by leaping down from one paddy field to the next." Of course, they admitted that their exuberance was probably due to the wine. "Happily, no one even sprained an ankle."

Dad's friends, Greenfield and Ahrendts, would go along on the picnics. When Greenfield was transferred to Hankow, he was replaced by a

Mr. Chapdelain. There is a picture of Chapdelain with the Shaw girls at one of these outings. Another picnicker was Shelley Brand, who was a Somerset Maugham character—at least, Maugham wrote about Brand in his book *On a Chinese Screen* (no name was mentioned but anonymity did not hide recognition). Brand had come out as a tea-taster, just at the time when Chinese tea was being replaced by tea from India and Ceylon. He tried his hand at being a merchant, an auctioneer, and a stockbroker, without much success, but he married a taipan's daughter and as a result was able to invest in a small hotel (really a guest house). It was the only other foreign hotel in Foochow beside Brockett's, and it was at Shelley Brand's hotel that Somerset Maugham stayed in 1920.

Brand was a short, portly figure with long, curly hair; according to Dad, he wore wide check trousers, a pea jacket, and a large sombrero hat. His greetings were sweeping gestures. He had a deep, resonant voice with which he declaimed rather than spoke. He confessed that he should have been an actor. "To be or not to be, that was the question," Maugham has him saying. "But me family, me family, dear boy, they would have died of the disgrace, and so I was exposed to the slings and arrows of outrageous fortune." My father said that Brand was fond of quoting poetry and remembered him one time reciting the whole of Tennyson's *Locksley Hall*:

> For I dipt into the future, far as human eye could see,
> Saw the vision of the world and all the wonder that would be;
> Saw the heavens fill with commerce, argosies of magic sails,
> Pilots of the purple twilight, dropping down with costly bales;
> Heard the heavens fill with shouting, and there rained a ghastly dew
> From the nations' airy navies grappling in the central blue ...

That was the passage that he let all the stops out of his vocal organ; the following was orated with less volume but as much dramatic emphasis:

> Till the war drum throbbed no longer, and the battle flags
>   were furled
> In the Parliament of Man, the Federation of the World.

It was at a concert that my father must have heard Shelley Brand recite the whole of *Locksley Hall*. There was usually entertainment of this sort almost every week at the Foochow Club or the Masonic Hall, and sometimes at one of the taipan's large houses. Amateur dramatics were very popular and, needless to say, Brand played a prominent role. The plays were mostly light drawing-room comedies of the period, long-forgotten farces, although attempts were made at more serious fare such as Barrie's *Admirable Crichton* and Stevenson's *Dr. Jekyll and Mr. Hyde*, and even Bernard Shaw's *Arms and the Man*, although the latter was considered to be very daring.

For an energetic young man like Stursberg, there were all sorts of sports: tennis was more of a social event, with tennis teas at one of the taipan's courts, but he could and did take part in team sports such as football and field hockey (he made no mention of cricket), played on a field in the middle of the race course. He was on the Foochow team, which had regular matches against squads from the visiting gunboats, and there seemed to be at all times one or more British gunboats at Pagoda Anchorage. While he made no reference to hunting or fishing when he was in Foochow, he did say in one of his first letters to Mary Shaw from his new posting in Yochow that he had gone out shooting "as usual" on Sunday: "I shot two duck and five teal but only recovered one duck and three teal."

After a blissful year and a half in Foochow, Arthur Stursberg, the Professor, began to realize that he was making little or no progress in his new career with the Chinese Post Office. He only worked half a day at his new job and, under the arrangement when he was appointed, spent the rest of the time teaching English at the two Chinese schools. Captain Shaw's death on June 8, 1908 seemed to jolt him into confronting reality—that and the fact that he had fallen in love with Mary Shaw. At any rate, he wrote to Peking that he would like to relinquish the lucrative school jobs and concentrate on postal work. His request was granted, and he was transferred to Yochow, a port on the Yangtse above Hankow.

This happened some weeks after the death of Captain Shaw. Actually, Shelley Brand, who did a spot of undertaking among the bits and pieces of jobs he had, looked after the laying out, and he called on the Professor, *aka* Arthur Stursberg, to help him wash the body. The colour bar was such that evidently a Chinese could not assist in the funeral preparations of a white man. This was a grim task for the young guest, who found that the old patriarch had quite a few bedsores. The burial was in the pretty little British cemetery which was not far from Terenure. It was a Masonic funeral, at Grandfather's specific request, and a young Anglican missionary, William Charles White, officiated. White was later to become Bishop of Honan, the great collector of Chinese art for the Royal Ontario Museum, Toronto, and a good friend of my father's, who got to know him well when he was Postal Commissioner of Honan.

6

PEKING DANCES

and the 1911 REVOLUTION

YOCHOW WAS 180 MILES ABOVE HANKOW (now part of Wuhan) at the confluence of the Yangtse and Hsiang rivers. The city itself was five miles up the Hsiang but the Customs compound was built on the bluff at the junction of the rivers. The substantial buildings of the Customs compound, surrounded by a brick wall, dominated the countryside and could be seen from miles. There was the palatial mansion for the Customs Commissioner, a similar though slightly smaller residence divided in two to provide semi-detached quarters for the Customs assistant and the harbour master, and the Customs House itself. All were two storeys high with wide verandahs, an architectural style favoured in the colonies. The compound was just above a Chinese fishing village where the Customs (i.e., the British) had jetties and other port facilities installed and where the river steamers called. The village became known as the Port of Yochow.

There were just seven foreigners in this large compound: Mr. and Mrs. Wakefield, the Customs Commissioner and his wife; Wilding, the Customs assistant; Gwynne, the harbour master; Haynes, a Customs examiner; a tide waiter; and the Postal officer. They were all British except for Haynes, who was American. The Port of Yochow was an isolated colonial outpost, the kind of closed society that young Arthur Stursberg, who had replaced Hungarian J. von Kompolthy, had never before experienced. "Ordinarily," he recalled, "the only Chinese with whom we came into contact were the Customs and Postal employees and our servants." Yet during his stay of nine months, there was never any discord.

As the new Postal officer, Arthur had quarters in the Customs House, but he was very pleased when he was invited to mess on a cost-sharing basis with Wilding. He felt sorry for Mrs. Wakefield "to be denied the companionship of even one other woman." There were other foreigners, missionaries, but they lived at Yochow city, some five miles away, which meant a long and troublesome journey in a sedan chair. Thus, little was seen of them, except for the medical missionary, Dr. Beam.

Social life was somewhat restricted, and the arrival of British or foreign gunboats—or, for that matter, any foreign visitor—was warmly welcomed. The Commissioner would usually give a dinner party, and, in the case of the naval officers, they would return the hospitality in their ship's ward room. In the absence of the inhibiting presence of female company, the younger fellows would resort to energetic parlour tricks like the one by a British consul who had stopped on his way up the Hsiang River to take up his post in Changsha: he climbed around the back of a dining chair without touching the floor.

When he first arrived in Yochow, Arthur was invited to play croquet on the lawn in front of the Commissioner's house; otherwise there was not much in the way of sports. He did go shooting every Sunday, as he told Mary Shaw, and his only other exercise was the picnics. While Mrs. Wakefield was carried in the Commissioner's sedan chair, the men would walk the several miles to a temple or Buddhist shrine. On one such excursion they were accompanied by the officers from the British gunboat *Snipe*.

Tragedy struck this isolated community when Haynes became seriously ill. Dr. Beam twice made the difficult journey from Yochow city to see him, and the second time decided that Haynes, who was in agony, should be taken down to the hospital in Hankow. Arthur was deputed to accompany him on the river steamer *Kian* (Jian) and was shown how to inject morphia; he did so twice during the night which, he said, "were the only times the poor fellow was free of pain." The steamer reached Hankow the next morning and Haynes was rushed to the hospital. Meanwhile, Arthur went ashore to see his friend Greenfield, whom he had visited some weeks before on the way up to Yochow to take up his new appointment.

That afternoon, he was stopped by an English man and ordered to return to the *Kian*. The steamer was being put in quarantine because Haynes had been diagnosed as having the pneumonic plague. The ship made for the outer harbour; the cabin that Haynes had occupied was fumigated, the bedclothes were burned, and Arthur washed himself in strong disinfectant. The dinner that night was a dismal affair, and the officers and the lone passenger fortified themselves with Scotch whisky. (The story of the quarantine would be recalled in detail because the captain of the Yangtse river steamer retired to Vancouver Island, where we were living, and every time he met my father, which was quite often, old Captain Torrible would remind him of the incident.)

However, the diagnosis turned out to be a false alarm and the *Kian* returned to the dock. The next afternoon Arthur disembarked. He arrived at Greenfield's quarters just in time to accompany him to the funeral of Haynes, who had died the day before. It was never clear what caused Haynes' death, although there was talk of blood poisoning. It is possible that the British authorities did not want to say how he died as it might cause alarm. They held a wake which lasted till 3:30 a.m. in the Russian Club. The next day, after attending to some chores, Stursberg and Greenfield took rickshaws to the race course, the centre of social activity in Hankow and a cool oasis in the humid heat. They had dinner, and then Arthur caught the *Kian* to return to his post.

Yochow proved to be a great training ground, as he was the only Postal officer and thus got to know every aspect of the work; he also took daily Chinese lessons. However, he had hardly settled back when transfers changed the makeup of this outpost. Wilding was the first to go—to Peking; he was replaced by two Customs assistants, Hyde, an American, and Muller, a German. Then Wakefield, the Commissioner, was moved to Changsha, and his job was taken by Kurosawa, the only Japanese of commissioner rank in the Customs service. The Wakefields were escorted from the residence to the jetty and the Customs boat that would take them up the Hsiang River to Changsha. My father took pictures of the procession, which was worthy of a viceroy; as the imperial representative, the Commissioner was really of that rank. First came the so-called cracker bearers who let off firecrackers, then an honour guard of Chinese soldiers from the nearby fort. Next came the official sedan chairs in which Mr. and Mrs. Wakefield were carried, followed by a squad of the settlement policemen and the Customs boatmen.

Stursberg himself was finally transferred to the Inspectorate General of the Post Office in Peking. He was very pleased and felt that his career was taking off, but he had to wait five weeks for his replacement, Caretti, an Italian.

It was a relatively short journey to Peking as there was a train from Hankow; it crossed the Hoang-ho (Huang-he), the Yellow River, on the way to the capital. Arthur, who had heard all about this great and sinister river, called "China's Sorrow" because of its devastating floods, sat up till midnight to witness the crossing. The train, he said, went "dead slow" over the mile-long bridge, "well illuminated by powerful overhead lights." He was met at the Peking Station by a couple of Postal colleagues, one of whom was a friend from Foochow days. It was typical of the manners of the Chinese Maritime Customs and the Post Office that they should see their officers going to a new post be met, shown every courtesy, and made to feel at home.

Arthur was put up in a small hotel on the edge of the Legation Quarter, the foreign enclave where the legations were located as well as the headquarters of the Chinese Customs and Post Office and the foreign banks. On three sides of the Legation Quarter was the *glacis*, a military term for an open space to provide a defence against an attack. The area had been cleared of buildings as a result of the Boxer uprising of 1900. The siege of the Peking Legations by the Boxers became one of those great colonial morality plays, like the death of Gordon at Khartoum or the relief of Ladysmith in the Boer War. My father recalled that a memorial service was held in St. Paul's Cathedral "for the foreigners massacred in Peking"; there had been sensational reporting to this effect which, as he said, "was not long in being proved false." There was no need for a glacis on the fourth side of the Legation Quarter since it was against a good defensive line, the south wall of the Tartar City, as that part of Peking was called.

It was with keen anticipation that Arthur Stursberg headed for his new job the day after he arrived in Peking. He crossed the northern glacis, entered the quarter through a portal between the Austrian and Italian legations, and walked down Marco Polo Road. On his right was the large headquarters building of the Customs and the French Legation, and on his left Rue Labrousse and the French Barracks, and Thomann Strasse and the German hospital. At the end of Marco Polo Street was Legation Street, the main thoroughfare in this fortified foreign settlement. (Another street was Morrison Street, named after the correspondent of the *Times* of London.) On the corner of Marco Polo and Legation streets was a single-storey brick building which housed the Inspectorate General of Posts; a little further along were the Jardine Matheson building, the Hong Kong Shanghai Bank, and other foreign banks and businesses. Beside these offices and the legations, the closely guarded enclave included some foreign residences, the compounds of high Customs and Postal officials, dining halls or messes, and the Peking Club, the centre of social activity.

When he arrived at the Inspectorate General of Posts, Arthur found he was to be Assistant Private Secretary to the Postal Secretary, Theophile Piry. Although the officers of the Customs and its offshoot the Postal service were of various European nationalities, with the British in the majority and the odd Japanese and Anglo-Indian, the head of the Post Office was always French. Theophile Piry was succeeded by H. Picard-Destelan. There was no protocol to this effect; it was more an understanding, a gesture, and it posed no threat to the British. In fact, the working languages of both the Customs and the Post Office were English and Chinese. The Chinese Maritime Customs was the first and most important imperial service as it was in charge of the country's credit and collected much of its revenue; the Post Office was just a branch, although it was soon to become a separate organization. The Inspector General of the Customs, or I.G., was always British.

Sir Robert Hart was the most famous Inspector General and indeed was the creator of the Chinese Customs service. As an empire builder,

Sir Robert could be said to rank with Sir Robert Clive, Lord Clive, the conqueror of India; Sir Stamford Raffles, the founder of Singapore; and Sir Frederick Lugard, later Baron Lugard, the architect and overlord of the African colonies. Hart, an Irishman who spent fifty-four years in China, became an advisor to the Manchu court at a time of chaos and disintegration. Besides suffering the humiliating debacle of the 1842 Opium War at the hands of the British, the Ching Emperor was faced with an internal revolt, the massive Taiping Rebellion, which had its roots in British and foreign contact.

Hung Hsu-chuan (Hong Xiuquan), a Cantonese teacher and mystic, was the instigator of the Taiping Rebellion. Although Hung had met an American Baptist missionary, he was mostly influenced, if not perverted, by Protestant tracts put out by a British mission; he came to believe he was the "younger brother of Christ." His Taiping creed, basically Christian and Protestant but tinged with Buddhist millennialism, forged the rebellious peasant masses into a fanatical fighting force. It was one of those moments in history when a seer of Hung's rabble-rousing ability could set off a conflagration that would envelop the whole of China. The rebels drove the demoralized Manchu armies out of the south and conquered the richest part of China, the Yangtse Valley. They took Nanking (Nanjing) in 1853. Hung made Nanking his capital and reigned there as Tien Wang, the "Heavenly King," for more than ten years.

At first, the British wondered whether the Taipings might be better rulers of China than the inept and corrupt Manchus. However, after the Second Opium War (1858–60), the occupation of Peking, and the burning of the Summer Palace, the emperor was in their hands and had given up more concessions and treaty ports. The British decided then that the rebels in Nanking, the "Christ Worshippers," were a troublesome lot and should be eliminated. The Manchu forces were reorganized, put under European officers, and led by a British major, Charles George Gordon. The "Ever Victorious Army," as it was called, was really a colonial force, a British-led Chinese Army, which was officered by British and other Europeans, comparable in a way to the British Indian Army. Nanking was retaken in 1864, and Hung's rule and his Heavenly Kingdom of Great Peace destroyed.

The Taiping insurrection was the greatest and bloodiest civil war in history. Twenty million people were killed, according to conservative estimates, and vast stretches of the country were laid waste; it took almost a century for some provinces to regain their populations. Yet this great uprising was the reason the British-run Chinese Maritime Customs was set up. The Manchu government officials had fled from the Taiping's ferocious onslaught, the Customs houses in Shanghai and other ports were abandoned, and in all the disruption and chaos, the British, French, and American consuls took charge of collecting duties and taxes "on behalf of Peking." This extraordinary *ad hoc* arrangement was supplanted by a colonial Customs service that was formally recognized in the 1858 Treaty of Tientsin, one of the "unequal treaties" and the one that, *inter alia*, legalized the importation of opium. Hart, who had been in charge from the beginning, was appointed Inspector General in 1863; by 1895 there were fully seven hundred British and other Westerners running the Chinese Maritime Customs.

At about the same time, the British took over the administration of the Salt Gabelle, or salt tax. Thus they had control of Peking's largest sources of revenue, leaving the Manchu Court with only the land tax, which it had to share with the provinces and municipalities, and other minor levies. The British maintained that the primary purpose of the Chinese Maritime Customs, and also of the Salt Gabelle, was to collect the indemnities imposed as a result of the Opium Wars (and later of the Boxer Rebellion) and to service China's recurrent foreign debt.

The disorderly state of the country in the wake of the complete breakdown in Peking's mandate made such a colonial takeover almost a necessity. There was little interchange between the officials of the Customs and those of the Salt Gabelle. The latter was strictly a tax-collection agency, whereas the Customs, under Sir Robert Hart's direction, developed a much broader role. The Customs sought to modernize and open up China to increased trade; it charted the rivers and coastline and put in lighthouses and buoys, took care of the harbours and pilotage, and had its own fleet of armed cruisers to guard against smuggling. And it formed a branch to look after the mail, which eventually became the Chinese Post Office. Customs was the imperialist organization that really ran China, and as one observer of the Empire said, the British Customs Commissioners felt they were helping the Chinese, just as the British Commissioners of the Indian Civil Service felt they were helping the Indians. According to Arnold Toynbee, Sir Robert Hart "in reality acted as General Resident for the Western Powers." (The Resident, under the British colonial system, was the supreme authority in a protectorate where the government was left in the hands of the natives.)

Shortly after Arthur Stursberg started work in Peking as Mr. Piry's Assistant Private Secretary, an entry was made in the Postal Secretary's Order Book stating that W.A. Stursberg had been promoted to the rank of Fourth Assistant C in the Chinese Maritime Customs. This meant that he was firmly established in the "indoor staff" and was on the ladder, if yet on the bottom rung, to becoming Commissioner. (The Postal service was still just a department of the Customs.) Arthur was pleased and excited as he knew that promotion was rapid in the new service. His optimism, however, as he wrote in his memoirs, was tinged with pessimistic possibilities. He wondered, "whether my health would sustain me. That cemetery scene in Hankow [the burial of the Customs examiner, Haynes] was still fresh in my memory." There was also his narrow escape from typhoid fever in Shanghai, and the stories the old China hands told of newcomers, hail and hearty one day and dead the next from cholera or some other endemic disease. While he realized that they were for the most part "ragging him," as he said, he knew of actual cases.

However, young Mr. Stursberg, the Fourth Assistant C, quickly overcame his despondency and got on with his career and the extensive social life in Peking. He was instructed in etiquette by one of his senior colleagues and told to call on the British Minister, the commandant of the British Legation Guard, and all married British ladies on their "At Home" days.

As in any capital, there were diplomatic receptions and parties, but in Peking, the Ministers Plenipotentiary and Envoys Extraordinary were concentrated in the Legation Quarter, which made for easy access. They were also not far from the Manchu Court in the labyrinthine Oriental palace known as the Forbidden City, to whom they were accredited although they had no contact with the emperor, Pu Yi, who was a three-year-old child at the time. The envoys had their own guards to provide security for their chanceries, as was protocol, but the difference in Peking was that there were thousands of foreign troops, mostly British and American, in nearby barracks. They were really an occupation force.

The first invitation the new Postal official received was to the British Legation's celebration of King Edward vii's birthday. There was dancing to the music of the Inniskillin Fusiliers band until the early hours of the morning. The guests included military and naval officers from the foreign occupation forces, "a glittering assembly of uniformed men and beautifully gowned women." The British Legation did not have as fine a ballroom as the Russian Legation, but Arthur noted that at their dance the Russians did not provide programs, the folded cards with a small pencil attached, on which one wrote down partners for the various dances. Instead, "it was a case of noting one's engagements on the stiff cuff of the starched white shirts that had to be worn with the male evening dress in those days." Since the ladies had no equivalent to record the dances they had promised, "misunderstandings sometimes resulted."

The Inspector General of Customs had a palatial residence with a staff of thirty servants including a famous chef who was adept at almost any cuisine. The residence had a garden "of princely proportions that far exceeded those of most legations." On New Year's Eve 1910, Stursberg attended a party there given by Lady Bredon (Sir Robert Hart was on home leave and Sir Robert Bredon was Acting Inspector General). The feature, he recalled, was a paper cotillion. Lady Bredon had assembled a collection of paper fans, sun hats, and lanterns in the shape of birds or animals, all the wonderful paper objects that the Chinese made, which the gentlemen would present to their partners. There were all kinds of hijinks. Six men competed for the dancing favours of three ladies by running through two hoops; the male guests stood behind a curtain so only their shoes showed, and the women picked their partners by their feet. The male wallflowers pelted the dancing ladies with confetti and paper ribbons. (There were never enough European women to go around, which was the case not only in China but in all the colonies.) A bomb blast in the garden announced the new year, and six guests dressed as clowns burst into the ballroom. Champagne flowed, a sumptuous repast was served, "Auld Lang Syne" was sung, and the party ended at 2:30 a.m.

It is surprising what a busy social life the newly arrived junior official had. In his letters to Mary Shaw, Arthur wrote of dining, dancing, or playing bridge at this legation or that, including the Japanese Legation, as well as at officers' messes, the Peking Club, and private residences. In fact, he complained of never having a spare minute and said in one letter, "I shall really be glad to get to a nice quiet place where one can lead a simple life and study Chinese." He had been writing to Mary Shaw every week, and sometimes more often, since he left Foochow. He called her "Mollie" and signed with his nickname: "Ever your devoted Professor."

At the decorous and well-appointed Peking Club, which was just across Marco Polo Street from the Customs headquarters, one played bridge for five cents Mex a hundred. The club rule was that score cards were turned in and the winnings or losses credited or debited from one's monthly account, so no money changed hands. The missionaries also held parties, usually tea parties or tiffin parties but not dances (although, Arthur wrote to Mary, some of the missionary ladies did go to dances, which was welcomed because of the shortage of European women). At these tea parties, the guests would play parlour games such as Up Jenkins, Stool of Repentance, and others of this genre, which have passed from the social scene like the aspidistra and the antimacassar.

There were also all sorts of outdoor activities in Peking. Polo was played on the eastern glacis, mainly by officers of the occupation forces who could call on their outfit's horses or ponies. The Peking Club had tennis courts which were flooded in the winter to form a skating rink; a *peng*, or mat-roof, covered the ice surface like a marquee and protected it from the cold winds and the sand blown by the frequent dust storms in the capital. The US Legation had a rink and so did the British, and even the Postal Club had its own small rink, all of them covered by *pengs*.

About the only team sport in which Stursberg participated was ice hockey. He was very enthusiastic and told Mary that it was "really about the finest outdoor game there is in my opinion." He played for the Peking Club, as did two others from his office, "so that almost one half—the full team only numbers seven—is Postal." Their main opponents were the American marines, although they were occasionally visited and walloped by a very strong team from the British community in Tientsin (Tianjin), the great port which was a couple of hours by train away from Peking. There was a big crowd of onlookers for the match against the American marines at the Peking Club's large rink. Arthur recalled "an agreeable custom": those who watched the game from the club's verandah (mostly women) were "served hot cherry brandy from the convenient club bar just inside the French windows."

At first, they had no difficulty in trouncing the US marines, but the Americans were determined to win, and Major Russell, the commanding officer, enlisted some new players. By the third game, the marines succeeded, much to the delight of their supporters. They had brought along their own cheering section of Marines, Arthur told Mary, and judging by his letter, he seemed to imply that this so astonished his Peking Club teammates that it put them off their game.

In the summer months, Arthur played tennis on the club's courts and used to go on walking tours of the sights of Peking. There were no automobiles, no hansom cabs, in those days, and the only transportation, aside from the rickshaw, was the bone-shaking, uncomfortable Peking cart. A Peking cart had no springs and was mounted on two large wooden wheels with a semicircular blue canopy over the passenger area; it was drawn by a large caparisoned mule. In any case, he wanted the exercise of walking; he liked to stroll down the quiet *hu-tungs*, lanes off the busy streets which were a feature of Peking. He visited the Temple of Heaven and stood on the stone in the centre of the Altar of Heaven where the emperor gave his annual obeisance to heaven. One of his pleasant memories was of beautiful Beihai Park, the imperial garden that Marco Polo had compared to paradise, and its great White Dagoba, a Buddhist tower built on a hill with a commanding view of the centre of Peking.

The Forbidden City, or Winter Palace, was closed to the public, but the Summer Palace was open. It was quite a distance to the Summer Palace but not as far as the Great Wall and the Ming Tombs. Fortunately, the first section of the railway from Peking to Kalgan, Mongolia, had just been opened, so Arthur and some friends were able to take the train to the Nankow Pass by the Great Wall. But it was still seven miles to the Ming Tombs and the Processional Way, which was lined with great stone carvings of animals and of a few men, prominent Ming Dynasty leaders,

✦ *The Dowager Empress'*
funeral pyre; photos
taken by my father and
published in The
Illustrated London
News, *October 2, 1909.*
The bow of the 180-foot-
long barge was in the
shape of a dragon's head
(right). Life-sized figures
dressed in silk propelled
the ornate ship over a sea
of paper lotuses (below
and next page).

was not paved in those days. Their transportation was by donkey for the men and sedan chair for the ladies, and by starting early in the morning from the small hotel at the Nankow Pass, they were able to see the Ming Tombs in a day.

As might be expected, Arthur took pictures of the Great Wall and the Ming Tombs, which were not much different from the pictures taken today. His photographs of the Dowager Empress's funeral were singular, however, and were published in the *Illustrated London News* on October 2, 1909.

Tsu-hsi (Ci Xi), the original Dragon Lady, had died the year before, but the funerary rites were not performed until some nine months later. A huge imitation imperial barge, 180 feet long, had been built on the open grounds outside the Forbidden City, on what is now Tiananmen Square; the bow was in the shape of a dragon's head. A number of life-sized figures were on board: women who seemed to be propelling the boat, priests, servants, all dressed in beautiful silk clothes. The fully furnished boat was surrounded by a narrow margin of imitation water, out of which grew a number of paper lotuses, the imperial flower of China. A giant *peng* protected this magnificent barge from the elements, which was passing strange as it was to be burned during the funeral ceremony, along with other goods the Dowager Empress might need in the afterworld.

The burning took place on "the fifteenth day of the seventh moon," August 30, 1909, apparently a propitious time; but the actual funeral, when the body was conveyed to the mausoleum on which Tsu-Hsi had spent vast sums of money, was not until the middle of November. Tsu-Hsi's was said to be the most costly of the Ching (Qing) Dynasty tombs, which were some ninety miles from Peking by the Great Wall and not far from the Ming tombs. According to one source, "The Hall housing her spirit tablet is dazzling, with walls, ceilings and pillars covered with gold leaf."

The last funeral of a member of the Ching Dynasty, which had ruled China for almost four hundred years, was a historic event, an extraordinary spectacle that would never be repeated. My father wangled a ticket to watch the cortège; he was without camera but with the required top hat. He noted, "the enormous catafalque borne by more than a hundred men, a great display of the [Chinese] Imperial color, yellow, and a number of Chinese infantry and cavalry troops in the procession." There was a full turnout of the diplomatic corps. Yet Arthur was not unduly impressed and thought some of it "looked tawdry"; he compared it unfavourably to the funeral of Queen Victoria which he witnessed as a schoolboy. The enormous catafalque and the cortège, somewhat reduced, took four days over a specially made road to reach Tsu Hsi's extravagant mausoleum amid the Ching tombs.

By 1911, there were rumours of revolution, and Stursberg was worried by reports that Foochow was in the hands of revolutionaries. A mutiny of the troops in Wuchang on October 10 had spread to city after city. However, in a letter dated October 29, he said he was relieved to read in the papers that there was no confirmation of revolution. He wrote to Mary, "I don't think I need have anxiety on your behalf as the rebels are taking such care to leave foreigners and their property alone, but if there is any disturbance take the precaution of going up to stay with the [Shelley] Brands." However, the Chinese on the staff in Peking were frightened, he said, and were assured by Mr. Piry that, in the event of trouble, they and their families would be put up in various Postal quarters: "What would you think of my having to share my rooms with a large Chinese family!" In this letter to Mary, he did not mention her mother, my grandmother; in fact, the only reference to Ellen O'Sea I could find in his correspondence was a postscript saying that he had asked Mission Press in Shanghai "to send your mother that little book" and they had sent it to him and that he would be forwarding it. Otherwise, both Mary and he seemed to ignore her existence.

In the middle of November, when the revolution was reaching its climax, the British Legation organized a corps of messengers whose job, if fighting broke out, would be to notify British nationals living outside the Legation Quarter and escort them into the quarter. Arthur Stursberg was enrolled as one of these messengers and was given "a revolver and twenty-four rounds of ammunition." He felt these precautions, including the packing and secure storage of Postal files, were unnecessary and alarmist, and he told Mary, "Really I am fed up with the whole business and the sooner things quieten down the better." It was not till three months later that there were any serious disturbances in Peking.

However, shooting and looting were certainly a by-product of the revolution. The child emperor had been forced to abdicate on February 12, 1912; three days later, the so-called Peking strong man, Yuan Shih-kai, became president of the republic and the arch revolutionary, Sun Yat-sen, who had set up a provisional government in Nanking (Nanjing), resigned "in order to unite the country." In a long letter to Mary, dated March 5, 1912, Arthur said that at first he thought the shooting was firecrackers, but when he finished dinner and went outside, he saw buildings on fire in the "Chinese city."

The British Legation was in some confusion and the elaborate arrangements for rescue parties had broken down. Nevertheless, Arthur and a couple of other fellows set out to bring British nationals to the safety of the Legation Quarter. They saw shops burning, and on Hatamen Street, one of the main thoroughfares, soldiers were smashing down storefronts with the butt end of their rifles and firing into the air. "It struck me as really extraordinary," he wrote, "that such a thing could happen in this enlightened age and that I should be witnessing it."

✦ *Revolution in Peking: beheaded civilian looters. These photos, taken by my father, were published in the* Illustrated London News *and the* Sphere, *April 1912.*

On their way back—most of the people they called on had already gone to the Legation Quarter—the young men came to a corner that gave a wide view of all the fires. They stood there for some time overcome by the sight of Peking burning. The British troops had been called out to guard the Quarter and a line of them were lying across one of the entry streets with their rifles pointing at the flaming city, and another line kneeling behind them. Elsewhere, the American soldiers had set up barbed wire entanglements; they had erected a barricade made of sandbags at the end of Legation Street and had a machine gun placed behind it. "They looked very business like but I really don't know what they thought they were doing," Arthur told Mary. There was not a chance of the Legation Quarter being attacked or besieged, as had happened in 1900 during the Boxer uprising. The looting and burning, much to the embarrassment of President Yuan Shi-kai, was by soldiers of his Third Division. They had gone on this devastating rampage because of the breakdown in discipline as a result of the revolution. They had also not been paid for months.

The next day, there did not seem much doing. Yuan Shi-kai apologized to the foreign community and vowed to restore order. However, that night the looting and burning went on in a different part of the city. The following day, Arthur heard there had been executions: civilians, caught looting by the rampaging soldiers who, in a reversal of roles, were now supposed to be restoring order, "had been beheaded on the street without ceremony." Arthur went around the city by rickshaw and took some grizzly pictures of the bodies that littered the streets. Some of them were covered up and there was not much to see, but in other cases "the head [was] either suspended from a bamboo by the queue or nailed by the queue to a neighboring telegraph pole—they presented rather ghastly sights." He felt "sorry for these poor wretches" who were less to blame than the soldiers—apparently only civilian looters were executed.

Then he learned that the mutinous Third Division was about to leave Peking, and he rushed to the railway station to photograph the soldiers boarding a line of open freight cars which they had piled high with boxes and sacks of loot. Some of the soldiers looked at him suspiciously, while others seemed pleased with themselves and were grinning. His photos of the beheaded civilians and the soldiers departing with their loot were published a month later in *The Sphere* and the *Illustrated London News*.

Faced with this total breakdown of law and order in Peking, the foreign legations finally decided to act, in a typical imperialist manner. The British and American troops and other Legation guards were assembled on the glacis. "It was quite a fine sight to see all the various detachments lined up [on the parade ground]," Arthur wrote Mary; he took pictures of this military display. The European soldiers from the local garrisons had been joined by a thousand extra men rushed up by train from Tientsin; they marched through the Chinese city as a show of force or "by way of a demonstration," as Arthur put it. A number of his compatriots, denizens of the Legation Quarter, walked around the city with the troops. They were astonished at the destruction.

A curfew was imposed on the Chinese in Peking with the result that "the streets are silent as the dead by seven o'clock ... now that the foreign troops are ready to take action and the Chinese know it, I don't think there is likely to be the least trouble." His Chinese teacher told him that the arson and looting was "much worse than what went on in 1900," during the Boxer Revolt.

7

My German

GRANDFATHER

WHILE ARTHUR STURSBERG was busily courting Mary Shaw by correspondence, he nevertheless found time to keep in touch with his family in London. He wrote weekly letters to his father, since his mother had died on March 13, 1907, just a year after he sailed for China. Before the advent of the Trans-Siberian Railway, the mail from England came by sea and took six to seven weeks to reach him, and often the news was out of date and queries bypassed by events. However, the connection of the Chinese Eastern Railway to the Trans-Siberian Railway meant that letters following this route, their envelopes marked "Via Trans-Siberian," took only a little more than ten days to reach their destination. This was "a wonderful boon to us expatriates," he noted in his memoirs, as it brought home so much closer.

Although he knew when he left England that his mother, my English grandmother, was ailing, her death had a traumatic effect on him. As her youngest child, he had been closest to her. He got the news just after he had moved to Foochow, and his new job with the Chinese Post Office and his new quarters with the Shaws helped to relieve him of some of his grief. It was a devastating blow for Grandfather, who was devoted to his darling Emily, the beloved wife who had borne him nine children and helped him make the transition from Germany to his new adopted land. She was buried in the City of London Cemetery, the headstone inscribed with the haunting words *Auf Wiedersehn*.

On April 18, 1911, more than four years later, Grandfather married again. When he got the news, my father was appalled. He spent some time "thinking it over," as he said in a letter to his fiancée, Mary Shaw:

> At first, I was inclined to blame him very much, but the more I thought it over the more excuse did I find for his action until now I have reconciled myself to the idea. Of this I am certain, that had he received the sympathetic treatment from his children that a father has a right to expect from them, he would never have thought of remarrying. As it was, however, the lonely life he had to lead would only tend to make him seek solace in the company of others ... You see, none of the boys ever properly understood him or he them (myself included) and during the past few years rather a large gap has come between them, I fear ... Otto [an older brother who was a missionary in India] and myself return our affection for him in the same way as when we were at home, but being separated by so many thousand miles we have provided him with no consolation in his loneliness.

In the same letter, he noted that Mary Conneeley, whom my grandfather took as his second wife, was "a maiden lady in her 57th year." Grandfather Stursberg described her as "an earnest true-hearted Christian and, as to her disposition, she is the nearest approach to your dear Mother which it is possible to find." Obviously Grandfather knew his second marriage would not be well received by his children, and he pleaded with them "to look upon my action in the same light as I do." He told them he would be much happier "when I have again a home of my own with a loving partner who I know will take all the loving care she can of me." My father's comment on this appeal, which he quoted at length in his letter to Mary,

was that Miss Conneeley's age was suitable for a man of his father's years: "I should certainly have never forgiven him had he married a young wife." My grandfather, Johann Peter Stursberg, was born at Garschagen in the Rhineland on February 10, 1840, although the 1881 British census gave his birthplace as the larger town of Lennep in the same general area. He could trace his family back to the fifteenth century to a Winolt Stursberg, whose date of birth was given as 1453. Stursberg is not a common German name, which is due partly to the fact that the spelling was not fixed in the early days and one branch wrote the name as Storsberg, another as Stoosberg, and some even as Strasberg. The Stursbergs were yeoman farmers and artisans. Grandfather's father, also named Johann Peter Stursberg, was born at the village of Stursberg in the early nineteenth century. At the end of the Second World War, I drove across Germany to Bonn and, in the pleasant and untouched countryside beyond the badly battered city of Dusseldorf, passed through two hamlets marked Stursberg I and Stursberg II.

Johann Peter the elder moved to Garschagen, where he worked as a silk weaver. He must have been of sturdy country stock, pragmatic, earthy, without a blemish of superstition, for his son, my grandfather, was the third Johann Peter to be born, the previous two having died in infancy. His parents refused to believe that there could be any bad luck attached to the Christian names they had chosen.

In the mid nineteenth century, the German states were in turmoil as the Prussians were going about the stern and often bloody business of building an empire. The foundation stone in this enterprise was the unification of the country of Germany, and some of the kingdoms and the ecclesiastical and temporal principalities, as well as the independent Hanseatic towns, had to be coerced into joining; others, such as Schleswig Holstein, had to be wrested from foreign rulers. There was interminable warfare. However, what worried the young Johann Peter—he had become an apprentice at fourteen years of age in the ironmongery business in the nearby town of Ronsdorf—was the Prussian succession. In 1861 William I had succeeded his brother, Frederick William IV, who had been deemed insane, as king. William had been brought up as a soldier and his first royal proclamation was that he would strengthen the army by increasing the annual levy of troops and extending the terms of service to three years.

A couple of Grandfather Stursberg's relatives had been wounded or killed in the conflicts with Denmark and Austria, or so the family claimed. At any rate, young Johann Peter was determined not to be conscripted so on April 6, 1861 he fled to London. It must have been a painful decision for him to leave his close and loving family: his father and mother lived for many years after his departure and, although his father visited him once in England, his mother never saw him again.

Johann Peter would be regarded as a refugee in this day and age, a draft dodger, with all that meant in the way of forms to be filled and questions to be answered. But going to London at that time was no different, except for the matter of distance and language and having to cross the Channel, than going to the nearby towns of Cologne or Dusseldorf. There were no passports then, no limitations on immigration to Britain in the mid nineteenth century. This was a paradox since the British had an inbred dislike amounting to contempt for foreigners, indeed, for all breeds beyond their shores, yet welcomed or at least allowed those who had escaped from Prussian rule and other repressive regimes a haven in their country. The most famous of these refugees was Karl Marx, who had been in London since 1849, but there were others: Spanish and Italian anarchists, Russian nihilists, even French Bonapartists.

When my grandfather first arrived in London, he must have been struck by the city's almost unbelievable size. Francis Sheppard indicates that "by 1871, [London's] population had reached the enormous figure of over three and a quarter million." It was, as one American visitor said, "a world within itself." The first underground railway, the Metropolitan Railway, was being built, and one of Grandfather's early sightseeing trips was to Paddington to gawk at the construction of this extraordinary project. Eventually, the Metropolitan was to be extended at both ends to form an "inner circuit" of underground railways, which became known as the "Inner Circle Line."

London was the great engine of the industrial age. And, as a result, Sheppard comments, "The air had become laden with the smoke of steam vessels, gasworks and the furnaces of a host of industrial establishments ... the noble prospect towards the City and the dome of St. Paul's had been ruthlessly sundered by the brick and iron of Charing Cross railway bridge." John Ruskin called London in the 1860s "that great foul city ... rattling, growling, smoking, stinking ... pouring out poison at every pore." An outcry, as only Ruskin could utter, against the ever-increasing pollution, the smog or awful "pea soup" for which London remained notorious until recent times.

Johann Peter Stursberg—he soon changed his name to John Peter Stursberg—was one of hundreds of thousands of immigrants who kept arriving in London, mostly from the countryside and small towns of England. Charles Dickens was one of them; when a boy, his family moved from Kent to Camden Town and he remembered his childhood in the country "with deep, almost despairing nostalgia." Dickens began to work a twelve-hour day in a boot-blacking factory just off the Strand at six shillings a week, but that was in the 1820s, and, of course, by the time Grandfather came to London, Dickens was a famous author.

While there was still great poverty and hardship, social conditions had improved by the 1860s so that the new German immigrant did not have to start work in a boot-blacking factory, or any other "dark, satanic mill." In fact, he had no trouble getting a good job. Although he had been an apprentice ironmongerer, he went to work for A.T. Geck, an importer of picture frames and mouldings. Augustus Theodore Geck was of German origin, and it is possible that he was known to the Stursberg family or their friends in Garschagen or Ronsdorf and assured them there would be employment available for the young man if he came to London. John Peter Stursberg was really a salesman, a commercial traveller, and he was so successful that he left A.T. Geck in 1872 to set up his own business: J.P. Stursberg, Merchant and Shipper, Dealer in Picture Frame Mouldings, Water Colour Drawings, 24/26 Banner Street, Bunhill Row, London; later, J. P. Stursberg & Sons at the same address.

On June 29, 1869, my German grandfather became a naturalized British subject. My cousin Mabel Stanley obtained from the Public Records Office in London a copy of the petition or memorial which with the testimonials of four British-born subjects and householders, covered eight foolscap pages, all in the finest copper plate handwriting. In the florid style of the day, the petition recognized that John Peter Stursberg "upon obtaining the certificate and taking the oath thereafter prescribed ... shall enjoy all the rights and capacities that a natural born subject of the United Kingdom can enjoy or transmit except that such alien shall not be capable of becoming one of her Majesty's Privy Council nor a Member of either House of Parliament." These restrictions existed in the 1847 Act, which was in force at the time but has long been superceded. Although John Peter was emotionally and overwhelmingly pro-British, there was a practical reason for wanting to become a naturalized subject. He had married a couple of years before, was starting a family, and had made an offer for "the purchase of a dwelling house for the residence of himself, his wife and family," and the petition averred that "he cannot legally become

✦ *Grandfather (second from left) and Grandmother (steering) Stursberg*
with relatives on a tricycle built for four

the owner of the aforesaid property without previously becoming naturalised."

The young native German, now more British than the British, married Emily Eliza Hague on December 23, 1866 at St. Mark's Church in Bath. Emily was the daughter of an innkeeper and victualler in Bath. Between 1868 and 1886, they had nine children, eight sons and one daughter, a typical Victorian family. My father, born on July 31, 1886, was the youngest; his brothers and sister were so much older that the nearest in the family to his age was his eldest brother Herbert's son, Cyril, who was his nephew.

My two grandfathers had not much in common except they were Victorians and ardent Empire loyalists. John Peter Stursberg had shaken the sod of Prussia from his boots and eschewed all things German; he never returned to his native land. He became an Englishman, and the Hagues replaced the family he had left behind. He spoke only English at home. While he did not reject his mother tongue and called the house he built in the Forest Gate suburb of London *Friedenheim*, then christened some of his sons with names like Otto, Hermann, and Carl, he did not encourage any of his family to speak German. None of them did, except for Otto, who earned a doctorate in Sanskrit at the University of Bonn and became a missionary in India. On language, John Peter Stursberg and Captain Samuel Lewis Shaw (who refused to allow his wife to speak Japanese) would seem to have had the same general objective, the assertion and expansion of English, the language of the Empire.

The Stursbergs delighted in all imperial and royal occasions, and one of my father's shining memories was of Queen Victoria's Diamond Jubilee in 1897. He was an eleven-year-old boy at the venerable City of London School, situated in the very heart of all the imperial celebrations. Eighty years later, he wrote in the school magazine that "we boys took full advantage of the broad steps in front of the school entrance to see the wonderful old lady riding in an open landau (drawn by eight cream-coloured horses) along the broad thoroughfare named for her, the Victoria Embankment." As for the rest of his family, they would have been in the crowds packed along the city streets leading to St. Paul's where the memorial service was held. They would have been thrilled by the great parade of some fifty thousand from every part of the Empire. No foreign potentates had been invited; instead, their places were taken in the golden carriages of state by the leaders of the Dominion of Canada and the other self-governing colonies of Newfoundland, New Zealand, Cape Colony, Natal, and the Australian states. Sir Wilfrid Laurier, who had been knighted for the jubilee, resplendent with his escort of scarlet-coated Mounties, bowed and waved his top hat to the cheering throngs. His carriage was followed by a picked contingent of Canadian troops. In the great procession were Indian princes in their bejewelled finery, turbanned Bengal lancers, cavalrymen from Australia, Bedouins on their camels, headhunters from Borneo, African warriors with their shields and assegais, Hong Kong Chinese policemen wearing conical straw hats, British guards in their dress uniforms, Highland regiments, and any number of bands. Yet this imperial pageant was really just a supporting act: the old

Queen, the Empress of India, who had reigned for so long, was the real show.

It was a famous day, the high day of imperialism, and it was celebrated throughout the British Empire. At dawn on June 22, 1897, Canadians in Ottawa were awakened by the clamour of church bells, factory hooters, and locomotive whistles. Ten thousand children waving small Union Jacks marched to Parliament Hill where they were addressed by the Governor General, Lord Aberdeen, an imposing figure in his blue vice-regal uniform with its silver epaulettes and belt. That evening a large crowd gathered at the same locale for a patriotic show and singsong where fairy lights spelled out *God Save the Queen* and *Dieu Sauve la Reine;* there were similar celebrations in other parts of the Empire. The Dominion issued special commemorative stamps that showed the young queen and the old queen, much admired and sought after by philatelists. In China, in Peking, in Foochow, there were memorial services, but no stamps.

"A less happy event that followed the Jubilee celebrations," my father recounted in the article he wrote for the City of London School magazine:

was the incidence of the Boer War and from the same point of vantage [the school steps on the Victoria Embankment] we saw pass by the regiment of the City Imperial Volunteers [CIVS] on their way to embark for South Africa to add to the regular forces engaged there (they had been suffering heavier than expected casualties). Those were the days when Kipling's "Absent-minded Beggar" (with music by Sir Arthur Sullivan) was sung in all the Moss music halls throughout the country, and during its singing showers of coins were thrown on the stage by the patriotic audience.

"The Absent-minded Beggar" may be all but lost to memory; here it is again, in part:

When you've shouted 'Rule Britannia'—when you've sung
'God save the Queen'—

When you've finished killing Kruger with your mouth—
Will you kindly drop a shilling in my little tambourine
For a gentleman in khaki ordered South?
He's an absent-minded beggar, and his weaknesses are great—
But we and Paul must take him as we find him—
He's out on active service, wiping something off a slate—
And he's left a lot of little things behind him!

Duke's son—cook's son—son of a hundred kings—
(Fifty thousand horse and foot going to Table Bay)
Each of them doing his country's work
(and who's to look after their things?)
Pass the hat for your credit's sake, and pay-pay-pay!

A short time later, Grandfather Stursberg, my father and the rest of the family were in Hyde Park for a sad and sombre royal event, the funeral of Queen Victoria. It was "a most impressive experience," he recalled. "A number of foreign sovereigns walked in the cortège when the Queen's remains were on their way to be entrained for ensepulture at Windsor."

Next there was the coronation of Edward VII, put off from June 26 to August 9, 1902 because of the monarch's celebrated appendicitis operation. By this time, my father was a boy clerk at His Majesty's Office of Works; with another boy clerk he assisted in the allocation of seats in the government stands at Westminster Abbey. When the work ended, "the two of us were each given a seat in one of the official stands. My co-worker was glad to sell his ticket for ten shillings and so, together with mine, my parents were able to see the procession in comfort. But they and other seat-holders had to rise in the early hours of the morning to get to town and make their way to the stands before the closing of the streets to all traffic."

John Peter and Emily Stursberg and their growing family moved every few years, it seemed, to a new house in and around Bath. As a commercial traveller, my grandfather was used to a peripatetic life, but my grandmother must have found it trying. However, in the 1870s, they settled in London, first at Regents Park, and then more permanently at

Lowther Villa, 358 Romford Road, in the growing new suburb of Forest Gate on the edge of Epping Forest. (It was in the 1890s on nearby Capel Road that Grandfather built *Friedenheim*, his peaceful home.)

He became a deacon at the Sebert Road Congregational Church in Forest Gate, a substantial edifice whose fine Regency proportions were marred by its drab Victorian brick construction. The church's interior was classical non-conformist with a balcony around three sides and a high stained-glass window that depicted Christ with the little children shedding a soft light on the rows of pews below and the simple altar table. The Stursbergs sat in the balcony. Across on the other side was another prominent family, the Kydds, whose *pater familias* was also a deacon. The families got to know each other and Fred Stursberg (Mabel's father) married Maggie Kydd. The Thorns also went to the Sebert Road Church and became friends of the Stursbergs. Otto fell in love with Lily Thorn. However, unlike Fred and Maggie, who were married in the church, Otto joined the London Missionary Society and was sent to India at the end of October 1897. Lily followed him out a month later and they were married when she arrived in Calcutta.

Arthur's sister, Lillian Emily, my Aunt Lillie, was a Victorian beauty, with a copper-tinted crown of wavy hair, violet eyes, and a peaches-and-cream complexion. As the only daughter, she was the apple in her father's eye. There was nothing too good for her. Not only did my grandfather send her to Miss Jotham's school for "young gentlewomen" in Southend but, since she played the piano and was musically inclined, he paid for her to go to the Royal College of Music. Furthermore, he saw to it that she travelled first class wherever she went.

Thus, it was a terrible blow for him and the Stursberg family when at the age of eighteen, Lillie eloped with a charming ne'er-do-well, Charles "Pip" Dunn, to the Registry Office at Gretna Green. The marriage certificate, dated May 23, 1898, showed that they had both falsified their ages: Lillie gave hers as twenty-one, and Pip, who put himself down as a "clothier," as twenty-two. (They were both underage to be married in Britain at that time.) Both stated that their fathers were deceased. It seems unlikely that Pip's father, a yeast merchant, was dead, and John Stursberg, listed as a "picture frame maker," certainly was not.

Nowadays, it is difficult to understand that a young couple running away to get married could be regarded as a scandal and a disgrace. However, manners and morals were much more rigid in those days. My grandfather Stursberg was a leading citizen in Forest Gate and a deacon in the Sebert Road Congregational Church. My grandmother Emily was an influential member of the British Women's Christian Temperance Association and had just been elected to the West Ham Board of Guardians (the board looked after workhouses and the poor). As good Victorians, they set great store by their status in the community, and they could not abide any gossip about their daughter's elopement. Further, Gretna Green had an unsavoury reputation for shotgun weddings and hurried marriages because of premarital pregnancy, although in Lillie's case it was more a premonition than reality. At any rate, my grandfather gave up his office of deacon, which had meant so much to him, and resigned from the church. He sold *Friedenheim*, and within three months of Lillie's marriage, the Stursbergs had left Forest Gate and London for Leigh-on-Sea.

Although Grandfather resigned from the Sebert Road church and fled from the gossip and prying inquiries about his daughter's sudden marriage, he did not have the heart to blame Lillie. She was too dear to him, and he felt sorry for her, for her misjudgement and folly. He became reconciled, and within a short time Lillie was back at home. How soon after the elopement? It must have been fairly soon because of the impecunious condition of her husband. Poor Pip Dunn! He had broken the golden rule of Victorian middle-class morality by getting married without having the means to support a wife.

The fact that the newly married couple had to live with the bride's father would have been the subject of more gossip and derision. So the Stursbergs moved from Leigh-on-Sea to Southend, but a year or so later returned to London, to Wanstead, the next borough to Forest Gate, but they never went back to the Sebert Road Congregational Church.

Lillie lived with her father for some years. She was with him when my grandmother died in 1907, but she and her family left him shortly after the funeral. Lillie had gone to work, largely because of her husband's lax and irresponsible attitude toward jobs, although he eventually settled down more or less in the clothing trade. In the world of business, Lillie's personality and drive proved to be remarkably successful. She reached the apex of her career during the First World War when she became the confidential secretary and personal assistant to Prime Minister Lloyd George. (There were also rumours that she was his mistress, but almost any good-looking woman who was close to Lloyd George was said to have been his mistress.)

At first, Grandfather was probably glad to see the Dunns go. There had been, in his own words, "much unpleasantness," presumably with Charlie. It was the first time my grandfather had been on his own, and he soon became dejected and reclusive with no one to share his bereavement. He had turned over his business to his sons, Herbert, Hermann, and Carl, although he kept his hand in by travelling to certain select customers in the United Kingdom. While he welcomed these trips, he found that sales were falling, and this depressed him. All of which led, after much soul-searching, to his decision to remarry. He had moved to Weston-super-Mare, a favourite seaside resort of his, and also of Emily's, and there, on April 18, 1911, he married Mary Conneeley.

It would be no exaggeration to say that this decision came as a dreadful shock to his family. My father was appalled; he spent some time "thinking it over" and eventually became "reconciled." The rest of the family were not as forgiving. They felt that he should never have remarried. There was even a suggestion of moral turpitude, that in taking a second wife he had dishonoured Emily's memory. My cousin Mabel observed that the words *Auf Wiedersehn* on our grandmother's tombstone "could have a more cynical message after grandpa married again than was originally intended!" Such was the harsh judgement of the times. Inevitably, the question came up of what to call her. Certainly not "Mother," nor "stepmother"; the consensus was that she should be known as "mater" or "grandmater."

When war broke out in August 1914, Britain's pent-up jingoism and racial superiority exploded. Shops and businesses with German names, and some without but purported to be in the hands of Germans, were attacked. There was looting. Stones were thrown and windows were broken. However, worse than any mob violence were the insidious rumours spread by the popular press that foreigners—who were obviously those with foreign names—could be spies. Forest Gate probably suffered more than any other London borough from this xenophobia because of its large number of German-speaking immigrants, not only from Germany but from Austria and Bohemia-Moravia.

In response, many of my Stursberg relatives changed their names. Some took names associated with the distaff side of their families. In 1915, Mabel's family changed their name to Stanley for no other reason than that the first two letters were the same as the first two letters of Stursberg and that Stanley was easy to spell and pronounce. Another cousin, who had been an army officer and fought in the war, changed his name in 1920—long after the patriotic tumult had died down.

In taking English names, the Stursbergs were in august company. Even the Royal family had to change its name, from Saxe-Coburg-Gotha to Windsor. On July 17, 1917, King George V finally bowed to popular pressure and issued a royal proclamation to this effect. The German surname had come from Queen Victoria's marriage to Prince Albert of Saxe-Coburg-Gotha. Victoria herself had a German surname, Hanover. The House of Hanover ended with her death in 1901, to be succeeded by the House of Saxe-Coburg-Gotha, which was transformed in 1917 to the House of Windsor. Another prominent aristocratic family also changed its name. Prince Louis Alexander of Battenberg was an admiral in the Royal Navy and held a high position in the Admiralty on the outbreak of war. Despite his friendship and close relations with King George V and the royal household, he was forced to resign because of the national hysteria. He and other members of his family living in England renounced their German titles and anglicized their name to Mountbatten. There was really no way of anglicizing Saxe-Coburg-Gotha, so King George V settled on Windsor, the site of his main residence, Windsor Castle. However the Stursbergs could have anglicized their name, if they had, it would have been Mountsturs.

Since Grandfather Stursberg and his second wife, our "grandmater," lived in Weston-Super-Mare, they escaped much of the virulent anti-German campaign. There was never a hint that he considered changing his name, as many of his children had done, and every indication that he disapproved of this change. My father did write to him and suggest that it might be better for business, which was not good, if he changed the name of his firm (J.P. Stursberg and Sons). However, Grandfather paid no attention; he was proud of his name and the name of his firm, and he refused to be moved by this racist hysteria.

Of course, my father never changed his name. At no time did he feel threatened for having a German ancestry in China where the British had hegemony. While he sympathized, in his letters home, with the lot of his brothers and deplored the discrimination they suffered, he never once mentioned that he had received any taunt or remonstrance because of his name. Nor did my uncle, Rev. Dr. Otto Stursberg. He continued with his missionary work in India, and no one at any time suggested that he might be a German spy seeking to turn his Bengali parishioners against the Raj.

8

MARRIAGE COLONIAL
STYLE *in* FOOCHOW

ARTHUR STURSBERG WAS IN HIS THIRD YEAR at the Postal directorate in Peking. Ever the upright and responsible youth, he had at last decided that he could afford to get married in the autumn of that year, 1912. He had been engaged to Mary Shaw for almost three years, which was a long time even by the standards of those days. On August 29, 1909, after his promotion to the officer rank of Fourth Assistant C in the Chinese Maritime Customs, he proposed to her in a rather stilted, formal letter. He was sorry, he wrote, that he could not go to Shanghai, where they had planned to meet, as he had a question that he had long wanted to ask her:

> Mollie dear, will you be my wife when I am in a little better posi-
> tion and have saved a few dollars? We have now known each other
> for well over two years and saw a great deal of each other in the first
> half of that period—what a happy time I had in Foochow and how
> I hated to leave without being able to tell you that I loved you and
> that some day I hoped to ask you to be my wife. On the salary that

I was receiving however it would have been awfully foolish to have done so. Of course I am only one step higher now, my salary being 95 Taels or $142.50 [1 Hai Kuan Tael was worth $1.50 Mex], and it is for that reason I am asking you to marry me when I am in a little better position—not sooner than two years hence.

...

Another thing, Mollie dear, which I must ask of you, if you feel that you could bring yourself to trust yourself for life to such a curious mixture as myself, is that our engagement be kept a secret—no one outside your own family being told of it. You may not perhaps know but in the Postal service there is a prejudice against juniors getting married and if it came to the ears of Mr. Piry that I was engaged he might put everything in the way of my marriage in consequence ...

"I am exceedingly dissatisfied with this letter," he wrote in a postscript, "and wish I could have seen you and spoken the substance of what I have here written. In a case like this writing seems awfully unsatisfactory. However I hope you will read between the lines and imagine what I would have said had I seen you."

This was such an important letter that he did not sign "Your devoted Professor," as he had done in so many other letters, but formally, with his full name, "With love, W. Arthur Stursberg." At the top of the letter, my mother had written: "Rec'd 8th Sept. 09; Ans'd 11th Sept. 09." I was sure that my father would have kept her reply, indeed would have treasured it, but I could not find it among his papers. However, there was no gainsaying its contents: she very happily agreed to the proposal.

This was not the first time Mary had become engaged. In a letter to "Dear dear Mary" dated August 3, 1902, Captain Shaw wrote, "Dear Ma and I are always thinking of you, we do indeed miss you so much [Mary was away at convent school in Shanghai] ... We have given our sanction to your engagement with Alfred and hope with the blessing of God that in a few months you will be a happy and contented wife. Anything you may require please ask." Mary Shaw was seventeen in 1902. Her fiancé to be, Alfred Begley, was twenty-three and was with China-Indo China Navigation Company.

What we don't know is what happened. Why was the engagement broken? Mary was a schoolgirl, but seventeen was not too young to get married at that time, and her father had given his consent. Alfred Begley had got to know Mary in Shanghai and never visited Pagoda Anchorage or met her family and did not know that her mother was Japanese. Perhaps when he found out, he decided that he could not go ahead with the betrothal. Another man, according to Julia, Mary's elder sister, wanted to wed Mary: a young Shanghai businessman named Kirk (Aunty J did not know his Christian name). Whether or not there was a formal engagement, nothing came of this tryst, perhaps because Kirk too learned that she was Eurasian. Perhaps these heartbreaks made my mother want to become a nun, which, when word got out, so shocked her brother, George, that he put an end to her association with the Roman Catholic institution in Shanghai.

Young Arthur Stursberg was not in the dark about Mary's Japanese mother, my grandmother; after all, he had lived at the Shaws' house in Foochow for more than a year. He was obviously so much in love that he had the courage to disregard this apprehended blemish in her breeding, although, he must have realized that it was a serious colonial issue. He seemed to have resolved the matter, as far as he was concerned, by wiping Ellen O'Sea out of his mind, which was to be expected considering his upbringing. My father came from a middle-class family with a traditional moral outlook and had absorbed the racial attitudes of the colonial society in China, especially after he left Foochow for the more rigid imperial environment of Peking. However, he did mention my Japanese grandmother in the letter asking Mary to be his wife. It had nothing to do with his proposal; he wanted Mary to thank her mother for the kimono she had sent him. "I am wearing it at the present moment," he wrote, "and like it immensely."

As was expected, Arthur informed the head of the family, George L. Shaw, who was then a rising young magnate in Antung, Manchuria, of his engagement to his sister. The news of this was well received, and in a

✦ *My father and mother before their wedding in Foochow, 1912*

letter dated October 9, 1909, George offered any assistance that might be required when they were married. However, he noted that "your salary is only HK Taels 95 per moon [*sic*], this is hardly enough income to keep yourself and your wife, but as you say your prospects are bright." (The HK Tael, or Hai Kuan Tael, was the denomination favoured for larger sums.)

George had no need to worry: Stursberg's expectations were fulfilled. After years of lessons, he had finally acquired a working knowledge of Chinese. He had even passed all the exams, which was a real achievement. He found it a most difficult language to learn because it is tonal and the meaning of a word depends on inflection. Ted Joliffe, who was born in China and spoke Chinese before he spoke English, maintained that few foreigners who learned the language as adults spoke really good Chinese. Children could pick it up easily, and it was a common occurrence, he said, "to hear the missionary child correcting a parent's deplorable Chinese." My brother and I learned Chinese through playing with the servants' children and probably spoke a better, if more vulgar, Chinese (with a Honan working-class accent) than Dad did. There are many examples of how mistakes could be made with the wrong inflection: for instance, *ma* means "mother" but it also means "horse"; *ping* means "soldier" but also "ice."

Some of the mispronunciations could be hilarious. One lady missionary thought she had told a Chinese woman, "I see your little baby is asleep" but found out that she had said the child was a poached egg (*shui jiao*, actually not a poached egg but Chinese for a boiled dumpling.) There was also a story of a missionary who ordered his Chinese servant to throw down the mission flag, which was on the balcony of the house, so that he could raise it on a staff in the courtyard. When the Boy did not respond, the missionary became quite excited and shouted again and again to him to throw down the flag. Finally, in desperation, the servant turned to the man's wife and said, "What am I to do? He keeps telling me to throw you down into the courtyard!"

Almost as difficult as learning to speak Chinese was learning to write Chinese. Each word is an ideograph; there is no alphabet and no substitute for an alphabet. The total number of Chinese characters was said to be more than forty thousand, but, of course, nothing like that number was needed to read a newspaper or write a letter. Only two thousand different characters were used in the translation of the Bible. My father knew a thousand characters, which was really a working knowledge, enough for ordinary communication and more than enough for him to keep up with the official paperwork in the Chinese Postal service. He had a learning method that many foreigners used: it consisted of small cards with a single ideograph or character on one side and the phonetic, or Romanization as it was called, and translation on the other side. These cards fitted into long oblong boxes, and he would go through them at regular intervals, memorizing the characters and their meanings. That was only way for non-Chinese adults to learn how to read and write Chinese, by rote; still, in this way, he became quite proficient.

Arthur's salary increased annually until it reached two hundred Taels per month, when he felt that he was sufficiently advanced in his career and in his earnings to support a wife. So, on May 12, 1912, he wrote to Mary that he would apply for leave to be married in the fall. He realized, he said, that the long engagement, the waiting and uncertainty, had been hard on her, and he apologized, but said that in all conscience he could not have taken the step any earlier.

The smooth tenor of Stursberg's work in the Peking office of the Postal service was broken by a row with his boss, Theophile Piry. It was all over T.P., as he was known, bringing in an outsider, a Customs officer, Pabst Jokl, to be his private secretary. Jokl, an Austrian, was fluent in English, French, and German; he was tall and handsome and made a popular figure in the social life of Peking as he was a violinist of professional calibre. On Madame Piry's "At Home" days in the Pirys' fine house on Legation Street, next door to the Belgian Legation, he was a regular visitor and would often be asked to play some of his favourite pieces, Brahms' Hungarian Dances being one of them, which he played "masterfully." He would often be accompanied on the piano by Piry's eldest daughter, Jeanne. The degree of intimacy T.P. showed toward the newcomer—to the extent of giving him a lift in his brougham to the office—was the subject of much gossip. "Papa," it was said, had him in mind as a future son-in-law.

Jokl's appointment over the heads of the three assistant secretaries, of whom Stursberg was one, was considered an injustice. However, when it was disclosed that Jokl, who had been on the same grade as them and at the same salary of two hundred Taels per month before his appointment, was given two raises, one shortly after the other, to three hundred Taels a month, there was outrage. The three assistant secretaries met clandestinely and wrote a joint letter of protest, composed largely by Stursberg, to Mr. Piry, which ended by saying: "We do not grudge Pabst Jokl his promotion; far from it, we wish him joy in his advancement, but we are disappointed in the thought that we are not considered worthy of similar treatment, and hence we submit this petition in the hope that you may find it possible to remove the cause of our grievance."

There was a brief, portentous interlude, then the joint letter was returned with the note, "Let each man write his own letter. T.P." The petitioning assistant secretaries, Hulme, Stursberg, and Poullain, wondered whether their boss was following Machiavelli's maxim of "Divide and Rule," but their solidarity was not broken. They sent back identical letters repeating what was said in the joint letter. This was followed by an ominous silence. T.P. behaved as if nothing had happened when one or other of the assistant secretaries, in the course of his duties, came in to see him. However, he was furious. He was biding his time while making plans to replace the assistant secretaries, which they knew about since staff changes had to go through their hands. About a month later, when the substitutes had arrived, he got rid of the troublesome trio by transferring them to places far from Peking.

Piry dispatched Hulme to Yunnanfu, which was as far from Peking as one could be sent; Poullain to Nanking (Nanjing); and Stursberg to Tsingtao (Qingdao). It was a policy of the Chinese Customs and the Post Office to send German nationals to Tsingtao, which was a German colony. Since there was no German of suitable rank available, Mr. Piry decided on the next best thing: a man with a German name. That was how Stursberg came to be transferred to Tsingtao. However, this was no outpost like Yunnanfu, in the farthest reaches of west China. In fact, it was considered the most desirable sub-district in the whole Chinese Postal Service, as it was a seaside resort and a comfortable German spa.

The journey to Tsingtao was by train with stopovers of a day or two at Tientsin (Tianjin) and Tsinan (Jinan). Stursberg had got used to the length of time spent travelling in China. Sometimes, he liked the leisurely pace as he would meet Postal colleagues and be put up at their homes, which was the colonial way of treating visitors since there were no modern European-style hotels. (No member of the foreign staff of the Chinese Customs or Post Office would be expected to stay at native inns—perish the thought!) However, the trip to Foochow in the fall of 1910 was most frustrating and tedious as he had to spend most of his three-week holiday travelling and only had ten days with his fiancée. Still, the trip was worth it to see his beloved again.

The Shaws had moved back to their house at Pagoda Anchorage; they had rented Terenure in Foochow to a newly arrived businessman. A photo was taken of the engaged couple in the garden beside the Sung Dynasty pagoda. They are sitting primly on a bench between orange trees heavy with fruit; my mother is in a long white dress, my father in a tweed suit with a stiff collar and bow tie. In the background, behind a picket fence, was the deep-water harbour. It was Arthur's first visit since he had left in the summer of 1908 and it was the last time he would see Mary before their marriage.

In contrast, the trip to Tsingtao was pleasant and took only three days. When Arthur arrived he was met by the local staff, who had arranged for him to have a room at the Prinz Heinrich Hotel, a typical German hotel. He recalled, in his memoirs, having a "truly mouth-watering steak" in the hotel's dining room. This fact is significant because beef was rarely on the menu in China; the steak meant cattle must have been raised in the colony of Tsingtao. He also remarked on the beer: the Germans had established a fine brewery and Tsingtao beer was renowned then—and is to this day. The town itself, Arthur Stursberg said, was European-looking "with a lot of very pretty lanes which very much reminded me of home." On some evenings a German military band gave a concert at a bandstand on the seafront. Near the hotel was a roller-skating rink which he frequented; it was a popular venue of an evening for foreign holiday-makers.

On several occasions he had dinner at the home of the Chinese Customs Commissioner, Herr Ohlmer, who was a German. In the order of protocol, Herr Ohlmer ranked next to the German governor of Tsingtao. Ohlmer asked after Sir Robert Hart; he was, he said, a great admirer of the founder of the Customs and of British hegemony in China. He was told that Sir Robert was not expected back from home leave— and, in fact, died a short while later. The younger members of his staff, who were mostly German, always addressed Frau Ohlmer as "Tante Emma." The new sub-district Postmaster felt he ought to take German lessons. He knew no German since his father had fled from Prussian militarism to England and did not encourage his children to speak German. Arthur took lessons from a colleague, but acquired no fluency in the language because all the Germans he met in Tsingtao spoke English.

The transfer to Tsingtao made no difference as far as plans for an autumn wedding. In fact, while he was there—and he spent only three months in the charming little German colony—Arthur Stursberg informed the Postal Secretary, Mr. Piry, that he intended to marry Miss Mary Shaw of Foochow and applied for three weeks' leave for that purpose. Although T.P. was furious over the joint letter of protest by the three assistant secretaries and said that he would "never forget" it, he made no attempt to hinder the wedding plans. The fact was that the action they had taken, as Arthur wrote to Mary, was supported by the rest of the foreign Postal staff in Peking, and Mr. Piry must have got to know about this. At any rate, Dad was granted leave and was told that at its expiration he would be transferred to Chefoo (now Yentai) where he would take up the appointment of sub-district Postmaster. Chefoo was a British seaside resort not far from the German spa of Tsingtao; both were in Shantung (Shandong) Province.

Most of the marriage arrangements had to be made by correspondence. Mary wrote to her eldest brother, George, the head of the family, about her trousseau, and he sent her a cheque for Taels 350, which came to about the $500 Mex that she thought she needed. At the same time, like any self-made millionaire, he insisted, "We are poor people, so do not be too grand." It was taken for granted that the daughter's family would pay for the wedding, and, apparently, George, as head of the family, was quite prepared to foot the bill. However, he did not reckon on it being so large. In a letter to him, Mary had suggested that the cost would be $2,000 Mex, which was the amount that a Foochow taipan had spent on his daughter's marriage. This sum, George said, took his "breath clean away." "It is a good job," he wrote, "that I have a strong heart, otherwise I might faint with heart failure or something like that."

George supervised the coming nuptials from his office in faraway Antung by the Yalu River with typewritten missives to both bride and groom. He approved of the wedding card but thought his name should not have been included since he could not attend. He had become the agent of a steamship, the *Yiloong*, by which he was sending the letter and his morning coat and vest; they would be delivered by the Chief Engineer, Mr. Forsyth. He was very proud of the ship, which was his first, and hoped that Stursberg (he never addressed him by his Christian name) would take a look at her.

"If my coat and vest do not fit you," he wrote, "please return by the *Yiloong*." They fitted. "The tragic part," my father recalled sixty years later, "was when sending them back, they got lost, and I had to pay for new ones." It was typical of George, the hard-headed businessman, that he would not waive their replacement for the brother-in-law who had scrimped and saved in order to marry his sister.

Timing was of the essence. Arthur had only three weeks' leave and had been informed by Mr. Piry that there would be a house for him in Chefoo. He and his bride would have to stop in Shanghai after the wedding to acquire the necessary household goods. He wrote to Mary that he expected to leave Tsingtao by steamer on October 5, due to arrive in Shanghai on October 7; if he were to make a connection with another coastal ship that day, which was highly unlikely, he could get to Foochow by October 9, but he thought it would probably be October 11, the day before the wedding.

At last the great day arrived, October 12, 1912. The fall, when it was sunny and cool, was the best time in south China. Mary, with the help of her sisters, was dressed in a tight-waisted, high-necked, long-sleeved, off-white wedding gown of heavy satin; she wore a traditional bridal veil with a crown of orange blossoms. Both sisters wore dresses made of the same off-white satin. Ceci, who was just out of convent school, was the bridesmaid, and in the absence of George and any of the other brothers (Willie and Robert were working for George in Antung, and, as the budding taipan said in a letter, they could not go to the wedding as he was short-handed), Julia gave my mother away.

This was surely an unusual arrangement. In George's absence, Ellen O'Sea, my Japanese grandmother, should have been the matron of honour. That would have been the usual etiquette. Instead, she seemed to have had no role at all at the wedding. Was she excluded? Or did she decide, in the self-effacing manner she preferred, not to take any part? There was a conspiracy of silence about her. Years later, in recalling her marriage, my mother never mentioned her mother; nor did my father. Did Ellen O'Sea go to the ceremony at the little British church? She is not in any of the wedding pictures. Perhaps my Japanese grandmother felt it was better for all if she remained in the house and looked after the reception.

It was a quiet wedding, as weddings went in the foreign community of Nantai. Arthur and Mary were wed in the small Anglican church with its tall Gothic windows and grey slate roof, like any other small church or chapel in England. Reverend Lewellyn Lloyd, the aged and long-serving minister at the small British church, officiated. He had baptised Mary and now would marry her. A business friend with a fine voice sang "A voice that breathed o'er Eden." Shelley Brand and Mrs. Brand were among the guests, and so were commissioners of the Chinese Customs and Post Office, their wives, and other European friends. No Chinese were invited. Mary arrived in a splendid covered sedan chair; its interior, my mother said, was upholstered in red velvet and there was a pile of red satin cushions on the padded seat; its exterior was lacquered black with gold decorations. The sedan chair was luxuriously comfortable but heavy and required four chair coolies, dressed in livery.

Except for the sedan chairs and the Foochow ambience, it could have been a wedding anywhere in the old country. However, the honeymoon was far removed from any such felicity in Britain. It was spent on a houseboat up the spectacular Yuanfu River Gorge: "Oh, it was so beautiful," my mother recalled on her diamond wedding anniversary. The newlyweds had spacious quarters, a living room, bedroom, and bathroom, and their own servants, a Boy and a cook. The houseboat had a crew of seven, the *laotai (lao-da)*, the head man or captain, and six men who rowed when there was no wind for the large, square sail. They rowed standing up on a platform in the bow of the houseboat, pushing their oars instead of pulling them.

The newlyweds started off their boat trip from Foochow, Mary arriving in the splendid sedan chair, Arthur walking, followed by their two servants and a line of coolies bearing their luggage. The Yuanfu's junction with the Min River was not far from the town but it was a very narrow passageway, and they only just squeezed through, the crew's oars scraping against the high banks and the old Laotai leaning on the steering oar and shouting instructions. Sitting in wicker chairs on the deck, the bride and groom watched the heavenly landscape glide by, the scenic splendor of bamboo forests and Buddhist shrines clinging to the steep rocky hillsides. It was the most romantic honeymoon, spent in a grand colonial style.

9

THE GREAT WAR

and SHANGHAI

I WAS BORN IN CHEFOO (now called Yentai), a treaty port and resort, on August 31, 1913. A few miles along the Shantung (Shandong) peninsula was the British naval base of Weihaiwei (now Weihai), which was also a popular summer resort, and further down was Kiaochow (Jiaozhou) Bay and the German colony of Tsingtao, where my father had spent three months in happy exile. Chefoo had a mild and salubrious climate with its shores lapped by the Yellow Sea. There were quite a number of German nationals there, probably because of its proximity to Tsingtao, and the newly married Stursbergs met them and other members of the foreign community at the Club, that imperialist gathering-place, which played a major social role in China and wherever the British held sway.

My mother told my wife (she would never have told me) that when she was in labour at the time of my birth, she asked the doctor for chloroform. There was nothing new about the use of this anaesthetic at the time of a difficult birth; in fact, Queen Victoria had started the practice. The attending physician replied, "Certainly, if you have the chloroform." It seems extraordinary to us today that the doctor should expect the patient to provide the chloroform, but that was the sorry state of medicine in colonial China at that time. All of the Western physicians and surgeons in the treaty ports and the interior, with the exception of Shanghai, were missionaries or quacks.

The real missionaries, those who had come out to China to spread the gospel and "save souls," only tolerated the medical missionaries, regarding them as a means toward the goal of evangelization. Furthermore, they resented the amount of money spent on dispensaries and hospitals. The early medical missionaries were ordained ministers, and their work was always a precarious balance between healing and preaching. However, the situation was changing with the arrival of young doctors who were ardent Christians but had no theological training. They were proponents of what became known as the Social Gospel (as opposed to the exclusive and fundamentalist approach of the evangelists). As time went by, their arguments won the day and overall missionary policy changed; and while there was no lowering of the Christian appeal, it was stated that for the missionary doctors "medical work must come first and be the very best possible." By the 1920s, there were modern, well-equipped hospitals in most of China, as well as universities with medical faculties, such as the West China Union University, founded by Canadians.

My father served only for thirteen months in Chefoo before being transferred back to headquarters in Peking. This was only a couple of months after I was born and so my christening was put off until we were settled in the capital. I was named in the traditional manner of the first-born, after my father and my grandfathers: Arthur Lewis Peter. My Grandfather Stursberg noted with an exclamation mark that my initials spelled ALPS.

The move to Peking was complicated by the fact that my mother wanted to keep the experienced amah who had been passed on to her by a friend and who had taught her a lot about the care of a newborn baby. However, the amah did not wish to go to such a distant and foreign place and was only persuaded to do so by an agreement to take our Chefoo cook along with us so that she would have someone to talk to (there was a different dialect and different customs in the capital). So I arrived, tucked under my father's arm, at the Peking station, to be greeted by quite a few of his old friends and colleagues to whom he introduced my mother and, I suppose, me.

After a brief stay in a hotel, the family moved into quarters assigned to them in the Chuan-pan Hutung, one of the *hutungs* or lanes which were a feature of Peking. It was a typical Mandarin's dwelling with its series of courtyards and an entrance on the hutung itself; there was a wall to keep evil spirits out as apparently they could not go around corners. On either side of the doors were representations of some fearsome guardian gods. The first courtyard was given over to the Chinese servants: the Chefoo amah and cook who had accompanied us to the capital, a locally hired Boy as well as an amah to do the sewing and washing, and the inevitable *dageng-de* or night watchman. In the next courtyard were the living quarters, the bedroom on one side and the dining room opposite. Facing the entrance with its threatening guardians was the main reception room.

There were beautiful formal gardens in the courtyards, and the hutungs were highly regarded as living quarters in Peking. Not far from us was the residence of Sir Robert Bredon, who had been Acting Inspector General of the Customs in the absence of Sir Robert Hart and who was now special advisor to the Chinese government. However, next door was a bar, which was much frequented by troops attached to various legations, and my father complained about the sound of raucous merriment at night. As a result, he was glad to hear that he would be moving into a two-storey, Western-style house on Hataman Street, which was quite a fine building and comfortable enough but with none of the indigenous attraction of our Chinese house on the Chuan-pan Hutung.

The Post Office had been cut adrift from its parent, the all-powerful Chinese Maritime Customs, and was now a separate entity. It came under one of the Central Administration Boards that the Republican Government in Peking had set up to assert its jurisdiction but which was but a pretence of authority. At first, there had been some confusion about titles, but finally the foreign directorate had adopted the Customs nomenclature, with Commissioners being the highest ranks under the top executive.

Theophile Piry was now Director General of Posts, or, to be completely correct, Co-Director General of Posts as there was a Mandarin who was a figurehead as the other Co-Director General.

My father was intrigued by the fact that he was returning to Postal headquarters and to his old job, which he had left under a cloud only a couple of years before when he had been "exiled" to Tsingtao. Evidently, Mr. Piry had had a change of mind, which might have been brought about by his need for an experienced secretary; the threat of war and the impending mobilizations had led to some of the young Germans in the service being called up.

Judging from the weekly letters that my father wrote to his father, my German grandfather in London, the talk in Peking, at the office, and in the club, centred on the war and its progress. The Germans who had been friends and colleagues just a few months before had been quickly turned into sinister and treacherous enemies. In a letter written in October 1914, Dad said that "a few days ago a contingent of 110 Shanghai Britishers who have responded to the call for volunteers have left for home by the *Suwa Maru* [a Japanese liner], paying their own passages—those who can, the others are being assisted by contributions. A few men have also left from Peking and Tientsin."

The Japanese were staunch allies and besieged Tsingtao; the British seemed to have played a minor role in this engagement, despite their naval base of Weihaiwei being so close by. Shantung's Postal Commissioner wrote that the Japanese were "only waiting for the concrete foundations of the siege guns to set before commencing the bombardment." It took only a couple of weeks for the German garrison in Tsingtao to surrender, and my father declared "undoubtedly the Japanese are wonderful military men." He added in another letter to his father, "It is said that they [the Japanese] let loose in the mined areas [around Tsingtao] 70,000 hares, and these little animals successfully cleared the way for them." He compared the humanitarian tactics of the Japanese with those of the Germans, who might have saved thousands of lives if they had done something similar at Liege [during their drive through Belgium]: "but then the German generals do not seem to care about sacrificing their men's lives from all one reads of the manner in which they send them forward in dense formation."

The Germans captured in Tsingtao, who were regular troops or reservists, were interned in Japan, while German and Austrian nationals in Shanghai and other treaty ports were treated in the same way as the British and French. They could not be otherwise since China was neutral at the time. As might be expected, the Peking government had been under pressure to join the Allies but was able to resist the demands of the British—a sign of growing independence and increasing American influence. China only heeded the appeal of the US government and broke off diplomatic relations with Germany in March 1917.

In a letter at the end of February 1915, my father said that a branch of the "League of Patriotic Britons Overseas" was formed at a meeting in the British Legation. Sir Robert Bredon was elected chairman. The purpose of the League, he wrote, was to get "Britons residing outside the King's Dominions, said to number 3,000,000, to subscribe toward the purchase of a battleship for the Navy and afterwards keep up the cost of maintaining it." (Such leagues were common throughout the Empire during World War One.)

My father was apparently absolved of his misdeeds during his previous stint in Peking and had become one of Mr. Piry's "brightest and best." At any rate, the Director General of Posts had seen that he received substantial increments to his salary and in the late spring of 1915 promoted him to the rank of Deputy Postal Commissioner. A short time later, Mr. Piry told Arthur that he was being transferred to Shanghai to take charge of the Postal Supply Department. There had been delays in moving into the house on Hataman Street, and my father recalled that "Mary and I felt disappointed in a way" that, after only a couple of months and all the labour of moving in, they would have to leave "and, of course, we are going right into the heat of Shanghai. Still my new position makes up for it." Indeed. He would be running his own show and would be Acting Commissioner. In a little more than eighteen months he had gone from lowly acting Sub-district Postmaster in Chefoo to Acting Commissioner in Shanghai. His advancement had been breathtaking and was partly due to the war and the departure of so many German officials from the service.

The move to Shanghai in June 1915 led my father to decide that my mother and I should go to Japan immediately. They had been talking

✦ *Family group taken in Japan, ca. 1915; my mother and her sisters, Julia and Ceci, in kimonos, my Japanese grandmother at the end of the bench, and me sucking my thumb*

about this for some time. We would spend the summer months there and join my mother's sisters, Julia and Ceci, and her mother at Kusatsu, a small spa in the hills some distance from Yokohama. The last part of the journey there had to be made on pony back, but it was worth the effort as my mother reported that it was "beautifully cool." The resort was where the group photograph was taken of my mother and her sisters, all dressed in kimonos standing behind the bench on which my Japanese grandmother sat. (The vacation in Japan occurred only shortly after Mum had been cut dead in the Peking Club, but, perhaps, she was not aware then of the racial nature of the snub. At any rate, this holiday was the last time she saw her mother.)

We left my father to fend for himself in the muggy heat of Shanghai. Not only was he moving into a new office but into a new house. As Noel Coward wrote,

Mad dogs and Englishmen
Go out in the midday sun.
The Japanese don't care to,
The Chinese wouldn't dare to ...

Dad wore a suit and waistcoat and a stiff collar and tie, which was *de rigueur* for an official in the colonies, no matter how hot it was. He found it difficult moving into a new house and unpacking by himself, "without Mary's help," but he was glad she was escaping the sweltering heat—"and we have not had it really hot yet," he wrote. At the end of August, he too left for Japan and joined my mother and me for a couple of weeks holiday there, before returning with us to Shanghai.

That was the way that the summers were spent. It was taken for granted that white women and children could not stand the Asian sun, so they were packed off for three months or more to mountain resorts (known as hill stations in India), while the men only escaped from the midday sun for a couple of weeks, either taking their families away or bringing them back, as my father did.

We went to Japan only once and spent the rest of our summers at the Chinese mountain resorts of Kuling (Guling) or Chikungshan (Jigonshan), or the seaside resort of Weihaiwei. These mountain resorts, with their clusters of Western-style cottages, were similar to resorts in the Adirondacks or the Laurentians. The only Chinese on the cool hilltops were servants. A whole industry grew up to serve families escaping the heat: there were houses to be rented and food and other supplies to be provided. Weihaiwei had beautiful beaches and I have a photo of my brother and me, with toy pails and spades, digging in the sand, like any boys at any seaside resort, only we were wearing large topees.

The summer heat in Shanghai was such that my father took to the office several stiff collars and another shirt and would change them when they became wilted and wet. He must have been relieved to go to Japan to fetch us back. He wrote in a letter to his father about sailing through the Inland Sea to Nagasaki and how beautiful it all was. Although he complained about having to move into a new house and unpack without Mary's assistance, he found it to be a fine residence: "it is, of course, the best house we have had up to the present." In fact, 17 Hart Road (named after Sir Robert Hart) was a suburban mansion. There were large reception rooms and verandahs, two lawns (one of which had been laid out for a tennis court), and a conservatory, the whole surrounded by a brick wall topped with iron spikes.

My childish memory of Shanghai, or the International Settlement where we lived, was that it was a European city where the only Chinese were servants. (Actually, a number of wealthy Chinese lived in both the International Settlement and the French Concession.) There were public gardens and parks which were not meant for the Chinese, and the gardens on the Bund had signs that read "No Dogs or Chinese." Hongkew Park, which was on the other side of Shanghai from 17 Hart Road, had a golf course, and my father wrote that he had been "initiated into the mysteries of golf" by his brother-in-law Willie. The International Settlement was a British-run municipality with its own British-officered police force, made up mainly of Sikhs who had an antipathy toward Chinese, as well as British magistrates. As might be expected, the French ran the French Concession, and both the settlement and the Concession were cordoned off from the cluttered mass of the native city.

Shanghai had such an allure for foreigners that it was known as the Paris of the Orient. As a result, there were many visitors to 17 Hart Road, which was just off the Bubbling Well Road, one of the International Settlement's main thoroughfares. My mother's brothers and sisters were often guests, and George, the rising taipan, stayed for weeks. Dad wrote that "Mary's sister, Julia, arrived on Sunday and we are expecting Ceci and her husband [she had married Melton Summers the year before] as well as Mary's brother, Willie, tomorrow night, so you see we shall be quite a houseful." Fortunately, he said, the Hart Road mansion had enough rooms and servants to accommodate them. Ellen O'Sea, my Japanese grandmother, never came to stay with us in Shanghai or anywhere else; she could have accompanied Julia, who was living with her in Foochow, but apparently the only journeys that she ever wanted to make were to her native land.

My father had taken to walking for exercise in Shanghai. He went on a nostalgic hike to the North Barrier Station where he had first served in the outdoor Customs as a uniformed tide-waiter. He found that not much had changed in nine years, and the old native houseboat that had been his temporary home was still doing duty as quarters for the two men stationed there. It was a ten-mile jaunt there and back, which left him tired and stiff but did not dampen his enthusiasm for walking. "From our house," he said, "it is possible to go for plenty of nice walks without encountering any Chinese houses and their attendant squalor and smell."

Then there was the problem with the servants, especially with the amahs who were so important for a young family (my brother, Richard, was born in the Shanghai house on January 30, 1916). It was difficult to get a satisfactory amah, who would not up and leave at a moment's notice. My parents engaged a new amah who came from Anhwei (Anhui) Province and spoke what my father called "an awful dialect of Mandarin." Our Shanghai servants could not understand her. If Chinese servants spoke different and incomprehensible dialects they usually conversed in the *lingua franca* of the Orient, pidgin English, but this amah knew no English!

Richard's birth was easier than mine. When the time came, my father simply telephoned for the nurse and the doctor. The fact that 17 Hart Road had a telephone was a sign of what a modern city Shanghai, or at least the International Settlement, was. While the English nurse was capable enough—my mother would never have had a Chinese nurse— she expected to be waited on hand and foot by the Chinese servants. She was always "growling" at them, Dad said, and added that if she had stayed much longer, some of the servants would have quit. Her behaviour, in treating the natives like dirt, was not an aberration but only too typical of many British in private employment at that time in China.

Shortly after moving to Shanghai, my father bought a Studebaker, a fine four-door touring car. He then hired a Chinese chauffeur who taught him to drive. I have a dim memory of sitting in the backseat of this auto-mobile which seemed so big to me, and there is a photograph of me standing on the running board. My father hoped to go for drives in the country, but there was only one road outside Shanghai, known as the Rubicon Road, a fourteen-mile stretch around the city which bordered Soochow Creek and passed the North Barrier Customs Station. Despite this, there were some 600 to 700 automobiles in Shanghai, which was as many as in any Western city of 50,000 to 60,000, the population of the International Settlement at that time (1915–16).

The war interfered with the smooth operation of the Postal Supply Department which, as its name implied, provided the service with all the supplies it needed, from furniture and uniforms to stationery and paper-clips, and even handled stamps, although this function was being gradually transferred to Peking. Much of the material came from Britain but as a result of hostilities, shipping was limited, resulting in embarrassing short-ages. The mailbags came from Wormwood Scrubs prison in England, but shipments were stopped for the duration, and my father had to scramble around trying to find other sources of supply for this essential postal equipment in Japan or the United States.

As the war went on, and there seemed no end in sight, Dad became somewhat conscience-stricken. He had joined the Shanghai Volunteer Force, but if his brothers in England enlisted, he felt, as he said in a letter to his father, that he was shirking his duty as he was so much younger than them:

Although I shall always regret not having done my bit in this great struggle, I must admit that I have not the courage to sacrifice my present position and opportunities. It would be a case of throwing up everything and beginning all over again if I volunteered—ten years [of] labour in a far country all wiped out in a moment. No more Britons are being allowed to leave China for the purpose of enlisting ... as the government considers that it will be playing into the enemy's hands to let British influence in China decline too much through the withdrawal of British subjects. However, I don't try to shield myself behind that excuse for if they were still encour-aging Britons to go home I should still not feel able to volunteer.

My father was not the only one whose conscience was pricked by the war. Shanghai had a fine racetrack, and there were some members of the Jockey Club who felt the race meets should be put off for the duration. However, after some discussion, the majority voted in favour of holding the races. They were ready to subscribe substantial sums to the League of Patriotic Britons Abroad for that warship, spend hours drilling with the Shanghai Volunteer Force, or do anything else to help the British war effort, but they would not stop the race meets. No: that would give the wrong impression of the Empire's decline!

As China was a neutral country, German nationals were free to come and go, although they were made to feel like pariahs in the International Settlement and were barred from various clubs and establishments, especially the race meets. They did not hide from the scornful gaze of the British and French, however, but carried on a secret war against them. They set up an agency "for the forging of passports, making of bombs, and the hatching of nefarious plots," or so my father wrote. The discovery of a cache of shells at a German residence led to the uncovering of this conspiracy which had as its objective "the blowing up of strategic points in the Siberian railway and the placing of bombs on board allied steamers." While the plot was broken, there was no way of dealing with the plotters, since a foreign offender in the International Settlement would be handed over to his consul to be dealt with. In this case, the German Consulate was deeply involved in the plot.

The chaos that had been China for a century continued: the revolution and the replacement of the empire with a republic settled nothing. The first president, Yuan Shih-kai, was no republican and had been "elected," really named to this post by Sun Yat-sen, the revolutionary leader because he was thought to be a strong man and would be a bridge with the past and continue the "immemorial traditions of China." My father wrote in one of his weekly letters to his father that the Chinese were "absolutely unfitted for a republican form of government" and this was certainly true of Yuan Shih-kai. He had had the highest imperial rank, that of viceroy and grand councillor, and made no secret of the fact, even after he was made president, that he favoured the monarchy.

In fact, Yuan Shih-kai saw the presidency as a way station to *his* becoming emperor. On December 12, 1915, he arranged for the monarchy to be proclaimed; the enthronement ceremony was fixed for February 9, 1916. This announcement aroused the fury of the provincial governments, which in most cases were military dictatorships, and one after another they declared their independence of Peking. As might be expected, the political turmoil brought about a financial crisis: many of the Chinese banks closed, which made running the Postal Supply Department even more difficult for my father.

The military governor of Yunnan started the revolt when his troops invaded neighboring Szechwan (Sichuan) Province and there was a certain amount of fighting with government forces. There was even trouble in Shanghai, and gunfire was seen and heard in the International Settlement. Dad set out to find out what was going on, as he had done in Peking, but he made no mention of having his camera with him. He took his car but only got as far as the border of the French Concession with the native city, where he was stopped and required to drive back. He learned later that it was a concerted attack on the arsenal, which was the stronghold of the Chinese government troops. Rifle fire could be heard, which meant there was a ground attack, while revolutionaries seized a Chinese gunboat and turned its guns on the arsenal. But another Chinese gunboat had come to the rescue, and the revolutionaries fled when they were shelled. The Shanghai Volunteer Force was called out at midnight, presumably to keep the revolutionaries out of the Settlement.

Yuan Shih-kai had to back down and at the end of April 1916 gave up most of his powers to the premier and the cabinet. However, that was not enough; his opponents, led by Sun Yat-sen, wanted him out. His humiliation was complete. On June 6, 1916, Yuan Shih-kai died. My father wondered whether he had been "put out of the way" and was afraid that there would be more trouble. Yuan's ill-fated attempt to become emperor loosened the country's tenuous bonds and opened the gate to the warlords.

Life in Shanghai was very different from that in most other treaty ports. It was less colonial, more like life in a large commercial city in Europe or North America. The club did not play the prominent social role that it did in Chefoo, Foochow, or even in Peking; in fact, there were many clubs. The Shanghai Club on the Bund, with its famous—or infamous—long bar, was the most prominent, but there were national clubs, commercial clubs, and sports clubs, the most prestigious being the club that ran the race course. My father must have been a member of some club or another because of his position, but he made no mention of it in his letters home. That did not mean that imperialism had somehow faded away. The municipal government was white supremacist and the Chinese were second-class citizens not only in Shanghai but in most of the cities of China as most of them had been taken over as "treaty ports."

Just before we were to leave Shanghai on furlough, my father, as a member of the Shanghai Volunteer Force, was called up to restore law and order on the streets. The Chinese were furious over the Versailles Peace Conference's decision to allow the Japanese to retain the German colony of Tsingtao and not return it to China. On May 4, 1919, students went on a rampage in Peking and in Shanghai, which forced all shops to close. They put up notices on their shutters; most of them, my father said, were merely patriotic slogans and harmless enough, but some contained threats against the Japanese such as "Kill the Dwarfs." This irruption became known as the May Fourth Movement which, with its strikes and boycotts, could be compared with the non-cooperation campaign that Gandhi launched at about the same time in India. With its involvement of students and its use of modern methods of protest and, ironically, Western political ideals of democracy and Marxism, this nationalist movement broke irreparably with the old Confucian past.

The white Shanghai municipal council decided to make the shops open, and the Volunteers were mobilized. My father was with a squad of sixteen who acted as an escort to "a most tactless [British] police officer" detailed to remove the posters and get the shops to open:

> He would attack the crowd with a stick because they happened to assemble to watch the proceedings ... we went down some side streets and here by his rough treatment of a shopkeeper the detective nearly caused a riot.

The squad retired and telephoned for help. My father elaborated on the situation in a letter dated June 11, 1919:

> We all thought the removal of posters indiscriminately whether inflammatory or harmless was a mistake and rather a loss of face for

the police for fresh ones were put up almost as soon as the old ones were removed—and the attempt to make the shops open was a dismal failure.

The closing of the Chinese shops was followed by a general strike. The telephone system was shut down, and the water and electricity supply was threatened. "In view of all this," my father recalled, "the Municipal Council decided to forbid students from coming into the [International] Settlement at all in any kind of uniform or carrying badges or flags." The Volunteers were called out again, but this ban had little or no effect at first. However, the Chinese shops gradually opened, after the shopkeepers demanded and got police protection, and, in a week or so, the closures and strikes petered out. Yet the whole incident lived on in the claims of the May Fourth Movement, which became a rallying cry for future campaigns against British hegemony.

IO

COMMISSIONER'S HOUSE

in OLD HONAN

WE LEFT SHANGHAI IN AUGUST 1919 *aboard the Japanese liner* Kashima Maru *bound for Victoria, British Columbia. It was the first furlough for my father since coming to China in 1906; he would have been entitled to home leave in 1914 but the Great War meant that it had to be postponed. At that time, the journey to England via Canada was probably as quick as the more direct way through the Suez Canal, but my father had another reason for taking this route: he was thinking of eventually settling in the Dominion. In England, we stayed with Grandfather Stursberg and Grandmater in their Weston-Super-Mare house and toured around in a motorcycle and sidecar, visiting numerous other relatives.*

My parents tried out a pretty blonde as governess, but decided that she was too young for China and hired instead the middle-aged and matronly Miss Daisy Hodgkin. Our return trip to China was delayed because our ship, the French liner Porthos, *had to have her boilers fixed. So we were stuck in Marseilles for three weeks. Finally, we were off on the long, hot journey, and I remember a burial in the Red Sea of a cook who had died from the heat. At last, there was the Bund rising dark and imperial out of the muddy waters of the Whampoo River.*

We were only in Shanghai for three or four days. My father had been appointed Postal Commissioner of Honan, the ancient province where so many dynasties had come and gone, and his headquarters would be in the historic city of Kaifeng, the capital of China from the tenth to the twelfth century during the Sung Dynasty, when it was known as Bianjing or Dongjing. In 1920 the provincial capital was in decline, its city walls being inundated by the sands from the Gobi desert.

My father's expense account shows that we had taken the precaution of hiring a Boy and an amah while we were in Shanghai. It took seven days in mid October 1920 to reach Kaifeng, first by river steamer from Shanghai to Hankow, then by trains with a change at the railway junction of Chengchow (Zhengzhou). The account lists first-class passages for us and third-class for the servants; there are also several items on payment of coolies to handle our 48 pieces of luggage, with a total weight, according to the expense account, of 2,210 kilograms. Our luggage had to be loaded on the steamer, unloaded, and transferred to the trains, a couple of times because of the change at Chengchow, and finally unloaded again when we reached our destination.

Presumably, the account covered the cost of the army of coolies who transported this great pile of luggage, which included crates of canned food, through the dusty streets within the city walls of Kaifeng to the mandarin's residence that was to be our temporary home while they finished building the Postal Commissioner's house. Since there was no Customs Commissioner in Honan—the Chinese Maritime Customs was confined to the treaty ports—my father was the senior colonial officer in this province of thirty million inhabitants. In fact, he was addressed as Commissioner and the plans for the new house were entitled "New Commissioner's Residence, Kaifeng." I thought our first home, the rambling old Chinese house with its series of small rooms and oiled paper windows (there was no electricity), was rather cozy. My mother did not like it and was glad when, in a couple of months time, we were ready to move. "Butter in the soap box," she said, "remember." And I have remembered to this day.

✦ *View from the tennis court of our house in Kaifeng; note the*
high brick wall around the compound

The Postal Commissioner's house was a large house in a large compound that covered several acres, surrounded by a high brick wall. There was a second house in the same compound, smaller but still big, for the Deputy Postal Commissioner. It became known as "Nan Guan" (south house) because it was to the south of Kaifeng and bordered the mud road that led to the South Gate. The style of architecture could be described as "Liverpool Baronial," with ceilings thirteen feet high (thirteen feet and three inches, according to the plans), and wide verandahs both upstairs and down. The Postal Commissioner's house dominated the landscape, as it was meant to do, and was an overbearing presence on the outskirts of the city with its narrow streets and mass of low grey buildings. Kaifeng had no outstanding features but for the thirteen-storey *Tie Ta*, the Iron Pagoda, which was made not of iron but of tiles that were the colour of rust.

Everything was new in the newly built house. The furniture, the beds and the bureaus, the tables, including the long dining-room table, and

chairs, the chesterfields, upholstered chairs, and sofas for the large drawing room, the desk and bookcases for the study, had all come from
Shanghai, straight from the European furniture factories there. However,
the tall white chairs in the children's room—we were too old for it to be
called a nursery—were probably locally made, as the cartoons of animals
were painted on their backs in bold red and black. Were they foxes in
those pre-Mickey Mouse days?

We had electricity from our own generator, but more than that, the
Postal Commissioner's and Deputy's houses were the only homes in the
whole of Honan to have flush toilets and hot and cold running water.
Across the mud road was the Southern Baptist missionary compound,
which looked like an American suburb plunked down in the middle of
China, but none of the Western-style houses had indoor plumbing. Still,
the modernism of our new house did not extend to electric fans—air
conditioning was unheard of then. Instead, a wide cloth punkah hung
above the dining-room table; it created a warm, gentle breeze when
pulled by the head Boy's son from his perch on the verandah.

For us, life was lived on two levels in Kaifeng. While we enjoyed many
colonial comforts within our compound, just beyond its perimeter lay the
medieval city with all its squalor and stench. The heads of recently
executed criminals and so-called bandits were hung near the main South
Gate and could be seen by my brother and me as we drove in our open
carriage into the city, despite my mother's best efforts to divert our attention. My friend Miriam Harris, the daughter of a Southern Baptist
missionary, actually witnessed an execution, even though her mother
quickly covered her head with the carriage rug. She recalled, "I saw a man
kneeling with his hands tied behind his back, and a huge man with a
sword chopped his head off." There were beggars and lepers on the streets.
One of my own gruesome memories is of a half-naked boy, covered with
sores, lying in his own excrement.

The city gates were closed at night. My father's office was in a low red-
brick building in the very centre of Kaifeng, but he was always home
before the gates closed and never had to climb over the city wall, as he had
to do some years later when he was journeying up the Yangtse to his new
post in Chengtu (Chengdu), in the great western province of Szechwan

(Sichuan). On that occasion, he had to visit an official in a town on the river's edge. By the time he had finished his business and left to rejoin his boat, the gates were closed and the gatekeepers adamantly refused to open any of them, so there was nothing else for him to do but clamber over the city wall and be lowered to the ground on the other side by a rope.

While conditions in much of China were as medieval and backward as those in Kaifeng, the 1911 republican revolution had brought about one major social change: the queues or pigtails that had been imposed on the Chinese people by the Manchus were banned. Queues were a mark of subservience, of humiliation; a drawing in a nineteenth-century British magazine showed a Shanghai policeman dragging a couple of coolies by their pigtails. However, the queues became part of the Chinese identity, like the beards of the Moslems or the hair of the Sikhs, and early missionaries who sought to be close to their fold tried to grow queues or wore false queues (Bishop White, for example, had a pigtail sewn into the back of his cap). The queue had been around for hundreds of years, and the common people had come to regard it as ordained by heaven and resisted attempts to remove it. Many of them, protesting and wailing, had to be dragged before the authorities to have their pigtails shorn.

In the Postal Commissioner's compound and the missionary compound across the mud road from us, the period was more the nineteenth century than the twentieth century, despite electricity. This was because we had to be almost as self-sufficient as the pioneers of Canada and the United States. It was difficult, if not impossible, to get fluid milk, since there was no dairy in Honan and few cows. So we kept goats and made our own butter and cheese—and ice cream, if we had ice. There was no refrigeration, and the ice, if it had not melted away in the heat of summer, came from the ice house, which most compounds had. Canned foods could be ordered from Shanghai but took weeks to be delivered, which was why we brought so much with us. Such staples as sugar and salt were available in bulk, in hundred-pound sacks, but had to be rendered by the cook to remove bits of straw and sand. Vegetables were mostly home-grown, and chickens and ducks were bought live and killed on the premises.

✦ A photo of my brother, Richard, and me in a donkey cart beside the entrance to the Kaifeng house, ca. 1922

Besides the goats, we had pigs and a donkey. My father liked to go for walks in the countryside and used to buy animals from the local peasants. The donkey was just a foal when we got him and he came to regard the billy goat as his mother and followed him around everywhere. Not only did we ride the donkey but we had a trap built for him, and my brother and I used to drive the donkey around the mud road between our house and the missionary compound. We soon discovered this was a source of entertainment for the crowds on the road. It was rather daring of us to go for such a drive, as we were not supposed to leave the compound, but the *mah foo*, the coachman, followed us around and saw that we returned safely. The *mah foo* looked after the livestock, and I remember him force-feeding geese by pushing sausages of grain down their throats.

The greatest danger was endemic disease. All drinking water had to be boiled. It tasted flat and was never cold enough to be a thirst-quenching delight. No vegetable was eaten raw. The summers could be fiercely hot and brought dust storms, really sand storms, from the Gobi Desert. The sky would become dark and menacing, and the whirling sand made a scratching sound as it beat against the windows and doors. Although they were shut tight and everything was battened down, there would be a thick film of dirt inside the house when the storm ended. The summers also brought an outbreak of cholera or a plague of some kind. Then there were no more picnics, no more driving around in the donkey trap, no more excursions in the springless Peking carts to temples or the banks of the Yellow River. Instead, we stayed in the house with the blinds drawn to keep out the heat and listened to the grown-ups talking darkly about victims falling dead in the streets, and of the amah's relative coming down with the cholera and what could be done about it? The amah was distraught. Was *Kao-lin*, a clay used in pottery, a cure or a suppressive since it lined the stomach? Was there any remedy?

We lived in splendid isolation. My brother and I kept mainly to the compound. We were never allowed to mix with the Chinese children on the road outside—our mother admonished, "You'll get lice if you do." I was envious of the ragged urchins playing in the mud road beyond the compound gate, especially when the Yellow River flooded and they were having such a happy time, splashing around and catching fish in baskets—and quite big fish too! That seemed incredible. But we could play within the compound with the servants' children, who were clean and apparently had no lice, and that was how we became fluent in vernacular Chinese.

Within the high brick walls of our compound, a park had been created with a tennis court at one end, surrounded by flowering shrubs and approached through a rose arbour, past beds of geraniums; there was also an extensive vegetable garden. The goats and other animals were kept in pens behind the coach house. Our other friends and playmates were the few missionary children in the Southern Baptist compound. That was why we enjoyed going to the mountain resort of Chikungshan where we met many more boys and girls of our age.

However, there were good times: "beautiful birthday parties," as Miriam Harris recalled, and wonderful old-fashioned Christmases. We made our own entertainment. When we were home on furlough, I had listened to a crystal set but not even the rumour of wireless had reached the interior of China. Miss Hodgkin, our governess, was good at organizing games and concerts. At one of the latter, my brother and I dressed up in goat skins and carried wooden staves for a rendition of Men of Harlech. My friend Hendon Harris, Miriam's younger brother, rather outdid us by appearing as Lincoln and reciting part of the Gettysburg Address. We had singalongs, with Miss Hodgkin playing the piano, usually of hymns, with the favourite being "Jerusalem the Golden."

The preparations for Christmas went on for days and that added to the excitement. We cut coloured paper into strips and fashioned chains and garlands with which to decorate the rooms. A pine tree was dug up and brought into the hall; it was covered with wonderful little ornaments that the amahs and the cooks made. Real candles provided the lights and were lit only once, on Christmas Eve with my mother and father and the servants, who had brought in a pail of water, standing watch.

The large public rooms in the Postal Commissioner's house lent themselves to official functions. My father entertained the senior members of the Postal staff and other high officials at Chinese New Year. There were several receptions, as New Year celebrations went on for days at the end of January and the beginning of February. My mother directed operations of an enlarged staff as all kinds of Chinese cakes and coconut and ginger and sesame sweets were prepared in the kitchen, but she had to keep out of sight, as no women were allowed at these parties. It was a hectic time. Gifts were exchanged, wrapped up in bright-red paper, and there was much bowing, but I was busy scurrying around, sampling the sweets and other delights laid out in lacquer dishes. However, the function that I remember best was when Dad entertained the *tu-chen*, the military governor, of Honan who arrived in an open carriage with an escort of cavalry. Chao-Ti was a fine old mandarin with a thin white beard. My brother and I peered down from the top of the staircase and watched my father and his deputy, a cheerful Corsican named Forzinetti, greet the *tu-chen* and his entourage. We were expected to look after the military escort, but that was done in the servants' quarters.

It was a memorable event at the end of an era. My father, resplendent in white tie and tails, was wearing the *Chia Ho*, the Chinese Order of the Excellent Crop. The *tu-chen* was of the old school and wore civilian clothes, a skull cap, and a dark watered-silk jacket with long sleeves that covered his hands over a satin gown; he spoke with elaborate old-fashioned courtesy. His province was ripe for picking for this was the period of the warlords. Only a few weeks after the formal dinner party in the Postal Commissioner's house, the old *tu-chen* with his entourage, and a bevy of wives and concubines, as well as his bodyguards, had decamped. One of the most famous warlords, the so-called Christian General, Feng Yu-hsiang (Feng Yuxiang), and his army of twenty thousand men, adjudged by Western observers to be the best fighting force in China, had crossed the borders of the province.

Before fleeing, Chao-Ti made a last, desperate attempt to negotiate. He appointed a five-man commission to ask for amnesty, and since he knew that the formidable Feng was a Christian, he made Reverend Hendon Harris, a leading Southern Baptist missionary, head of the commission. Pastor Harris was the father of my friends, Miriam and Hendon Jr.; he was a tall, good-looking Southerner, an active man who was a keen tennis player, and he and his wife often played on the court in our compound. It would be a dangerous undertaking, but Mr. Harris, who spoke Chinese fluently, could not refuse. The commission was given a train—an engine on which large white flags were mounted, a coach, and a dining car—to take them to the border town of Chengchow, a railway junction, that the Christian general had seized.

Despite the white flags, the train was fired on as it approached Chengchow. Bullets blasted through the coaches, and the missionary and other members of the commission dived for the floor. The train stopped. A courier, who, Mr. Harris told Dad, was one of his Post men, bravely went forward on foot with a white flag to explain that this was a truce mission. The train was allowed to proceed to Chengchow, where Hendon Harris had his first encounter with the famous warlord. He found him to be a huge man by Chinese standards, six feet, two inches tall, which was about the American's own height, but heavier; a charismatic figure, dressed in the cotton uniform of an ordinary soldier. When Harris put forward Chao-Ti's plea, General Feng spoke directly without any convoluted courtesies: "No! No compromise! We are marching on Kaifeng!"

It took two days for the army to reach the provincial capital, and they were two days of chaos and anarchy, a classic example of what happens when the ruler has fled and all order and restraints have collapsed. The return to savagery was almost immediate. There was widespread looting and rioting; the old *tu-chen's* troops, routed, abandoned, left to fend for themselves, turned into murderous gangs. They robbed flour mills, food stores, and factories. They stole for the sake of stealing. One missionary saw cavalry men with stacks of hats on their heads; they had obviously raided the local hat-maker's shop. The soldiers went on a wild rampage of destruction. My father's office in the centre of Kaifeng was broken into and wrecked; I saw a photo of the damage which Dad had taken to let headquarters in Peking know what had happened.

The interregnum disorder, the gunfire outside the walls of the compound, made us take shelter in the large central hall of the house. The windows by the staircase were barricaded with mattresses. We slept in the hall, and I could hear the sound of shooting that seemed to grow louder at night as if there were a pitched battle going on. The servants were frightened and huddled in their quarters, and seemed to be moaning. Miss Hodgkin kept asking my father in a quavering voice for assurances that we would not be killed. I can only remember being excited: this was like an adventure story that I had read about being besieged by natives in Africa or somewhere; was it by Rider Haggard or Henty? The next morning—and it seemed such a beautiful day after the wild night of rioting—I picked up spent rifle shells in the flower beds beside the high brick wall.

We were allowed out of the compound to watch the long lines of General Feng's soldiers marching up through the wheat fields toward the city's main South Gate. They seemed better disciplined, better dressed in their grey uniforms than the ragtag troops of the old *tu-chen*. My mother was impressed: "They even had handkerchiefs," she recalled. The day was bright and sunny, and everyone seemed relieved and pleased at the sight of these troops, especially the missionaries from the Southern Baptist compound across the mud road from us, who were also out to see them arrive. I waved to Miriam and Hendon Jr. Their father had gone to the South Gate and would be one of the first to greet the Christian general when he made his triumphal entry into Kaifeng (May 14, 1922). The missionaries of all Protestant denominations, Anglican, Methodist, Presbyterian, and Baptist, hailed Feng as "an example of the power of the Christian message," but the Catholics stood aloof: he was not one of them. Many foreigners, not just the Protestant missionaries, thought Feng might be the Constantine of China, but there were a few cynics who compared him with another Christian zealot, Hung Hsu-chuan of the bloody Taiping rebellion.

General Feng brought about some much-needed reforms during his time as *tu-chen*, and it must be said that he was a much better governor than his predecessor, Chao-Ti. He was a warlord all right, but at that time he was an exception to the run of other warlords, most of whom had evil reputations as predators and parasites, and overtaxed and tyrannized the people under their control. The Christian general rode around Kaifeng on a bicycle, much to the astonishment of the populace and foreigners like my father. This was all part of his carefully cultivated image of a nationalist soldier who was close to the people. Feng did attempt to stamp out corruption. He improved education generally in Honan, he converted many temples into classrooms, and he opened the first public library in Kaifeng. He sought to ban opium smoking, prostitution, and gambling, and tried to enforce the rules against foot-binding, which was still prevalent in the province.

As might be expected, Feng Yu-hsiang returned the missionaries' high regard for him by co-operating with them and enlisting their help in his endeavours. He was close not only to Pastor Harris of the Southern Baptist Mission but also to the Canadian Anglican clergyman William C. White, the first Bishop in Honan, who conducted services for his troops. So did a firebrand preacher, Reverend Jonathan Goforth, from the Canadian Presbyterian Mission in Changte, or Anyang, the dynastic seat of the three-thousand-year-old Shang or Yin Dynasty in North Honan. In fact, Dr. Goforth acted for a time as the chaplain of Feng's army.

General Feng's methods for promoting Christianity were military. We were invited to one of his mass services; I remember sitting on bleachers on the edge of a large parade ground outside the city walls. The troops marched in, regiment by regiment, singing gospel hymns: "Onward

Christian Soldiers" was one I recognized. At a command from the officer conducting the service from a high platform, the men waved small bibles (New Testaments). It was a sight that thrilled the missionaries. "The sea of open testaments," as one of them described the scene, "every right hand of every soldier in the great audience of 4,000 young Chinese men holding forth the Word of God." It was also a harbinger of the Red Guards and Chairman Mao's little red books.

The summers in Kaifeng were burning hot, and the summer the Christian general was governor was one of the hottest. The earth was parched and no crops grew. There was drought and famine. The city was besieged by thousands of poor people begging for food. We had gone to the mountain resort of Chikungshan, but my father remained behind. There was great distress and disease in the crowded streets. Feng did what he could to relieve the suffering; he opened relief camps but there were not enough of them. Only rain could resolve the situation, and every effort had to be made to propitiate the elements. So the god of Kaifeng City, in its role as the Rain God, was trundled out. This was an enormous idol, some ten feet high, on a flat, eight-wheeled cart that was dragged by a large number of men, sweating profusely in the sultry heat, through the city streets to the baked fields outside. Although the Rain God was shown the effects of the drought for three days running, the sky remained a blazing blue.

Finally, Feng acted. Posters were plastered on the city walls inviting the populace to come on a certain day to a certain park to pray for rain. A large platform was built at one end of the park, which served as a pulpit for the Christian general on the day of the prayer meeting. He was not alone but had with him his officers and all Protestant missionaries in the Kaifeng area—my father was not invited—who joined with him in his supplications. Feng's timing was impeccable. The sky was overcast. The prayers and lamentations were interrupted by rain, a torrential downpour. The great multitude of Chinese at the prayer meeting were soaked but overcome with wide-eyed astonishment. The missionaries ran for shelter with joy in their hearts. God had saved the land, or as one of them said, "Ask, believe, and it shall be given."

It looked as though General Feng Yu-hsiang would soon fulfill the great expectations that the missionaries had for him. Kaifeng was but a way station on his drive for Peking and power. He left after being *tu-chen* for less than a year, much to the dismay of the locals and the missionaries, who knew that his reforms would be overturned. Six months after his army's arrival on the outskirts of Peking, the Christian General joined in a conspiracy with enemy forces to take the capital. What was worse, according to his biographer, James Sheridan, was that the "coup by Feng Yu-hsiang—long reputed to be bitterly anti-Japanese—was actively supported, probably financed, and perhaps conceived" by the Japanese. For a short time, Feng was the *de facto* ruler of China. He replaced the president and forced Pu-yi, the last emperor, out of the Forbidden City, where he had been allowed to live although deposed in the 1911 Revolution. Next there were reports that Feng had started talks with the Nationalist Party, the Kuomintang, and with its founder, Sun Yat-sen, the father of the Chinese revolution.

These reports were borne out by the fact that Sun Yat-sen came to Peking to confer with Feng Yu-hsiang as the first step in establishing a new regime. From the perspective of the missionaries, especially those who had known him in Kaifeng, God's plan seemed to be unfolding as the first quarter of the twentieth century was coming to an end. Sun, however, was terminally ill with cancer and died on March 12, 1925, before the negotiations had reached any conclusion. This was a devastating blow, as the discussions with the nationalist leader gave the Christian general some legitimacy; now he was just another warlord, and his enemies combined and drove him from Peking. Later, he made deals with Chiang Kai-shek, and eventually, he broke them. Feng then sought help from the Soviets, much to the consternation of the missionaries, and went to Moscow, but turned against the Chinese Communists.

He was an opportunist, a "picturesque ruffian," as Emily Hahn called him. By now he had lost the support and admiration of the missionaries. Perhaps "Rice Christian" would be the wrong term, but Feng used Christianity for his own military purposes, as Sheridan says; he believed the gospel produced better and more reliable fighting soldiers, and this was the reason for the indoctrination of his troops. My father never liked him. As the Postal Commissioner and senior British officer in Honan, he had called on him in Kaifeng, but Feng never returned the call, which was an insult. "His way of throwing his support first on one warring faction and then on the opposing group," my father wrote, "only confirms the form of treachery that was his innate nature."

The Christian general, the medieval setting of Kaifeng and the province of Honan, and our colonial lifestyle in the Postal Commissioner's House were all part of my education. So were the missionaries and missionary children like Miriam and Hendon Harris. However, the formal lessons in the children's room, now known as the schoolroom, were a blank in my memory.

What did our English governess, Miss Hodgkin, whom Miriam called "Miss Pigpen" as a girlish joke, teach us? What books did she use? Of course, it was pretty straightforward stuff—reading, writing, and arithmetic. I remember having a den in a cupboard underneath the staircase in the great hall where I wrote and illustrated stories about pirates and American Indians, about whom I knew nothing except what I had absorbed from books, but never a line about the Chinese, about the *mah foo* or the servants' children with whom we played. I read avidly Richmal Crompton's *William* books, beginning with *Just William*, which had an English setting that seemed ideal although far removed to a boy growing up in Kaifeng. Still, Miss Hodgkin seemed to have done an adequate enough job as she left my brother Richard and me sufficiently well versed to be equal to our peers when we did go to school.

Education was in some ways a heart-rending problem for many foreign families in the Far East. There were schools, usually boarding schools, for missionary children—Miriam Harris and her older sister, Helen, went to one of these in the mountain resort of Chikungshan—but these were mainly small, makeshift arrangements with one or two missionary ladies looking after twenty or thirty children, and the classes did not go beyond sixth or seventh grade. As a result, most British parents in China, as in India, had to part with their children at the tender age of seven or eight and ship them home to be educated. Gordon White, Bishop White's son, was only five and a half years old when he was sent to school in England; he only saw his parents every five years when they were on furlough.

There were a few English-language high schools, the most famous being the Chefoo School. It provided a classical English education from prep school to the sixth form, the equivalent of Grade Twelve, where graduating students took matriculation or the Oxford School Certificate exam. The Americans had a couple of high schools in the larger centres such as Shanghai, and it was in a convent in Shanghai that my mother was educated. There was a Canadian school in Chengtu, Szechwan, which was run by the West China Methodist, later United Church, Mission, the largest Canadian mission. It followed the Ontario curriculum, with students writing Ontario exams. The Chengtu School, with forty or fifty boarders, was much smaller than the Chefoo School but had the same high standards. When its most famous graduate, Ted Joliffe, returned to Canada at age seventeen, he had no difficulty getting into the University of Toronto; he was the Ontario Rhodes scholar for 1931.

My father became a good friend of Bishop White's. He had first known him as an Anglican priest in Foochow who had conducted the Masonic funeral of Captain Samuel Lewis Shaw. White was consecrated as Bishop in Honan in 1910, and afterwards moved to Kaifeng to set up the Canadian Anglican Mission. There were other missions, such as the Southern Baptist Mission across the mud road from our compound and nearby the China Inland Mission. My friends Miriam and Hendon Harris were with the Baptist Mission, and there was an older boy, Raymond Joyce, whose parents were with the CIM, but he was only home for the holidays as he was at the Chefoo School. Yet the Canadian Anglican Mission was closest to us, not only because my parents liked the Whites but because of its doctors and its small hospital. (I remember having a tooth out there although when I was operated on for adenoids I went to a larger Nanking hospital.)

Bishop White had become an ardent sinologist with a passionate interest in Chinese history and culture, and was cognizant of the fact that there were remnants of a Jewish community in the capital of Honan. The Jews, who had been merchants and traders, had come to Kaifeng, then the capital of China, in the twelfth century during the Sung Dynasty, and apparently took up residence there and stayed. Their descendants had been completely assimilated, however. They looked Chinese, spoke Chinese and knew no Hebrew; some were even illiterate, yet Bishop White said they called themselves Jews. He wanted to build the Anglican cathedral on the site of the ancient synagogue, now a pond of dirty water, but "the price asked by the Jews was prohibitive." However, he was able to obtain the synagogue's memorial tablets, dated 1489 and 1679, and had them erected on either side of the entrance to his church, which he called Trinity Cathedral. We attended the opening service of the cathedral, which had taken a long time to build. It was a handsome red-brick building which seemed out of place amid all the greyness of the old Chinese city.

The early twentieth century was a time of turmoil in China, of marauding bandits and warlords, and of a total breakdown in government; yet it was a time of widespread construction. The Lunghai Railway, the great north–south line that ran through Kaifeng, was being built by a European consortium. Work gangs were digging up all manner of antiquities and archaeological treasures, for the whole of Honan and the North China plain was a vast burial ground. Bishop White, who was fascinated by early Chinese artifacts, particularly bronzes, began collecting. He later remarked that if he had not done so, the historic works of art that he had acquired would have been lost. And much of what was uncovered was destroyed or discarded because, in the chaos that was China then, there was no organization, no museum, for holding and preserving these records of the past.

When my father died in 1979, among his effects was a thin tin box which, when opened, disclosed on a bed of cotton wool the cracked plastron of a turtle with characters etched on its surface. (I was quite excited as I realized this was an oracle bone.) My father must have got this relic from Bishop White since he did not know Dr. James Menzies, the Canadian Presbyterian missionary who was the real discoverer of these bones, "the first evidence of Chinese writing." While out for a walk near his home in Changte (Anyang) in northern Honan, Dr. Menzies stumbled on the remains of a most ancient dynasty, what he called "The Waste of Yin"—the Yin, or Shang, Dynasty ruled China from 1600 to 1100 BC.

With his high regard for Chinese culture, the Bishop was keenly interested in oracle bones and also collected them.

Although William C. White remained Bishop in Honan until he retired in 1934, his major interest shifted from church affairs to collecting for the Royal Ontario Museum. Perhaps he felt he had completed his life work as an Anglican missionary with the construction of Trinity Cathedral, which had been a stressful and difficult task and had taken up so much of his energy. At the time in China there was no control over export of antiquities—this was the period of the warlords when the mandate of the central government did not reach far beyond the capital and the only country-wide authorities were the British-run Customs and Post Office. As a result, White was able to provide the Museum with what became one of the greatest collections of Chinese art outside China. It included early bronzes, stone carvings, Tang Dynasty figures, early pottery, and magnificent Taoist and Buddhist murals.

II

THE 1927 STEP TOWARD
IMPERIAL OBLIVION

WE LEFT KAIFENG IN THE EARLY SPRING OF 1924 *and again returned home (to England) via Canada. As soon as we arrived in Victoria, my father acquired a seven-acre holding at Royal Oak, about seven miles from the Parliament Buildings and the Empress Hotel. I went to a three-room wooden schoolhouse, a mile and a half down the switchback West Saanich Road and opposite the small Royal Oak Municipal Hall. It was the first school I had ever attended and I loved it. But I was not long at this carefree rustic academy as Dad had decided that my brother and I should go to Bedford School, the British Public School that my mother's youngest brother, Leo, had attended; in fact, he had already enrolled us. Why did my father buy the Royal Oak property, since we lived there for only a little more than three months? Perhaps it was his way of securing a foothold in Canada.*

Bedford School was a typical British public school. It was not as elitist as Eton and Harrow, but like Rugby, Oundle, and Hailerbury (founded by the East India Company), Dulwich, St. Paul's, and Merchant Tailors (an offshoot of the London guilds), schools with whom Bedford played games. The public, really private, schools had been called the "nurseries of empire," and they could still be called that in the

1920s. Since the Great War, the Empire had become larger with the acquisition of former German colonies and trusteeship territories; it was a grossly overgrown, rickety political structure, shaken by the rising tide of nationalism. Yet despite all this, the British public-school boys could expect a virtual lifetime of work in the colonial services.

A POLITICAL AND SOCIAL STORM WAS BREAKING when Dad returned to China on his own in 1925, leaving us with our mother as day boys at Bedford. An extraordinary leader had arisen in India: Mohandas Gandhi, a moralist and religious reformer, more saint than politician. He radicalized the Congress Party and used it to rally the people in non-violent campaigns against the British Raj; these rallies often turned violent. Meanwhile, a different kind of leader, the exact opposite to Gandhi, had emerged in China: Chiang Kai-shek, a tough, ruthless soldier. He had become head of the Kuomintang, the nationalist party, and directed its anti-imperialist, anti-British "northern campaign," which led to the 1927 exodus from China.

Father sailed from Marseilles on February 21, 1925 and reached Shanghai on March 26. He stayed with Aunty J, who had married and moved from Foochow to Shanghai where her husband, Harold Carey, had a job with an American firm. They talked about old times and she must have mentioned that her mother, my Japanese grandmother, was crippled by arthritis. Some three or four years later, my cousin, Basil, and his mother, Aunt Ceci, visited Foochow and stayed at Terenure. Basil said that our grandmother could not walk and had to be carried around by an amah.

However, Dad made no mention of this in the letters he wrote Mum, although there was a cryptic remark about Ellen O'Sea in one of them. At school, my brother and I were being called "Chinky." As might be expected, this racial epithet upset us, and Mother wrote to Dad to tell him about it. His reply surprised me: while noting our reaction to this epithet, he suggested that Mum should inform us we had a Japanese grandmother. She never did.

The sojourn in Shanghai was short-lived. My father was to be Postal Commissioner for Western Szechwan (Sichuan), but before he could take up the appointment he had to spend some months in Nanking (Nanjing) relieving the Commissioner there. As a result, it was not till the last days of August that he was able to begin the long journey up the Yangtze to Chengtu. The first of the river steamers, ss *Huangpu*, which was to take him to Hankow, brought him face to face with the social upheaval that would reach a crescendo in 1927. The Chinese crew was on strike and had been replaced by white Russians. The steward, according to the Irish captain of the *Huangpu*, was a Polish duke, and some of the others were ex-generals. My father was skeptical, but some of the Russians had held high positions; he told Mother, "At the same time there are some rather villainous-looking rascals among them."

A second steamer, ss *Shasi*, took Father from Hankow to Ichang (Yichang), the stretch of the Yangtze known as the "middle river." At Ichang, he boarded the "upper river" boat for Chungking (Chongqing), a short, stubby American vessel, the ss *I Ping* (most of the rest of the Yangtze river steamers were owned by such British firms as Butterfield and Swire, and Jardine Matheson). The *I Ping* had powerful engines to battle the whirlpools and stiff currents of the gorges; there were only nine passengers aboard, including four American "bluejackets" who were on their way to join US gunboats at Chungking and other stations up-river. The steamer entered the first of the Three Gorges early in the morning, and Dad remarked, "The scenery the whole day has been wonderful." It was evening and they were in the Wind Box Gorge when he wrote the letter, "It [the scenery] has impressed me as much in its way as the Rocky Mountains did."

After two weeks and three steamers to make the journey from Nanking to Chungking, there was still a further two weeks of travelling to reach Chengtu. Father spent nine or ten days on a native boat dragged by trackers up the Kialing (Jialing, which was the way it was pronounced), a tributary of the Yangtze, to a place called Suining, then five days overland by sedan chair to his final destination in Western Szechwan. He could have gone all the way to Chengtu by boat, but it would have taken much longer.

This was the way the early missionaries travelled, only there was no upper river steamer then and their boats were hauled by teams of trackers scrabbling along paths cut in the steep sides of the gorges from Ichang to Chungking. Accidents frequently occurred. One missionary counted a dozen wrecks on his trip up the river; he saw one boat go "scudding past with end stoved in and boxes rolling out and floating down the rapids." This also happened on the Jialing. Dad noticed "one boat that was some little distance in front of us" suddenly shoot out and go careening down the river with its tracking rope trailing, "and a minute after the trackers came into view tearing along the bank." It was a dangerous but thrilling experience.

In the old days the native boats were comfortable, if not luxurious, as one missionary recalled: among the public rooms was a well-furnished dining room which had a large map of China on one wall and a large Union Jack on the opposite. But that sort of fine accommodation was far from the boat that Father hired in Chungking. In fact, he told Mother that she wouldn't have liked it a bit, that it was nothing like the houseboat they had on their honeymoon. He complained of the cramped quarters he shared with a couple of the thirty cases and trunks that he was taking with him. He had one servant, a cook who doubled as a Boy, and also an escort of a couple of soldiers provided by the local magistrates. The boat, the Postal flag flapping on the masthead, "inched" forward with the crew of a dozen trackers bent double bucking the powerful current. Such travel was monotonous, tedious, he said. He was glad of a book of crossword puzzles Mother had sent him; he read to pass the time, and also wrote letters that formed a detailed daily diary.

Whenever he could he left the boat to walk along the riverbanks or climb the steep cliffside paths and watch the trackers at work. At the worst rapids, his boat's crew of a dozen men would be joined by reinforcements from the locality who, for a little cash, would add their muscle to moving the boat. "It was quite a sight," he wrote. The men would yell as they pulled the long bamboo rope, and the *laotai* would scream encouragement. The *laotai*, or "old man," was the team leader. He would rush ahead, kneel down, and kowtow to the trackers, then he would run back along the line, beating his stick on the ground and chanting.

The boat's trackers were naked, "without nether garments," as they were often wading. They used their oars mostly to cross from one side of the river to the other, and each time they crossed, they were swept downstream, which Dad found "very discouraging." To make the best of this slow process, my father would go ashore and collect butterflies, a popular hobby at the time. One of the soldiers always accompanied him and carried the net and the "killing bottle."

My father's impatience with the slow progress probably led to a further delay. He kept urging the *laotai* to go a little faster, with the result that the *laotai* spoke so harshly to the trackers that they quit, and he had to find a new crew.

At Suining, the new Commissioner was met by a delegation from the Post Office, including the Delivery Inspector who had been sent from Chengtu to accompany him on the rest of his journey. His boxes were off-loaded and also the sedan chair he had acquired in Chungking. Forty coolies had to be hired to carry the luggage and chairs. It was quite a procession, with the "loads carried chairwise attached to two bamboo poles" usually by a couple of men and my father, like a general, bringing up the rear; the cook with the food and kitchen utensils in another chair went ahead and got "my meal ready at a place agreed upon beforehand so that when I come up there is no waiting." As on the boat, Father had an escort of soldiers, four of them, perhaps because of the long baggage train. Most of the time he walked and, as he wrote, "collected some interesting caterpillars."

The countryside was fully cultivated and the road they were on was paved with blocks of stone "but only wide enough for two chairs to pass." It was a busy road with lines of coolies carrying all manner of freight, both coming and going. Every day, a courier arrived from Chengtu, bringing bottles of water and beer, bread, and other foodstuffs, as well as mail; and my father remarked that it was a tribute to the Chinese Post Office that he got letters from England on this ancient highway "2,000 miles in the interior of China." He stopped the night usually at local inns, one of which, he said, would have given Mother "the creeps." He reached Chengtu and the residence of the Postal Commissioner, Mr. A. Ortolani, whom he was relieving, on September 22, 1925; it was almost exactly a month since he had left Nanking. A few years earlier, the journey would have taken three months.

Chengtu was considered a senior appointment, as it was the capital of Szechwan, the great western province. The largest province, Szechwan had a population at that time of forty-five million. Yet it was a world apart, with only a swift flowing river and that primitive pedestrian track to link it to the rest of China; the city, like the province, was isolated by the gorges of the Yangtze. Perhaps because of this, the main means of transportation was the sedan chair. This was very different from Kaifeng, where we had a carriage, and reminiscent of the old days in Foochow. The difference in Chengtu was that Father had to have a couple of body-guards accompanying the chair. All they did, he wrote to my mother, was to "march in front of the chair and shout when people don't get out of the way"; he considered it a "ridiculous custom." Much of the time he walked with the chair following him. He eventually got a bicycle but used it mostly for recreation.

Although deep inland, the climate in Chengtu was semi-tropical, and all manner of fruits and vegetables could be grown on the rich alluvial soil of the countryside. Dad noted on his overland journey that he "saw the first pomelo or orange tree today." Despite being almost as unreachable as Lhasa, Chengtu was a great deal more cosmopolitan than Kaifeng, although Kaifeng had a good railway connection with the rest of the world. There were foreign consulates, the West China Union University, and a cinema which surprised and pleased my father. On the day after arriving, he followed protocol and called on the British, French, and Japanese consuls.

The university was founded by the Methodist (United Church) Mission, the largest Canadian mission in China; the campus was in the suburb of Nantaissu outside the city wall, and Father remarked on its Western-style buildings with their curving Chinese roofs and on the fine suburban houses of the missionaries (professors and administrators) clustered around its grounds. The university was remarkable for its faculty of dentistry, the first and only one in China; in Ted Joliffe's view, it was the greatest Canadian initiative: "I don't know of any other mission that sent out dental missionaries of all people." Dad noted with some satisfaction that Chengtu had missionary dentists. Such missionaries were a sign of how far the Social Gospel had progressed, so that the mission's work was more to do now with modernizing than evangelizing China.

As was expected, the new Commissioner took over the quarters of the old Commissioner. It was a fine Mandarin house, which had been the palatial residence of a high official of the Szechwan government. Dad was impressed: "the living rooms were quite well fixed up with floors and foreign style doors and windows; altogether it is a very nice place." The photographs that he took showed representations of the same fearsome guardian gods that were on either side of the doors to our dwelling in the Peking *hu-tung*, only the entrance and the walls surrounding the Chengtu house were some twenty-five feet high. There were lush gardens and palm trees in the courtyards and, in one of them, a crooked bridge across a lotus pond; Father counted a couple of orange trees. The grounds were so extensive that they included a tennis court, "enclosed by the house [drawing room verandah] on one side" and high walls on the three other sides.

Only a few days after he had taken over as Commissioner, Dad had to deal with the chaotic, lawless conditions that were peculiar to Szechwan. The Post Office had a profitable business shipping silk parcels out of the province to the coastal cities, but it had to be suspended. A general at Suining was seizing whole boatloads of these parcels and demanding the payment of taxes on them. My father had actually run into this minor warlord on the overland journey to Chengtu: his troops tried to stop him from crossing a river. Apparently, they were imposing a toll or tax on the wretched populace, but after a heated altercation, they were ordered to let the foreigner and his caravan pass.

There was a marked difference in the anguish felt by the provinces of Honan and Szechwan during the warlord period. On the one hand, Honan was the prey of only one warlord at a time, and only occasionally was there any battle. On the other hand, Szechwan was divided among seven warlords and several renegade military commanders, and fighting, while localized, was almost continuous. The fighting could be vicious and bloody: the town of Loshan on the Yunnan border was taken and retaken five times in the early 1920s. Ted Joliffe, who lived there as a boy, watched from a window of his house a bitter battle for the Pung-tu Bridge where a thousand men were mowed down. "We knew it was a thousand men," he said, "because my father [Rev. Charles Joliffe] was vice president of the local Red Cross and he knew that the Red Cross had buried more than a thousand men the next day."

Bandits were also plentiful in Szechwan. They had disrupted the postal service, and my father grumbled that the six or seven generals, as he put it, who were running the province were only interested in making as much money as possible, "and don't care a rap about the bandits."

My father's social life in Chengtu was an unending round of tiffins and dinner parties with the same group of people: the consuls, the Roman Catholic and Protestant missionaries, his deputy Forzinetti (who had been his deputy in Kaifeng), and occasionally a foreign businessman or high Chinese official. Dad became very friendly with the British consul, Affleck, and vice-consul, Lamb, who were both single as he was, and admired their stately English house. The dinners were usually followed by bridge or mah-jongg, which could go on to the early hours of the morning; there were few dances due to the usual dearth of white women in colonial outposts such as Chengtu, but many more dances than in Kaifeng. "It's strange isn't it, to find [Protestant] missionaries dancing," he wrote. "We should have been glad if they had done so in Kaifeng." Generally speaking, he found the dinner parties to be "a futile business"; he liked playing bridge, "otherwise I get bored stiff."

He knew that he would have to return the hospitality, and it worried him because he had no confidence in his servants. He called them "hopeless fools" in one letter to Mother. They were "raw" and "untrained." He had inherited these servants from his predecessor, Ortolani, who had told him that with his wife there to supervise, he did not really need better servants and in fact eschewed them as they were likely to be members of the "Union of Foreign Servants." This was the first time that Father had ever heard of such an organization; it was an indication of how far nationalism had reached in Chengtu. Still, he was determined to hire, at the very least, a good cook.

The cook, really a chef, had to be adept at Western cuisine and capable of putting on an eight-course dinner for a dozen to twenty guests. As in Kaifeng, there was no Customs Commissioner, and thus Dad was the senior British colonial officer in Chengtu and, as in Kaifeng, he had to

*✦ My father with British consul Affleck and vice-consul Lamb
on the steps of his Chinese house in Chengtu*

entertain the Chinese authorities. Except there was not one general but
seven. As might be expected, the *tu-chen* or military governor of Chengtu,
and his assistant were generals; but the civil governor and his assistant
were also generals. Then there was the delicate problem of seating them
because "these generals are all much on a par as regards their relative
importance." Furthermore, there were rumours that they were at logger-
heads and any mistake in protocol could result in conflict. However, all
went well, and the new cook outdid himself in producing a ten-course
dinner. (At least he did not have to feed the generals' escorts as we had to
do with the old *tu-chen's* entourage in Kaifeng.)

Since many of the Canadian missionaries lived by the university in
Nantaissu, they had to entertain at lunch or tiffin parties. The city gates
were closed at six o'clock in the evening and would not be opened for anyone until the morning. However, even a Protestant missionary tiffin was
a four-course meal—and this was short rations compared with a tiffin
party of the Roman Catholic mission in Chengtu. There were at least
eight courses, and my father wrote, "they served red and white wine [with
the meal] and champagne and cognac with the coffee," as well as cigars.

He had got to know a number of the priests and began taking weekly French lessons from Père Laroche.

During 1925, there was a revolutionary upsurge in China that lasted some three years. On May 30, British police opened fire on a large political demonstration in Shanghai, killing twelve people; and on June 23, the British and French used machine guns against a much larger demonstration in Canton, killing fifty-two and wounding a hundred. (A prime mover of that demonstration was said to be Chiang Kai-shek.) The resulting general strike and boycott practically shut down Hong Kong and Shanghai and lasted for more than a year.

Mother was supposed to join Dad in 1926, and many of the letters he wrote her from Chengtu were taken up with detailed instructions on what she would have to do before leaving. She would have to put my brother and me in a boarding house—but what about holidays? It was finally arranged that we would spend them with relatives in Highgate, London, and my father expressed the hope more than once that they would take us for part of the time to "some bracing seaside place." The question of a guardian was worrying. There were minutiae such as our pocket money, how was it to be paid, whether we should have savings accounts. In later letters he dealt with her travel plans and even suggested booking a passage on the *Kashima Maru*. Obviously, Mother was looking forward eagerly to rejoining him, but he warned her that "China is not the place it used to be and never again, I think, will be the pleasant place we used to know."

Aside from the mail being interrupted by bandits and the depredation of that renegade warlord at Suining, my father had not experienced much anti-foreign feeling in Chengtu. However, he had been told by Dr. Joseph Beech, an American who was head of the West China Union University, that there were student strikes (often said to occur at examination time). What was, in some ways, worse was the militancy of the servants with their union; they walked off their jobs the year before, Dr. Beech said, and left the missionaries in the lurch for days. That is why Dad said that the "dear old China" that my mother longed for "won't be worth living in for a foreigner in a few years' time."

On June 7, 1926, Edith Harrison Sibley, a Canadian missionary, went for a walk on a crowded Chengtu street. She and her husband had come from the outlying station of Junghsien (pronounced Yu-shien) some 150 miles away for medical and dental checkups and were staying with missionary friends in an inner-city compound; the Sibleys were well-known members of the Canadian Methodist Mission in Szechwan. Mrs. Sibley was returning to the compound for lunch when a man came up behind her and struck her a single decapitating blow with a broadsword. After she fell to the ground, he hacked off her head and threw it into a latrine. The ghastly crime occurred not far from the main Post Office and some of the clerks heard shots fired and saw the murderer killed by soldiers. Later, my father went out to take a look at the body. It so happened that at that time Bill Sibley was paying a courtesy call on the Commissioner, but it was only some time afterward that Dad realized who he was.

As might be expected, he wrote to my mother about the terrible incident. He was afraid the news would get out and be "misrepresented as something anti-foreign." It was not that, he said, but the work of a "dangerous lunatic." However, the murderer, who was dressed like a coolie, turned out to be a member of the Red Lantern Society, a holdover of the secret societies that gave rise to the anti-foreign Boxer uprising of 1900; furthermore, he had come to the city with intention of killing a foreigner. Father had second thoughts that afternoon and, in a letter typewritten in the office, he wondered about the "desirability or otherwise of your coming out." It was obviously a painful question for him, as he had been so desperately lonely and was looking forward so much to their reunion. He had said so in an earlier letter: "I hope you will make a new man of me when you come out for I am a poor miserable creature without you." He could not face up to telling her not to come, and he left it to her to make the decision. She would have to make it soon, as she was supposed to be leaving in September and putting my brother and me in a boarding house for the term starting that month. He had thought of wiring her not to make any final travel arrangements "until you receive my letter of 8th June" but felt that it would unsettle her too much. Still he would like her to cable him yes or no.

One thing that this tragic affair had done, he told her in the typed letter, was to make him write to the director general, H. Picard-Destelan, about his early retirement. "If you do come, I don't want to keep you out here longer than I can help. If you don't come, there is all the more reason for my wanting to leave early." The funeral of Mrs. Sibley on June 9 was, he wrote, "a most harrowing affair." Heartfelt eulogies were paid to the murdered missionary; four men spoke of her Christian work and her love of the Chinese people, "and all of them had difficulty in controlling their voices." The British consul, Affleck, read Dad the strong protest that he was sending the military governor. However, as days passed, calm returned, with the foreigners comforting themselves with assertions that the "dastardly outrage" was the work of a madman and not the result of nationalist furor.

Father changed his mind again on June 17 and wired Mother: "SHALL PROBABLY ADVISE YOU NOT TO COME WAIT MY LETTER EIGHTH LOVE." He was evidently afraid she would make some permanent arrangements in the month that it would take the letter to reach her, such as giving up our comfortable apartment which was so close to Bedford School, arrangements that would be difficult to reverse. He returned to the work of directing the postal services with its usual frustrations due to the unsettled conditions in the province, and to the tedious round of dinners and tiffins with the same people; he played tennis on the university courts at Nantaissu which he rather enjoyed. The murder of Mrs. Sibley had brought to the fore all the concerns he had, and on July 6 he wrote that "China is getting more and more Bolshevized and the staff more and more difficult to control ... chaos is increasing." On the following day, perhaps because he had received no word from Mother, he sent another cable: "CONFIDENTIAL INTEND TO RESIGN MARCH YOU STAY WITH BOYS."

In July 1926, Chiang Kai-shek began his so-called Northern Expedition. The National Revolutionary Army was made up of half a dozen army corps and at least one hundred thousand men—a tenth of the size of the warlord forces opposing it. However, with Soviet advisers, the nationalist army moved forward steadily from Canton. The advance was on three fronts: toward Hankow (Wuhan), Nanking, and Foochow. The middle column, with Nanking as its objective, was commanded by Chiang Kai-shek, while the column heading for Hankow had most of the Communist cadres and the chief Russian advisor, Borodin. Dad's only hint of these goings-on was that Mother's letters were taking a month and a half to reach him instead of the usual month. He learned from two-week-old Hankow English-language papers that the delay in the mail was caused by what the reporters described as a "new war"; the main railway lines, he told my mother, "were being blocked for a time by military movements."

On September 5, 1926, the Wanhsien incident occurred. Some days earlier a Butterfield and Swire steamer had rammed a junk loaded with soldiers, most of whom drowned. The local warlord, Yan Sen, was furious, and seized two B and S steamers at Wanhsien and demanded reparations. No one is sure exactly what happened next. The British tried to board the ships, and there was a fire fight in which some of their officers were killed. As a reprisal, the British gunboats HMS *Cockshafer* and HMS *Widgeon* bombarded the city, starting fires and killing, according to the Chinese, some three thousand people. The Shanghai English-language press hailed the "Wanhsien Epic" and said that foreign prestige had been reaffirmed and the Chinese taught a lesson and "put in their place." Dad received the official British version of what happened, and with it a hand-written note from the vice-consul, Lamb: "It's a wonderful show on the part of the navy, but we can never forgive these bloody Chinks for ... the loss of so many British lives."

Wanhsien was the quintessential gunboat diplomacy, and it could not have come at a worse time. Chiang Kai-shek's Northern Expedition had become a triumphal march through the great cities of the lower Yangtze; and Wanhsien, when the massacre became known, could only add to the nationalist anger and desire for revenge. Father let my mother know about the incident; he sent the letter "via Suez" so that "he could speak freely about the Wanhsien affair." He was suffering from the paranoia of so many of the British about the Bolshevik menace and was afraid that his letter might be opened if it went "via Siberia." Up to now, he wrote, "everything has been quiet [in Chengtu]" but he had packed a suitcase just as a precaution. He had received a wire from Mellows, his fellow commissioner in Chungking, saying "SITUATION GRAVE PRACTICALLY ALL BRITISH SUBJECTS LIVING ON BRITISH STEAMERS STOP

READY TO LEAVE AT SHORT NOTICE STOP ALL FOREIGNERS LEAV-
ING WANHSIEN."

Chungking seemed to be in nationalist hands, and Mellows sent a second wire on September 18, 1926, saying that his wife and most European
women had left for Ichang and asking my father to inform the director
general. Dad was surprised at this request and assumed that, for political
reasons, the telegraph office in Chungking would not accept wires for
anywhere outside Szechwan. There were all kinds of wild rumours that
"the Cantonese," as he called the Nationalist forces, were in retreat, then
that they were advancing and had reached Hankow. Once again he assured
my mother, "everything is quite quiet here." But there were ominous signs:
the Reds, as he said, were trying to organize his Postal workers. A meeting in a local tea shop had been broken up. The servants who had gone
on strike the year before were threatening to walk out again and did so at
the time of the exodus in 1927. Father was not taking any chances and was
packing his butterflies in a box for early shipment.

"All depends on what happens in Central China," he wrote in November.
Christmas 1926 was celebrated in the usual colonial style with an endless
round of dinner parties that Dad found so boring—Chengtu was cut off,
without mail or news. But early in 1927 the British consul got word of
serious trouble. The foreign concessions in Hankow had been taken over
by Chinese troops, and Affleck said that "people [there] are told to be
ready to leave." Sian (Xian), the ancient capital of China, was in the hands
of anti-British forces. Feng Yu-hsiang had joined in the nationalist campaign, and his troops had gone on a wild rampage in Honan. It was
distressing for the missionaries, as they had aided and abetted the nationalists, and here were their protegés, so to speak, attacking their compounds,
destroying their hospitals, looting, and burning. Some idea of their wan-
ton fury could be seen in the way that soldiers had smashed and trampled
into the ground the thousands of oracle bones that Canadian missionary
Dr. James Menzies had collected.

On January 9, 1927, the consul received a dispatch from the British
Minister in Peking ordering him to advise all British subjects to leave
Chengtu. My father had informed the director general that he would leave
only when the consul left. He actually arranged for the latter's departure

through the Post Office's boat contractor. He left the day after Affleck did, on January 24, and got the many boxes that he had been packing since the beginning of the year onto a junk, the same sort of native boat on which he had come to Chengtu. It was a miserable trip, he wrote to my mother, cold, rainy, and uncomfortable. He was with seven missionary boats, the last of the thirty-eight boats that were used in the evacuation of the Canadian West China mission. At night, they would often tie up together so that he could break the monotony of the voyage with a visit. One of the missionaries he knew was on a boat no larger than his with his wife, two children, and a mother-in-law. "It must be a terribly cramped affair," he said in this letter to Mother, "and how the calls of nature are attended to under such circumstances, I don't know."

On February 5, after a night's stopover in the British Postal Commissioner's house in Chungking, which was stripped of furniture as Mellows had already left and his deputy was preparing to leave, my father boarded ss Chi Chuan which had been requisitioned for refugees. Besides himself, there were thirty-one foreign passengers including seven children and one sick man, and only three double-berth cabins; many of the missionaries had to be put up in the second-class Chinese cabins which were bare cubicles with wooden bunks. Dad was lucky in that the captain let him sleep on his camp bed in the enclosed bridge; the steamer anchored every night. The small saloon had four sittings for meals and was used as sleeping quarters by the wife and daughter of a French official with the Salt Gabelle. A couple of days later at Wanhsien, they all changed to a middle river boat, the ss Shasi, which was a bit bigger. My father had to sleep on the settee in the saloon while Dr. Joseph Beech had a camp bed in the same public room.

A party of Canadian missionaries from Chengtu had left Chunking some days earlier; their small steamer was just as crowded and, if anything, conditions were worse because they were fired on. One of the missionaries recalled, "I don't know how many times we had to leave a half-eaten meal or whatever we were doing, and either go down to the bottom of the ship or get behind the heavy reinforced steel plating on the deck. I think there were sixteen bullet holes in our cabin." Dad's boat was stopped by a military launch and boarded by "soldiers of the Southern Army who conducted a search which lasted one and half hours." When he reached Hankow, the situation seemed normal; "the only difference," he wrote, "is that one sees Cantonese soldiers with fixed bayonets on guard at street corners and outside the doors of all firms in the British concession." He also noted that the Kuomintang flag was flying over the Post Office, Customs, and other government buildings. Hankow was the last stop for him and thousands of other foreigners fleeing to the protected haven of Shanghai.

However, not all foreigners sought refuge there. Many, including the Canadian missionaries in Honan, were evacuated to the treaty port of Tientsin (Tianjin). This meant a two-day trip by train, and some of them had to make the journey in filthy cattle cars that had been used for transporting Chinese cavalry horses. Dr. James Menzies was one of them. He had had to leave behind his great collection of oracle bones, and it was the soldiers of the Christian general, Feng Yu-hsiang, who occupied his house and, in an act of sheer vandalism, destroyed the entire collection.

Shanghai had become an armed camp, and Father was pleased to see the array of foreign warships in the Whangpoo (Huangpu) River as his boat steamed slowly towards its wharf. He put down the names of three Royal Navy cruisers that they passed—*Vindictive, Enterprise,* and *Hawkins*—and noted that next to them were a couple of ships loaded with British and Indian troops. (The British had dispatched a battle squadron to Shanghai, of which the 10,000-ton cruiser HMS *Hawkins* was the flag ship.) The Americans were also there in force and, standing outside his hotel, my father watched a march of 1,500 US marines, six abreast, through the main streets of the foreign quarters. The liner SS *Megantic* arrived with the crack British regiment, the Coldstream Guards. Barracks were hurriedly built at Jessfield Park on the perimeter of the International Settlement, since all schools and available public buildings had been taken over to house the thousands of refugees; some of the missionaries had to make do with temporary quarters in a warehouse that had no windows and was thick with dust.

The nationalist army seized Nanking on March 24 and its troops went berserk, attacking British, American, and Japanese consulates, killing seven foreigners (mostly missionaries), and looting foreign property. In order to rescue their nationals, US and British gunboats laid down a barrage, killing fifteen Chinese soldiers and four civilians. Father referred to the "terrible time the foreigners of Nanking have been through" in a letter to my mother and wrote, "You need have no longing to return to China, darling, for it exists no longer as you knew it, and most of the foreigners out here now loathe it." Yet, despite this outrage and a general strike that threatened to shut down the International Settlement, life went on much as usual and the famous long bar in the Shanghai Club was packed with businessmen and other foreigners for drinks before tiffin. Dad met a few old friends; the atmosphere was congenial, he said, "and there was a most tremendous babel of voices."

His friends and others at the club's long bar could feel secure because of the muster of a formidable number of foreign troops in Shanghai and the arrival of so many British and American warships. Some political observers felt that such a strong force meant the Western Powers were contemplating an armed intervention in China. They were encouraged in this view by the sabre-rattling English-language press which was demanding revenge for the Nanking "massacre." Winston Churchill certainly supported such an intervention and urged the "systematic bombing of the Chinese army as well as the use of poison gas." James Endicott, a Canadian missionary with Communist sympathies, asserted that the 1927 exodus was planned by the British since, in the event of a march on Hankow and Nanking, "they did not want thousands of foreign hostages in the interior of China."

However, despite the war cry of the old imperialist Churchill, the question was whether there was ever any intention to mount an offensive against the Nationalist Forces. There were some forty thousand foreign troops in Shanghai, mostly British and Indians from the British Indian Army, and several thousand more in Tientsin and other treaty ports. They constituted a much stronger force than the eight-nation Allied army that had suppressed the Boxer rebellion and captured and sacked Peking. However, the situation was quite different from what it had been twenty-seven years before. For one thing, the Great War had eliminated three of the Imperial powers that had taken part in the 1900 invasion—Russia, Austria, and Germany. In 1900 the West was at the height of its power, while in 1927 the remaining European imperialists were in decline and only hanging on against colonial unrest and uprisings in China and elsewhere.

Thus, they were prepared to make a stand in Shanghai, the "citadel of imperialism," but would venture no further than the boundaries of the foreign quarters. They were in no mood to mount an expedition against the nationalists, as they had done in the past; instead, they offered appeasement. They were ready to give up their concessions in Hankow which were, in any case, in the hands of revolutionary forces—the "Reds," as my father called them. He had seen fully armed "Cantonese soldiers" patrolling the streets of Hankow and on guard at its main buildings.

Hankow was the first foreign enclave to be recovered by China. It was the first step to imperial oblivion, albeit not much of a step. The Western powers would make no further concessions. They did not have to, since Chiang Kai-shek had come on side. He had turned on his Communist allies in the National Revolutionary Army, expelled Borodin and other Soviet advisers, and slaughtered leftists within and outside the army. The Chinese bankers and merchants were alarmed at the general strike of the Communist-dominated labour unions and the way they had taken over the Chinese city in Shanghai, where red flags were flying. They approached Chiang Kai-shek and agreed to pay him millions of dollars to "restore law and order." This he did, and, with the covert support of the British and French, struck the Communists such a blow that they did not recover for years; hundreds of union officials and workers were rounded up and killed. Although Dad had seen and written about the red flags, there was nothing in his long letters to Mother on the bloody Shanghai coup as he had left before it occurred.

Had he remained, he would have known all about it since the gunfire and the smoke from burning buildings could be heard and seen on the Bund and in other parts of the international settlement. In fact, Chiang Kai-shek assembled his motley force of storm troopers, mobsters, and thugs from the Shanghai underworld, members of the notorious Green and Red gangs, on the borders of the sacrosanct foreign quarters. At any rate, it was from the International Settlement that the murderous assault on the Chinese city was launched at four o'clock in the morning of April 12, 1927; my father had boarded the *Empress of Canada* on the night of April 4.

12

REPRISE

No Foreign Bones in China

FOR THE THIRD TIME, Dad returned to England by way of Canada. It would be the last time and the prelude to our immigration. He got a job as a development officer with Canadian Industries in Montreal, and we moved there in 1928. For a time we lived in NDG, Notre Dame de Grace, the name of which seemed to be the only thing French about the suburb. I went to McGill, then a private university, the pride of the English Canadian establishment and modelled on the Ivy League universities in the United States. French was taught as a foreign language, and I took German. I was seventeen when I became a freshman, a callow youth who neglected his studies for the social life on the campus.

My inglorious college career was brought to a close by the Great Depression. My father's job petered out in 1931. Canadian Industries had to let him go: development was dead, and the order of business in the 1930s was survival. It was a desperate time. In May 1932 Dad decided to take refuge in the small holding on Vancouver Island, the sweet pine-scented retreat we had almost forgotten. I followed some months later as I had a summer job; I got a free ride as a guard on a CPR "Chink Train," the vulgar name for the colonist car carrying Chinese in bond from the United States to Vancouver and the China-bound Canadian Pacific liners.

Oh, the awful dreariness of the Depression, its aching dullness. For two years, I did anything to earn a buck: I picked fruit, I worked in the woods. Finally, I got a job on the Victoria Daily Times. *It was an ideal small-town newspaper on which to learn journalism, as one did everything. Through the exchange program of the Empire Press Union, I did a stint on Fleet Street, on the* Daily Herald, *the first British paper to reach 2,000,000 circulation. I returned just before the outbreak of war and joined the* Vancouver Daily Province, *then switched to the* CBC. *My big break came when I was made a* CBC *war correspondent. But my greatest assignment was the 1946 Paris Peace Conference, as I met Jessamy at its beginning and we were married before its end. I served as a roving foreign correspondent then, later United Nations correspondent in New York, and finally Ottawa Correspondent.*

CHINA WAS ONLY A MEMORY NOW, but there were reminders. When I returned home for Christmas 1944 to do a cross-country speaking tour for the Canadian clubs and to make a film promoting war bonds, I was asked to lunch by Bishop White, whom we had known so well as the Bishop in Honan. He was living in Toronto and we had a very pleasant family lunch. Afterward, he showed me his collection in the Royal Ontario Museum and the magnificent gallery named after him, where the superb thirteenth-century murals show Buddha reigning supreme and Lao Tse leading the Taoist processional with the Jade Emperor and the Empress of Heaven. He gave me a copy of his book, *Tomb Tile Pictures of Ancient China,* and inscribed it to me "in memory of your earlier days in Kaifeng"; he put down the date as "February 17th 1945."

Bishop White told me then that, after the war, he would like to return to Kaifeng and the diocese of Honan, if his services were wanted; a few months later, in September 1945, he received an urgent call to help in the restoration of the Canadian Anglican Mission which had been devastated by war and famine. He was excited at the prospect of revisiting Kaifeng but his return to the mission that he had established was not a happy one. He had left China in 1934 and so much had changed that it was no longer the country that he knew and loved.

He reached Shanghai in midsummer 1946. It was a time of turbulence and chaos with inflation raging completely out of control. His return to Kaifeng was delayed for weeks because the fighting in the civil war had moved into Honan. He found the mission in a shambles; his beloved cathedral had been hit by Japanese shells. He worked hard, making funds available to feed and clothe the starving, but he was frustrated at every turn. He could get no assistance from the national government, and the Communists, whom Bishop White had refused to take seriously and considered to be a "passing phase" in China's long history, were closing in on his mission. The heavy demands on him, the hopelessness of the situation, affected his health. Finally, Bishop and Mrs. White left Kaifeng in May 1947 to return home.

The Southern Baptist missionaries, Pastor and Mrs. Hendon Harris, the father and mother of my boyhood friend, Miriam, also returned to Kaifeng at about the same time. Shortly after I became CBC correspondent at the United Nations, I got a letter from Miriam. She was married and living in Grand Rapids, Michigan, and had heard my broadcasts on Communist China and the Korean War. In her letter, she reminisced about the old days and said that "Mother and Father were chased from Kaifeng three years ago by the Communists." We kept up a desultory correspondence, and she sent me a book that her mother had written about their work and life during their forty years in China, to which Miriam had contributed a foreword.

Pastor and Mrs. (Florence) Harris were held up for weeks in Shanghai, as Bishop White was, "because the Communists had dynamited large sections of the railway lines disrupting travel until repairs could be made." Finally, they reached Kaifeng and the Southern Baptist compound which was across the mud road from our former home. The Japanese had occupied their compound and their first task was to clean up the mess they had left behind. That was easy compared with the trouble they had with the United Nations Relief and Rehabilitation Agency (UNRRA), which had occupied, "illegally" as Florence Harris put it, "many of our residences and school buildings." Most of the personnel of UNRRA were Americans who were "defiant and insolent" when they were asked to vacate these places which were sorely needed by the mission. She wrote, "The Kaifeng head of UNRRA had the effrontery to say that his relief program was more important to the Chinese than the missionary endeavors."

It was a classic case of rivalry, of the old Christian missionaries pitted against these new international relief agency missionaries for the hearts and minds of the Chinese people. Mrs. Harris was bitter and wrote scathingly how UNRRA had sent piles of wooden tent pegs but no tents; she "wondered what benefit these were to China's starving people, except to be used as firewood!" Food came by the trainload from the United States, but much of it, she said, "was unacceptable to Chinese taste," including cheese, sauerkraut, baking soda, and canned fruit. Then there was the surplus war supplies of machinery that UNRRA had brought in. Florence Harris claimed that for a mile along the Lunghai railway track "scores and scores of 'donkey engines'" were left to rust as there was "absolutely no use for them" in Honan.

There were some fifty thousand nationalist troops in Kaifeng. As the main Communist forces approached, they began digging trenches by the Southern Baptist compound and made openings in the wall, giving the mass of undisciplined soldiers easy access to the mission's residences and schools. "These lawless, idle and frightened soldiers," Mrs. Harris wrote, "were creating a chaotic situation, making life almost unbearable." The Postal Commissioner's house, our old home in Kaifeng, was in the centre of this war zone. Robert Hart, a UNRRA representative, showed me snapshots he had taken of Nationalist troops digging trenches beside the compound's high brick wall.

In the years after we left the Postal Commissioner's house, it changed hands several times. My father was succeeded by an Englishman, D. Mullen, whose family moved into the house on our departure. However, by the mid 1930s, the last foreign commissioner had left, not to be replaced, because of the threat of warfare with the mounting Japanese campaign. From then until the end of the Second World War, the house was occupied by a Japanese general, the commander in the area, and his staff. Then UNRRA took over and twenty officials, including Hart, were billeted in our old house, and another ten to twelve in the Deputy Commissioner's house in the same compound.

Chou En-lai (Zhou Enlai) stayed in the Postal Commissioner's house. UNRRA was engaged not only in famine relief but in rebuilding the dykes along the Yellow River that had been destroyed during the war, and Chou had come to Kaifeng to discuss this work and the threat that civil war posed to containing the flood waters. The Communist leader arrived by plane, walked past the lines of nationalist bombers and fighters to the UNRRA jeep, and was driven to the compound. Hart had assigned him a bedroom and suggested it might be safer for him to sleep indoors. But no, Chou didn't want that. It was hot, and he would sleep on the exposed upstairs verandah, which he did.

The next day, he went to see the nationalist military governor. "We offered him a convoy," Hart said, "a couple of jeeps with United Nations flags flying, but he refused." The Communist leader preferred to walk. "Everybody knows I am here and who I am," he said, "and they won't touch me." He walked past nationalist guards at barricades and sandbag emplacements along the road to the main South Gate and into the city which was stiff with nationalist troops. No one touched him. "It astounded all of us," Hart said. Was his conference successful? Probably. Chou was a legendary figure as a negotiator before the Communists took power and he became premier.

Robert Hart was the liaison officer for UNRRA with the nationalist and Communist authorities. He had in his jeep two hats, one a nationalist peaked officer's cap, the other a Communist forage cap with a red star, and he would literally change hats when he changed sides. The agency, he admitted, had "tremendous difficulties" with the Kuomintang forces. They had to pay "squeeze money" but were able to keep the bribery and corruption below ten percent of total costs. The problem Hart had with the Communists was finding their leaders. He had a regular contact who would pass him on to another man some miles away who would take him to a third person who might know where the command headquarters was. The Communist leaders were always on the move; this was the precaution they had to take while awaiting the arrival of the main forces of the People's Liberation Army (PLA), as it was now called.

As the UNRRA representative who could move around at will and was trusted by both sides, Hart had a remarkable eyewitness view of the Chinese civil war. The nationalists were holed up in the cities; they were islands in the ocean of the countryside which was in the hands of the Communists, the ocean that would eventually rise and submerge them. Honan, on the North China plain, was the main channel down which the PLA field armies would travel to conquer the whole of mainland China. However, if the island was small enough, and the ocean was in flood tide, it could be overcome. Hart saw this happen to the small walled town of Chowchiaokuo, some eighty miles from Kaifeng. The nationalists had some five thousand troops inside, and the Communists had about thirty thousand outside. Hart watched thousands of men padding over the fields in single file hour after hour, carrying scaling ladders, even artillery, with the wheels on bamboo poles, so they would leave no tracks. When the Reds were ready, they sent in a note demanding surrender which was rejected. Then there was a great sound of gunfire. The guerillas attacked from three sides, leaving the fourth open so the nationalist officers could escape, which they were allowed to do so long as they left the soldiers and their arms and equipment behind.

By the end of 1947, the PLA field armies had engulfed Kaifeng and the whole of Honan. On December 12, with the boom of cannons in their ears, the Harrises left. A church friend had a truck and drove them along a dirt road through "guerilla-infested territory" to the railway junction of Chengchow (Zhengzhou), some sixty miles from Kaifeng, where the Lutheran mission had sent planes to evacuate "marooned missionaries or Christian workers." "The next day," Mrs. Harris wrote, "I had my first plane ride." They left China for the last time and returned to Hendon's home in Clinton, Mississippi. Robert Hart and two of his staff stayed behind in the Postal Commissioner's house until UNRRA ordered them to leave and sent a plane to take them out. Some nationalist officers and their wives and children forced themselves at gunpoint onto the plane which was the last flight from Kaifeng. It was grossly overloaded, but Hart worked with the pilot to move the panic-stricken passengers to the middle of the plane for the takeoff; roaring and shaking, it just got airborne at the end of the runway.

Early in 1948, Sam and Lewis Shaw came to dinner. It was the first time I had ever met my Japanese cousins. They were in London to collect reparations for the loss of a couple of freighters the British had requisitioned during the war. Uncle G, Sam and Lewis' father, who had made a fortune as a merchant in Manchuria, had become a ship owner in the 1930s. I recalled at that dinner his coming to Canada in 1934 to buy two freighters. We went down to Victoria's Rithet Pier to meet him, and there he was, a corpulent figure looking the very model of a big businessman in his cashmere overcoat, standing on the bridge of the *Empress of Russia* as the liner glided slowly toward the dock. The acquisition of these ships was a form of insurance for George L. Shaw, as he knew he would eventually have to leave Antung and Manchuria now that the Japanese had taken over. In 1919, when he was working in Korea, the Japanese had imprisoned him on a charge of aiding and abetting Korean revolutionaries; British protests brought about his release after six months in jail, but he knew he was still in Japan's bad books.

My Japanese grandmother, Ellen O'Sea, had died in 1934. All that was known of the cause of her passing was that she had been crippled by arthritis for years. While Uncle G did not move to Foochow until some time later, he must have known about her illness and death. He must have told my mother, because he stayed with us for a couple of days before going on to Vancouver to acquire the ships. However, I never heard either her name or that she had passed away. Grandmother died as she had lived, quietly, almost invisibly. She was buried in the little British cemetery beside Grandfather's grave; hers was a simple tombstone beside the elaborate monument to Captain Shaw, the marble angel with head bowed in mourning, which, in a way, was a reflection of their relationship.

The 1934 trip to Canada was really the beginning of George becoming a ship owner. There were altogether six freighters, according to his son, Lewis; they were of two to three thousand tons and plied the China coast. However, in a 1939 New Year's card to my mother, Uncle G wrote, "Have all our five ships coming here." Since the ships were registered with the British, they were requisitioned at the outbreak of war with Japan, but apparently there were only two ships left; the others must have been lost before Pearl Harbor.

At any rate, Sam and Lewis collected only ninety thousand pounds in reparations for two ships. The reason they were in London to pick up this indemnity was that their father had died suddenly on November 30, 1943. He was sixty-three years old and had appeared in the prime of life; Lewis blamed his death on the inadequate medical services in Foochow. George was buried in the British cemetery beside his father's and mother's graves.

Julia remained in Terenure. She had been living in Foochow since the late 1920s and had looked after her mother during her long crippling illness until her death; she was George's housekeeper when he moved down from Antung. (Julia was separated from her husband, Harold Carey, who had returned to the United States.) When her brother died, she lived alone in Terenure with only an old servant for company. She was alone when the Japanese swept into Foochow in October 1944; they left a few months later, in May 1945. She was alone when the Communists, the PLA, finally reached Foochow in August 1949. "Really all in all," she said in the 1971 Hong Kong radio interview, "both the Japanese and the Communists were very kind to me."

During the time that Aunty J lived under Communist rule—and she stayed there longer than most foreigners—she was in Terenure. She rented the second floor of this elegant Regency-style house to a local Communist leader, which was a wise move as it provided her with protection, and divided the ground floor into three apartments, occupying one of them. She wrote regularly to my mother about life as it developed in the People's Republic. There were campaigns, campaigns against flies and fleas, campaigns to increase production, campaigns about Chairman Mao's thoughts, campaigns on cleanliness and stopping spitting (very unsuccessful). In one campaign to eradicate smallpox, they vaccinated everyone street by street; but when they came to Julia, they said she was too old.

The British kept after her to leave. They did not want the bother of being responsible for a little old lady in the depth of Communist China. But she was reluctant to go: Foochow was her home. However, the Chinese were making life difficult for foreigners, and she finally left in 1961. It took some four days to reach Macau. She chose the Portuguese colony rather than Hong Kong because a Foochow friend was there and had offered to put her up.

As she recalled in 1971, Julia had left "with only her clothes." She was penniless. My father and mother supported her, and, at one time, Dad had the idea that she might move to Victoria to be with her sister. He looked into whether there was a suitable home for her in Canada but found nothing, which was fortunate since Julia seemed less than enthusiastic about leaving Macau. Later my brother and I contributed to the welfare of our old aunt.

When my father sought shelter from the Great Depression in the small holding at Royal Oak, Vancouver Island was becoming a haven for displaced imperialists, old China hands like himself, burra sahibs of the Indian Civil Service and their mem-sahibs, retired Malayan and Hong Kong policemen, former tea-planters from Ceylon and rubber-planters from Borneo, gunboat commanders who knew the road to Mandalay was the Irrawaddy River, traders and missionaries from the Far and Near East. A China-Japan Society used to meet regularly in Victoria, mostly for tea and bridge and mah-jongg, but Dad never joined. He stuck to his seven-acre property in Royal Oak.

He corresponded with some of his colleagues in the Chinese Post Office, particularly with T.H. Gwynne, who had joined the Service some years before him and had stayed on to the bitter end. I knew about this since Gwynne had sent him stamps from the Shanghai Post Office's philatelic list of May 20, 1946, which was among his personal effects. Although he never said anything about it, my father must have wondered whether he should have continued in the Post Office, as his old friend had done. He had been overcome by emotions in Chengtu and had been too hasty in quitting the Service during the troubles that brought about the 1927 exodus. He realized this when he reached Shanghai and saw the relative calm and the determination of the British to remain. He wrote to the director general, Picard-Destelan, asking if he could withdraw his resignation, but it was too late; it had been accepted and that was final.

My father was forty-five when he took refuge in Royal Oak. Later, during the war, he subdivided and sold the property, and my parents moved to Victoria. Aside from some accountancy, he never worked again. He did what other displaced imperialists did during the forty years they lived in this comfortable outpost of empire: he pottered around the garden and played bridge and mah-jongg. He tried to keep up his Chinese and maintained a consuming interest in all that happened in the country of his glory days.

China had changed dramatically. From the humiliation and subjugation of the Opium Wars in the nineteenth century, that "age of contempt" for the country my grandfather knew, from my father's time when it was virtually a British colony, China had emerged as a great power. When I was the CBC correspondent at the United Nations, I covered the debate on "condemnation of Communist China for aggression," which was important in that it tested the post-war sentiment of the "world federalists" and other liberals that an international organization such as the UN could censure and bring to order the government of a major power. Of course, it failed, but it did confirm China's eminence. Chinese troops had poured across the Yalu River into Korea and driven the American forces back in defeat. China became a nuclear power sooner than anyone had expected, and there were war scares over Formosa, where the nationalists had taken refuge, and the coastal islands of Matsu and Quemoy. Red China, the Red Menace, was not jeered at now but feared. All was dark and mysterious; a bamboo curtain had fallen, making it a forbidden land.

IN THE 1960s, I made several attempts to visit China, but to no avail. My requests were rejected usually because it was "inconvenient at that time." I wondered darkly if I was being refused because I was born in China. Then Canada began negotiations, which were held mainly in Sweden, on recognition of the People's Republic, and the diplomatic atmosphere changed from hostility to one of compromise.

I knew Chester Ronning, having met him at the United Nations in the 1950s when he was with the Canadian delegation. Ronning was the last Canadian representative to Nationalist China before the Communists took over and only left Nanking in 1951 after his recommendation to recognize the People's Republic was rejected by Ottawa. He spoke Mandarin fluently; he had got to know the new government and was on friendly terms with Chou En-lai. He was an ardent advocate of the recognition of the People's Republic and its admission to the UN.

Ronning was in Ottawa at the time that agreement was reached on the recognition of the People's Republic, and, as the last Canadian representative in China, I sought him out for an interview. He told me that he would like to pay a return visit to what was his native land; it was twenty years since he had last been in the country. I asked him if I could accompany him with a camera crew, and he said that he would find out. Days, weeks went by, but finally I got word that the trip was on, that we were invited to spend a month in China in the spring of 1971. Somehow news of this got out, and I was bombarded by requests from the American television networks to include one of their reporters in our party. They would do anything: "How would you like to have Walter Cronkite as a cameraman?" I laughed, but I think the caller was serious. The Americans were that desperate to breach the bamboo curtain and enter the forbidden land.

Although it was twenty-two years after the Communists had come to power, the country still seemed in a revolutionary state. Mao Tse-tung (Mao Zedong) had seen to that by launching the Cultural Revolution in the mid 1960s; it was said to have ended in 1971 but was still going on. We were taken to a May 7 school on the outskirts of Beijing. This school mainly retrained bureaucrats to be farmers, and great emphasis was placed on making them do the dirtiest jobs. Collecting buckets of human excrement went a long way, the commissar running this May 7 school asserted, "to shake the superior air of being an official or intellectual."

Chairman Mao, the Great Helmsman, was to be seen everywhere on signboards, in larger-than-life images. The soldiers of the People's Liberation Army had no rank badges, but there was a way, somewhat esoteric, of telling an officer or a general by the number of pockets in his drab khaki uniform, or so I was assured. The Customs House on the Shanghai Bund, that former centre of British power where my father had worked briefly, had a landmark clock tower with a carillon which was said to have played "Rule Britannia" in the glory days of Empire; now it sounded out the "The East is Red," which might be considered to be the Communist equivalent.

Then there was Norman Bethune, the Canadian doctor who joined the Communist Eighth Route Army when it was fighting the Japanese

✦ *Peter Stursberg in China*

and had died while caring for the wounded in November 1939. His ven-
eration as a hero of China was assured when within five weeks of his
death Mao Tse-tung wrote the essay *In Memory of Norman Bethune*. It
appeared in one of the little red books which were published in the mid
1960s during the Cultural Revolution; the books were reprinted in many
languages, and my English copy was dated 1966. Bethune's name was on
the tongue of almost every official we met during our visit. We had to
visit his tomb in the town of Shichiachuang (Shijiazhuang), about a hundred miles from Beijing; his remains had been moved to a big memorial
park there. Bethune dominated this vast cemetery, which might be
described as the Arlington of the People's Republic; there was the large
"Norman Bethune International Peace Hospital," the Norman Bethune
Museum, and his monumental tomb. When we walked to the gravesite
with its statue of the doctor, the sun was shining and I noted groups of
children sitting in the shade of trees nearby; their lips were moving, and
they seemed to be praying to Norman Bethune. Oh no, I was assured,
they were reading Mao's eulogy to him in the little red book.

I was in Beijing for May Day that year. From early morning, columns
of workers and soldiers marched down the wide Chang-an Boulevard
past our old Peking Hotel, an imperialist relic, to Tiananmen (The Gate
of Heavenly Peace). By afternoon, all streets leading into the huge square,

which covered forty hectares or about a hundred acres, were closed to traffic. At night, it was a great spectacle, a crowd of half a million lit by the glow from the beams of searchlights probing the dark sky. The great concourse moved with the gentle swell of a sea, and on a score of platforms, reaching far back to its distant edge, excerpts from the half-dozen revolutionary operas were being performed. It was thrilling sight, and I remembered it as the sort of pageantry that was meant not for an emperor but for a conqueror, a Genghis Khan. And the mighty assembly erupted when Mao Tse-tung finally appeared. The sound was deafening. His arrival on the Gate of Heavenly Peace signalled the beginning of the fireworks, which were magnificent, as expected—after all, the Chinese invented fireworks.

When we were in Beijing I sought out the Chuan-pan *Hu-tung* where I lived as an infant. It seemed rather dusty and run-down, and I could not see what was so attractive about it. In Shanghai, there was no sign of our large house with its wide lawns at 17 Hart Road; as far as I could figure out, a factory or warehouse stood where the house had been. At least they gave Hart Road, named after the great imperialist, Sir Robert Hart, a fine Chinese name, *Changde*, meaning "perpetual virtue." The Bubbling Well Road, which was our main route to downtown Shanghai and the Bund, was now known as Nanking Road West.

We visited Fancheng, a country town in Hupei (Hubei) Province, where Chester Ronning was born. Ronning's father had worked here as a Lutheran missionary and Ronning himself also worked as a missionary teacher in the 1920s, leaving China, as my father had done, in the exodus of 1927. The local population had not seen a foreigner in years, and the crowds gaping at us and pressing their noses to the window of our car made it difficult to get around. Chester's mother had died in Fan-cheng, and he wanted to see her grave, but all the officials could do was to show him the gravestone. I did not realize the significance of this at the time—that there was no grave, only a gravestone.

At the beginning of the China trip, I looked up Aunty J in Macau. I telephoned her from my Hong Kong hotel and said that I would be coming over on the hydrofoil the next day (April 25, 1971).

"That's my ninetieth birthday," she said, "and I'll meet you at the hydrofoil station."

She took me to lunch at the Hotel Lisboa, a wedding cake of a building that had three floors of gambling. At the end of the trip, I went to see Julia again; she gave me a pendant for Jessamy and made me promise to bring her the next time. I swore I would do so on her hundredth birthday.

I never thought that I would have to keep my promise to Aunty J, but 1981 came and in January, I went to the Chinese consul in Vancouver to arrange for a visit to the People's Republic. We would see Julia, we would attend her hundredth birthday party, but just as Chester Ronning had gone to Fancheng, where he was born and which meant so much to him, so Jessamy and I would go to Kaifeng and Foochow, the places that meant as much to me.

China seemed no different from what it had been ten years before. Bicycles were everywhere: regiments of them in the big cities, riding six to ten abreast. The odd automobile, usually an official car, and the occasional Soviet-model truck were like elephants amid the teeming masses of pedalling humanity; the traffic jams, such as they were, were bicycle jams. The hotels were badly run, and many were relics of the past. In Beijing, we stayed at the old Peking Hotel where I had stayed in 1971, and in Shanghai at the Jinjiang, a large hotel built by the French in the early 1930s. Jessamy found the rooms dirty. However, it was the service that was truly awful; if anything, it was worse than it had been ten years before. When I complained about this, I was told that there were fewer of the old waiters left, and the hotel staff was made up of young people, products of the Cultural Revolution, untrained and actually taught to consider service demeaning.

This attitude became a serious problem for the People's Republic as it wanted to increase the number of tourists, especially American tourists. The officials in Beijing came to realize that the hotels could not be run by government boards or revolutionary committees. The politicians, the commissars, had to be ousted and professional management restored. The best way to do this was by joint ventures with foreign hotel chains, and the first of these was being built. That was one difference from 1971; there were others.

Chairman Mao had disappeared from the streets. There were no more statues of him, and the only painting of him hung over the Gate of

Heavenly Peace, where he had proclaimed the establishment of the People's Republic in 1949. Mao had died in 1976, and his body lay in a crystal coffin in the newly built mausoleum, the Chairman Mao Memorial Hall, as it was called, at one end of Tiananmen Square. With his death, the Cultural Revolution really ended. The Gang of Four, which included Chiang Ching, Mao's wife and cultural dictator, was quickly overthrown. Norman Bethune also was left in peace in Shichiachuang; nobody mentioned his name on this trip.

The Cultural Revolution had done untold damage to the country. You can't play at revolution for years without suffering the economic consequences, as has been said. China had lost "a generation," according to Deng Xiaoping, the new Vice-Chairman and emerging paramount leader. It was due to Deng's guidance that the Communist Party, at its most recent plenary session, had broken with the past and Mao's revolutionary dictates and had adopted a policy of modernization and economic development. This was a shift of historic importance and the beginning of the move from moribund socialist industry to a vibrant market economy; it would release the great entrepreneurial skills of the Chinese people. Already in 1981 there was a lot of construction, and our attention was drawn to it; in later visits I would see building cranes everywhere. (A third of the building cranes in the world were said to be in China at that time.) Productivity and development were such that historian Harold Evans predicted that while the British dominated the nineteenth century and the United States the twentieth century, "the Chinese may cast a long shadow on the twenty-first."

Our Chinese guides could not have done more to find the places that meant much to me and my family. They had no difficulty locating Terenure in Foochow, since Aunty J lived there till 1961 and people remembered it as Mrs. Carey's home, but the Postal Commissioner's house in Kaifeng? Mr. Li, our guide, shook his head. Fortunately, I had brought a picture of it, and I showed it to him in the guest house where we were put up. There was no hotel in Kaifeng, which had declined even further and was no longer the provincial capital; Chengchow, the railway junction which had become a big city, had been made the capital of Honan in the 1950s. Kaifeng's one claim to fame now was that it was the headquarters of the troops guarding the Yellow River, and Mr. Li recognized the Postal Commissioner's house from the photo and said it was in the military cantonment. He would have to get permission to visit it, which he did.

And there it was, the great ugly house made uglier by a bricked-in verandah. It was being used as an officers' transit camp, and I noted twenty-two places laid in the dining room. Dad's ground-floor study had two beds in it. Up the grand staircase, carpetless and worn, under which I had my den, was the children's wing, the schoolroom and bedroom and Miss Hodgkin's room, and in between a bathroom with the bath taken out. My mother and father's bedroom had been divided into a couple of bedrooms, and their bathroom had been converted into another bedroom. We walked on to the upper floor verandah, one that was not bricked in, and looked out over the compound. There was the high brick wall and the garden, a riot of weeds, and where the tennis court had been were barracks. Mr. Li asked if our house in Vancouver was as big as this. "Oh, no," Jessamy said, "not nearly as large." Mr. Li seemed puzzled. "So you've come down in the world," he said.

Bishop White's house had been turned into a junior school, and his beautiful garden was a dusty schoolyard. Trinity Cathedral, which had been his proudest achievement, was a pile of rubble; its destruction was the work of the Cultural Revolution, or so we were told. However, the Jewish stele that White had obtained and placed on either side of the entrance to the Anglican cathedral had been saved. They were in a city yard full of stone carvings and other relics which the provincial museum (now in Chengchow) apparently did not want. These memorial tablets, all that was left of Kaifeng's ancient synagogue, one of them dated 1489 and the other 1679, were in an open shed, and their only protection from the elements was a tin roof. Among this haphazard collection was a grey granite tombstone:

In loving memory
Reverend George E. Simmons, D.D.
Canon of Trinity Cathedral
Born July 3rd, 1877
Died September 11th, 1936.

Canon Simmons was a ghostly figure from the past. I remembered him coming around with Bishop White to our house, the Postal Commissioner's house, at the Chinese New Year receptions. But where was he buried? Another gravestone without a grave.

We had tea in Terenure with the voluble and mysterious Mrs. Wu, who said she was a great friend of Mrs. Carey's, although Aunty J, at her hundredth birthday party, did not seem to know who she was and how she came to be living in the Foochow house. We had tea on the verandah, but I could not imagine my grandfather taking the sun there on the last year of his life or my grandmother waiting on him, or my mother and father, two young people in love, sitting there admiring the flowers in the garden. The verandah had been filled in, and we had tea in a makeshift room. The floorboards were bare, the walls dirty and peeling, but behind Mrs. Wu was some fine antique furniture which must have belonged to the Shaws. The garden where my mother picked roses was full of vegetables and night-soil pots and had an unpleasant odour. Nine families had been crammed into the house during the Cultural Revolution, according to Mrs. Wu. Its awful dilapidated state was not improved by outdoor kitchens and lean-to sheds along the side of one of the mouldering, crumbling walls. Terenure had become a slum.

The small Anglican church where my father and mother were married was not far from Terenure. We walked over and found it had become an army construction dump. A truck was being loaded with bricks in the handsome gateway where my mother had arrived in a sedan chair for her wedding. How had this happened? I asked Moses Hsieh (Xie), Bishop of Foochow, a tall ascetic figure who had been educated at Oxford and Belfast Universities. After all, the Communists had returned the churches to the congregations in 1979, and were spending millions of yuan in restoration work. Bishop Hsieh agreed, but said that the British church, St. John's, as he called it, was too small. It had pews for at most a hundred people, whereas the nearby Methodist Church, which had been returned to the parish and renamed the Tien An Church (the church of heavenly peace), could hold twelve hundred worshippers and often had that number at Sunday services.

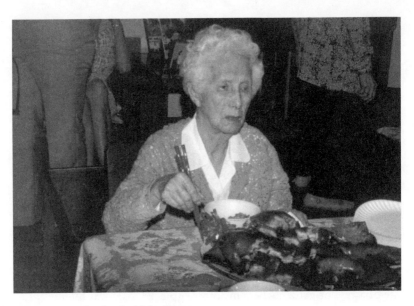

✦ *Julia, my Aunty J, at her hundredth birthday party*

There was another and more important reason for coming to Foochow, and that was to see my grandfather's and grandmother's graves— especially Grandfather's, with its monument of a mourning angel that I had only seen in photographs. When I asked Mr. Li if we could see the graves, he consulted a local official and said that the British cemetery was "covered," as he put it, by a middle school. But what about the ornate tombstone? Surely it had been moved and stored somewhere? Mr. Li and the official looked embarrassed: it had vanished, they said and implied it had been destroyed during the Cultural Revolution. In this case, there was neither grave nor gravestone.

Aunty J had a different account of the destruction of Captain Shaw's grave. At her hundredth birthday party, on April 15, 1981, I told her about our visit to Foochow and the officials' claim that Grandfather's grave had been destroyed at the time of the Cultural Revolution. In all the hubbub of the party, it was difficult to hear what Julia was saying, but she was talking about Grandfather's grave. Its desecration, she said, was the work of students during the Korean War; it had nothing to do with the

Cultural Revolution. She knew because she was living in Terenure during the winter of 1950–51.

"Late one night," she told me, "there was a noisy demonstration, then they marched on the little British cemetery, toppled the gravestones, and dug up the graves." The students, Julia said, shouted, "No foreign bones in China." It was a slogan they yelled time and time again: "No foreign bones in China." Later she visited the cemetery and saw the devastation: graves dug up, bones scattered, the bones of her father and mother, my grandfather and my grandmother, and the bones of her brother, George, and the marble angel toppled from its base and lying broken on the torn ground. It was ghastly, horrible, like a scene from the Last Judgement.

The Korean War was a time of anti-foreign fury in China. It resulted in the expulsion of all the remaining Christian missionaries, three thousand Protestants and two thousand Roman Catholics (among whom were six hundred Canadians). There had been an indication that the missionaries, since those that were left were largely doctors, agronomists, or teachers, would be allowed to stay, but the ill-fated American advance to the Yalu prompted the Communists to decide to clean out all foreign influence, no matter the cost. American participation in the Korean War, coming as it did only a year after the People's Republic was proclaimed, and United States hostility to the new government were bound to arouse suspicion and xenophobia. Militant youths took to the streets, not only in Foochow but throughout the country, and attacked the foreign cemeteries, so that there were no foreign graves left, or, as they would have said, "no foreign bones left defiling the sacred soil of China."

When Mary Goforth Moyan, daughter of noted Canadian evangelist Dr. Jonathan Goforth, returned for a visit in the late 1970s, she looked for the graves of her five brothers and sisters who had died in China. She could not find one. The son of another missionary, C.H.S. Luttrell, searched in vain for his sister's burial place in Honan. When he died in 1934, Dr. Davidson Black, the discoverer of Peking Man, was interred in the British cemetery in Peking, which was by the city wall; the last that was heard of his grave was when the wall was levelled to build a ring road and the cemetery was covered. Many missionaries, missionary children, and other old China hands took the opportunity of the lifting of the Bamboo

Curtain to return to their old haunts, but not one of them found the graves of their loved ones.

In their destruction of the foreign cemeteries, of my grandfather's and grandmother's graves, the rampaging youths of the early 1950s were expressing an age-old belief that the soil of China belonged exclusively to the Chinese. Any intrusion on the part of outsiders, of the "foreign devils," was a debauchery and a defilement. It was not a holy land, in the sense that Palestine is, but the pre-eminence of ancestor worship in China meant the land was especially dedicated to the family and the clan.

While the People's Republic did not approve of ancestor worship, or any other form of worship, it did give a Marxist imprimatur to the bond between the Chinese and their soil. In any settlement of foreign property claims, the government refused to pay for the land, saying it belonged to the people. This was made doubly clear when the Communists decreed that no one could ever own real estate in China, an edict that excluded not only the "foreign devils" but also the Chinese. The appearance of China's cities has changed dramatically: from medieval walled cities with their masses of low buildings to modern arrays of skyscrapers with the walls turned into motorways. Many of these skyscrapers were built by foreigners, by overseas Chinese, by Taiwan Chinese, and are owned by these entrepreneurs, but they are all on land leased from the government. Thus, in the end, they belong to the People's Republic.

The militant youths who destroyed my grandparents' graves could trace their lineage back half a century to the Boxers who were out to cleanse China of imperialists and their "running dogs." These youths were also the forerunners, if not the forebears, of the virulent Red Guards of the Cultural Revolution. It was the pent-up emotions of years of humiliation and shame that drove them to acts of desecration. The debacle of the Opium Wars and subsequent colonial subjugation, the rape and plunder of the country by British and other imperial forces, were a deeply held part of the collective subconscious. All foreign influence had been expunged with the Korean War, the last Christian missionaries had been sent packing, but the young nationalists wanted more, still more. They insisted on the final retribution of clearing out the last Western remains, so there would be no foreign bones in China.

Notes

Chapter 1

The day I joined as a little boy (p. 9): As quoted in Robert K. Massie's book, *Dreadnought*.

The stench of the slave ships was appalling (p. 11): In 1947, when I was a correspondent for the *Daily Herald*, London, I followed the route that Grandfather had taken around the hump of West Africa, only in a plane rather than a ship. It was the last days of empire, and we passed over Spanish Morocco, French Morocco, Spanish Ivory Coast, French Mauretania, French Senegal, British Gambia, Portuguese Guinea, British Sierra Leone, American-influenced Liberia, French Ivory Coast, British Gold Coast, British Togoland, French Togoland, French Dahomey, and British Nigeria. In the Gold Coast, now Ghana, I visited a slave castle called El Mina. I took a look at its dark dungeons and holding cells and also at the nearby graveyard with its mouldering tombstones, and derived a certain morbid satisfaction out of noting how soon after their arrival so many of the slave traders died.

CHAPTER 2

He would have made regular trips up the Irawaddy (p. 24): When the British
annexed the whole of Burma as a result of the Third Burmese War in 1885, the
audience hall of the royal palace was taken over by the Upper Burma Club,
while the throne room became the garrison church—but this was almost
twenty years after Grandfather had left Burma and the service of the King.

You are such an unreasonable creature (p. 29): Some of the letters from this
period were difficult to decipher because they had been "cross-hatched," an irri-
tating, penny-pinching, Victorian habit of writing across what had been written
previously in order to save notepaper.

CHAPTER 3

The greatest race (p. 40): When my wife and I were holidaying on the Hawaiian
island of Maui, we found in a Lahaina art shop a print of Montague Dawson's
dramatic painting *The Pagoda Anchorage*, which is of the clipper ships preparing
to leave. I like to think of it as a depiction of the *Taeping* and the *Ariel* before
they set off on the great tea race. There they are, these tall ships, like ghostly
galleons, with all sails set, waiting in the dim light of an early dawn for the tide
to turn, oil lights burning, and beside them sampans and junks watching and
waiting too for the clipper ships' release from the anchorage and the start of
their long voyage home. And in the background is the dark, grey mass of the
shore and the tall landmark of the old Sung Dynasty pagoda and beside the
pagoda the shadowy outline of the house where my mother was born.

Among the most popular for the British market (p. 41): The curing of the tea
has not changed in eons and the large concrete shed that stood on the outskirts
of Foochow when I was there was probably the same one that prepared the
leaves for export a century before. When I visited, the tea was spread outside
on the cleanly swept ground as it was a sunny day; usually it was spread on the
concrete floor inside the shed. Jasmine tea is made by covering the layer of tea
with jasmine flowers, and then adding another layer of tea and another lot of
flowers, and so on. Within a short time the scent is transferred to the tea leaves
and, in the case of the best jasmine tea, the withered flowers are picked out
by hand.

CHAPTER 4

Practically all marriages were arranged (p. 53): Uncle G, the eldest son, acted as head of the Shaw family even before Grandfather died in 1908, and my father wrote to him in October 1909 for permission to marry my mother.

The role of women was seen (p. 54): The Meiji restoration did little for the emancipation of women, and even to this day, although they may be more independent because of education and employment, women are still treated as social inferiors. Everything is done for men. In my Japanese hotel, I noted that not only were soap and towels provided in the bathroom, but a razor, comb, and toothbrush, and in the bedroom, a nightshirt and slippers so that all a businessman need take was his briefcase, and, perhaps, a clean shirt. I talked to a friend in Tokyo who told me that it was quite usual for secretaries to accompany their bosses to the golf course and be available to take notes of the inevitable business discussions. Things were, of course, much worse in the 1860s when my grandmother was young.

She was alone (p. 55): Although the opera *Madame Butterfly* is set later, at the turn of the century, the story of Cio-Cio-San (*San* is an honorific) is like that of my grandmother. Madame Butterfly gives up her Buddhist religion to marry the American naval lieutenant, Pinkerton, much to the disgust of her fellow countrymen, and, according to the opera, was true to his faith and the United States. It is interesting to note that Butterfly comes from the same southern island of Kyushu as O'Sea did. "Did she come with Ruth's sad heart / From all familiar things to part?"

There was an incident Julia recalled (p. 59): When questioned in the interview on Hong Kong Radio about her amazing memory, Aunty J said that she had heard it talked about so much that "it remained in my mind."

CHAPTER 5

My father woke to find a nun on her knees (p. 66): My father began writing his memoirs in the late 1970s when he was in his nineties. It was too late and he only completed a couple of chapters and left rambling notes on the rest. The account of the dream and of his coming down with typhoid is from the first chapter.

Yet the old man was persuaded to go on a picnic (p. 74): My father had become intrigued with the relatively new hobby of photography while he was still in England, and when he arrived in Foochow, he wrote to one of his brothers, who was a keen photographer, to send him a stand camera. He wanted a stand camera (like a modern portrait camera) "so that I could see exactly what I was doing." The camera came with a tripod and a plate holder. Photography in those days was very hard work. He had to have a darkroom, which in Terenure was the cubbyhole under the stairs, in order to change the plates and do all the developing and printing, and he had to have the equipment and the chemicals to carry out the whole process.

CHAPTER 6

On the corner of Marco Polo and Legation streets (p. 83): Needless to say, all of this, the glacis, the Legation Quarter and its foreign-named streets, and even the Tartar City wall, has gone.

The Manchu forces were reorganized (p. 84): Charles George Gordon, later known as Chinese Gordon, was to be killed by Muslim rebels in Khartoum and become a martyr of the Empire.

Hart was appointed Inspector General in 1863 (p. 85): The archives of the British-run Chinese Maritime Customs are stored by the People's Republic in Nanjing. They consist of 53,672 volumes of administrative records from 1861 to 1949, when the last foreign Inspector General, Lester Knox Little, fled to Taiwan with Chiang Kai-shek. The archives are said to be largely in English. The journals of Sir Robert Hart, comprising seventy-seven volumes, are kept in the library of Queen's University, Belfast.

He played for the Peking Club (p. 88): At the turn of the century, ice-hockey teams had seven players, reduced to six in 1911.

Tsu-Hsi's was said to be the most costly (p. 92): The extravagances of the Dowager Empress were legendary. She spent an enormous amount of money from funds set aside for the building of a Chinese navy on restoring the Summer Palace. The Palace had been twice badly damaged by riotous British and other European troops in 1858 and 1900, the sort of barbarous acts that the Chinese would ascribe to "foreign devils." Tsu-Hsi used the naval funds under the pretext that she was building a naval training site; the Palace was never once used for this purpose. She did put up a marble boat as a token or gesture to the navy, but this beautifully carved "ship," one of the great tourist attractions at the Summer Palace, was built as a pleasure dome for the Dowager Empress.

According to one source (p. 92): The source of this quotation, *60 Scenic Wonders in China*, was a tourist booklet published by the Chinese government in 1980. It describes the Dowager Empress as being "notorious for tyranny and extravagance" and drew attention to an intriguing feature of her tomb, the reversal of the phoenix and dragon roles in the carvings. "The dragon, which symbolizes the emperor, is usually depicted as amusing himself with the phoenix, which represents the empress. Here it is the phoenix who is playing with the dragon."

The last funeral of a member of the Ching Dynasty (p. 92): The last emperor, Pu Yi, ended his life as a gardener in Peking (Beijing) and was given a gardener's funeral in 1967.

CHAPTER 7

My grandfather, Johann Peter Stursberg, was born at Garschagen (p. 99): Lennep is now a suburb of Remscheid, with which it was incorporated in 1920.

"The Absent-minded Beggar" may be all but lost to memory (p. 105): There were four verses to "The Absent-minded Beggar" and the chorus varied somewhat but always ended with the last line: "Pass the hat for your credit's sake and pay-pay-pay!"

However, in the 1870s, they settled in London (p. 106): My father had a long way to go from his home in Forest Gate to the City of London School. He took the Great Eastern Railway train to the Liverpool Street station and then a horse-drawn bus. "The buses of those days," he recalled, "had inside and outside accommodation. There were two parallel benches to sit on on the roof and one passenger could sit on a seat in the front alongside the driver. (The roof fare was one penny.) To prevent the streets becoming a morass of horse droppings, a small army of men and boys, armed with a three-sided kind of pan, did the cleaning up. Their collections were then dumped into a permanent container alongside the kerb for the ultimate release doubtless to the farming community not then so far away from the city centre."

He sold *Friedenheim* (p. 108): The Sebert Road Congregational Church, which had been the pre-eminent centre of social and religious life in the London suburb of Forest Gate during the late nineteenth and early twentieth century, declined as the Empire declined. There were fewer and fewer members, and the balcony where the Stursberg family sat was virtually empty. In 1974, the church was sold to a local gospel mission and renamed the Miracle Church. The demographics had changed so much that Forest Gate was likened to Kingston, Jamaica. The children at the school across the road from the church were almost all black. The Jamaican pastor was proud of the fact that, aside from some banners, he had preserved the plain Protestant interior of the old church.

There was really no way of anglicizing Saxe-Coburg-Gotha (p. 110): Actually, it had been anglicized slightly, as the German name of Prince Consort Albert was Sachsen-Coburg und Gotha. In the same way, it could be assumed that, as a result of Queen Elizabeth's marriage to Prince Philip, the Prince of Wales and her other children would have the surname Mountbatten. However, the Queen decreed that Prince Charles and the other royals should continue to be members of the House of Windsor, much to the chagrin of the Mountbattens.

CHAPTER 8

This was such an important letter (p. 114): At that time, Christian names or first names were not used in familiar communication between adults, and it was not till they left China and the traditional etiquette of the rather stultifying colonial society that they called each other Mary and Arthur, both privately and publicly. Some people who grew up in the nineteenth century never accepted the commonality of Christian names, even when they were married. Such formality did not apply to the way that parents addressed their children, however.

In a letter to "Dear dear Mary" (p. 114): In fact, Julia, my Aunty J, typed the letter. Captain Shaw apparently found the weather oppressively hot, too hot to write.

Piry dispatched Hulme to Yunnanfu (p. 119): Yunnanfu, the modern Kunming, was the terminus of the Burma Road in the Second World War.

Reverend Lewellyn Lloyd (p. 123): Arthur, the cautious swain, was afraid that, because of his advanced years, the Reverend Lloyd would not register the wedding properly at Somerset House, London, and so, to avoid any possible legal difficulties, decided to follow the church ceremony with a British consulate marriage. However, there was no time for this in Foochow and it had to await the couple's arrival in Chefoo.

CHAPTER 9

I was born in Chefoo (p. 125): Chefoo was famous for its school, founded in 1881, the oldest and best known of the English-language missionary schools in China. Old Chefusians included such luminaries as author and playwright Thornton Wilder; founder of *Time* magazine Henry Luce; and Canadian Senator Alister Grosart, who was given credit by Prime Minister John Diefenbaker for the Conservative election victories of the late 1950s. It was ironic that the Chefoo School should be modelled after Eton and other elitist British public schools because it was founded and run by the China Inland

Mission (now the Overseas Missionary Fellowship), which was non-conformist, if not fundamentalist, and whose members tried to live like the Chinese and eschewed the luxuries of the missionary compounds with their Western-styled houses, tennis courts, and rose gardens. Broad playing fields surrounded the ivy-clad school buildings, which were on the waterfront and across the road from the beach. Sports were compulsory, as they were in British public schools. "You played soccer [or another sport] three times a week," Grosart recalled. "It didn't matter whether you were good, bad, or indifferent, you went to the notice board and there you were on a team." Swimming lessons were compulsory, and a normal boy was expected to be able to swim three miles by the time he was fifteen years old.

All of the Western physicians and surgeons (p. 126): As I noted in Chapter 5, the Shaws moved into Foochow when my grandfather was eighty-five years old and growing weak because the only "doctor" at Pagoda Anchorage was an engineer.

He compared the humanitarian tactics of the Japanese (p. 128): My father's remarks typified the sort of love–hate relationship that the British had for the Japanese even at that time. "The Japanese," as he was to say after a holiday trip to Japan, "are not loved very much out here either by the foreigners or the Chinese, but one has to admit that they have done wonders with their country in the short time that has elapsed since they were behind the Chinese in civilization. The greatest contrast between China and Japan is, I suppose most will agree, in the squalid ways of living of the one people against the cleanly habits of the other."

My childish memory of Shanghai (p. 132): I was just a tiny tot, less than two years old, and I have no memory of Peking. But I do remember Shanghai—not our life there, but incidents, like snapshots, such as a typhoon that shook the trees until the branches came crashing down and made such a fearsome sound that I hid under the bedclothes. Another curious incident was of some little boys and myself climbing on to the roof of a row of houses—my mother and father must have been visiting friends—and I was astounded when one of the boys let down his trousers and defecated.

However, after some discussion, the majority voted in favour of holding the races (p. 134): Stopping the races would not have put many people out of work since there were no racing stables in Shanghai. The custom, my father wrote, was to "buy griffins [sic] a few months before the races and sell them again afterwards." (Griffin was an Anglo-Indian word meaning a "horse making its first race.")

CHAPTER 10

Instead, a wide cloth punkah hung above the dining-room table (p. 142): We had eleven servants including the gardeners and the *mah foo*, or coachman. The number of servants was proportionate to one's rank, and when my father was on his own as Commissioner in Szechwan, a senior post, he had twelve servants, which he felt was excessive and a burden.

Bishop White, for example, had a pigtail (p. 143): In the nineteenth centuries, the early missionaries, whatever their nationality, whether they were Protestant or Catholic, wore Chinese clothes; they felt that they would get rid of their foreignness (foreigners were regarded as devils by the Chinese) and be closer to those that they wanted to "save." However, there were the queues, and few could grow their hair long enough to be plaited into pigtails, so most of them, like Bishop William C. White, the first Bishop in Honan, sported false queues. By the twentieth century, they had given up trying to hide their foreignness. Ironically enough, when the missionaries left China for good, they were expelled by the Communists and they wore Chinese clothes. A couple of Canadians, who were among the last to be ordered out, arrived in Hong Kong in April 1952 wearing Mao uniforms.

My father, resplendent in white tie and tails (p. 146): The British-run Chinese Customs and Post Office followed the practice of British colonial services everywhere in awarding their officers decorations when they reached a certain level in the hierarchy. Dad's Memorandum of Service shows that he received the sixth class of the Chia Ho when he was secretary to the Director General of Posts in 1914, the fifth class when he became head of the Shanghai supply department in 1916, the fourth class the following year, and the third class, which was usually the highest class awarded foreigners, on becoming Commissioner in 1920.

He sought to ban opium smoking (p. 149): The binding of women's feet began in the tenth century during the Sung Dynasty whose capital was Kaifeng, and soon became a common practice throughout China. It was seen as a mark of gentility and, quite obviously, anyone with bound feet was quite unable to work in the fields or do manual labour. The binding began in childhood and was painful and crippling. The standard of perfect beauty, according to Chinese records, the "Golden Lily" was a foot reduced to three inches in length from heel to toe. These tiny crushed limbs had a sexual attraction. The Christian missionaries regarded foot binding as barbaric, and took credit for bringing about its end. But it was really the overthrow of Oriental despotism by Western imperialism that resulted in opposition to the practice where it counted, among the Chinese upper classes. However, feet could not be unbound, and there were old women hobbling around the streets of Beijing in the 1980s.

The prayers and lamentations were interrupted by rain (p. 150): In *Chinese Warlord*, his biography of Feng Yu-hsiang, James Sheridan confirms that Feng did call a "special prayer meeting at which he prayed for rain." His account, however, is not as dramatic as the missionaries'. "The next day," he says, not the day of the meeting and in the midst of the supplications, "the rain fell in torrents." Still, the people were greatly impressed, and declared that "Feng is wonderful in prayer."

His way of throwing his support (p. 152): Feng Yu-hsiang, who had supported the Communists, then turned against them, was on his way to join them when he died. He had left China in 1946 for the United States. In the summer of 1948, he boarded a Russian ship to return home by way of the Soviet Union. Then, suddenly, TASS announced that Feng had died as a result of a fire aboard ship in the Black Sea. His remains were returned to China where some years later they were buried with full honours. He had been rehabilitated in the eyes of the Communists, perhaps because his wife, Li Te-chuan, served as a minister in the government of the People's Republic.

When its most famous graduate, Ted Joliffe, returned to Canada (p. 153): Joliffe became a prominent labour lawyer and had a remarkable political career as leader of the CCF in Ontario; he almost became premier as result of the 1943 election.

I was quite excited as I realized this was an oracle bone (p. 154): The purpose of the oracle bone was divination. A question was inscribed on the shin bone of a deer or the breast bone or plastron of a tortoise. It might ask: "If the King goes out against the Yee barbarians in the eighth moon with a thousand men, will he be successful?" It was not always portentous and could deal with a prince wanting to know whether it was the right time to go hunting. A red-hot poker was stuck in a hole bored in the back of the bone, and the way it cracked provided the answer.

CHAPTER 11

Dad noted that Chengtu had missionary dentists (p. 162): There was no dentist in Kaifeng, and if I had a toothache, I had to go to the Anglican mission hospital, where the knowledge of dentistry did not go beyond extraction.

They approached Chiang Kai-shek and agreed to pay (p. 174): The sum was $10,000,000 according to Harold Isaacs, but other authorities put it closer to $15,000,000. Chiang Kai-shek and his henchmen extorted millions more from the wretched Chinese bankers and businessmen who found they had made a pact with the devil. The treachery and carnage of the Shanghai coup were the subject of several books, including Andre Malraux's novel *Man's Fate*.

Chiang Kai-shek assembled his motley force (p. 174): Chiang himself was said to have belonged to the Green gang.

CHAPTER 12

Robert Hart, a UNRRA representative (p. 178): I met Robert Hart (no relation of Sir Robert Hart, the empire builder) in Ottawa where he was a civil servant. He was a key official with UNRRA and opened its office in Kaifeng. He knew the Commissioner's house well; in fact, he had lived there.

She was buried in the little British cemetery (p. 181): My cousin Lewis visited the cemetery and saw her grave, and, as he told me, "kicked himself" for not noting whether her tombstone had inscribed on it her birthplace, which had been such a mystery.

He stuck to his seven-acre property (p. 183): In time, my father did find friends from the old colonial days, such as Charles Lee, the head of the Salt Gabelle in China, who built a fine house on a hillside near us, and Captain Torrible, the old Yangtse riverboat captain, to name a couple.

We were taken to a May 7 school (p. 185): May 7 schools were so-called after the date at the beginning of the Cultural Revolution when Mao promised to turn China into a "great school," where peasants would study politics, soldiers learn to run factories, and bureaucrats acquire farming skills.

Then there was Norman Bethune (p. 185): When Norman Bethune returned from the Spanish Civil War in 1937, the Montreal doctor, inventor, and political activist had become famous for organizing a mobile blood transfusion unit, the first of its kind to operate at the front. He had come back to raise money for the anti-fascist cause in Spain, but within a year he was off to China to join the

Communist forces there fighting the Japanese invaders. The work was overwhelming at the front in the Wutai Mountains and Bethune, who was short of supplies, had no rubber gloves. He cut his finger during a rush of operations; the resulting infection proved fatal. He died in a peasant hut on November 12, 1939; his body was carried back through the grieving ranks of the Eighth Route Army to a temporary burial place from which it was later removed to Shichiachuang.

We visited Fancheng, a country town in Hupei (p. 187): While Chester Ronning was born in China, he grew up in Alberta and completed courses at the University of Alberta before returning to China as a missionary teacher in 1922. He was principal of Camrose Lutheran College in Alberta from 1927 to 1942. Beside being *charge d'affaires* in China, his other Canadian diplomatic appointments were ambassador to Norway, 1954 to 1957, and high commissioner to India, 1957 to 1964. He was on special missions to Hanoi in 1965 and 1966 in attempts to mediate the Vietnam War. He was awarded an honorary degree by the University of Alberta. Chester Ronning was ninety years old when he died in Camrose, Alberta on the last day of 1984.

I swore I would do so on her hundredth birthday (p. 188): It was my father who had told me that Aunty J was living in Macau and that I should visit her. My mother and father spent the last four years of their lives in a seniors' home in West Vancouver (they left Victoria to be near my brother, Richard). They died shortly after we left Ottawa to retire to West Vancouver; however, we were in time to celebrate their sixty-seventh wedding anniversary. They were ninety-four and ninety-three years old when they died within three weeks of each other at the end of 1979.

It was due to Deng's guidance (p. 189): In 1981 I interviewed Huang Hua, who had been the first Beijing ambassador to Canada and later its first representative at the United Nations, but was then Foreign Minister and Deputy Premier of the People's Republic. It was during this two-hour-long interview that the historic change in Communist Party policy was revealed, the party's move away from revolutionary tactics toward modernization. My article entitled *Restructuring Chinese Policy in the Wake of Chairman Mao* was published in the May-June 1981 issue of *International Perspectives*.

It had pews for at most a hundred people (p. 191): It was largely due to the Communists that the various Protestant denominations were amalgamated into "the Church of Christ in China." The warring sects, as a Chinese bishop said, made for Christian confusion. Incidentally, in China, the Protestants were called Christians whereas the Catholics were known as Catholics, *not* Roman Catholics, as if they were a completely different religion.

They insisted on the final retribution of cleaning out the last Western remains (p. 194): There were exceptions. For instance, Norman Bethune, whose monumental tomb dominates the great memorial park in Shiachiachuang, the vast cemetery of the Communist war dead; and the American writer Agnes Smedley—but these people were heroes of the People's Republic. A Canadian diplomat in Beijing confirmed that there were no foreign graveyards in China now; he told me this during my 1986 visit when I was at the Embassy's Canada Day party. If a foreigner died here, he said, the body could be shipped home, or cremated, or interred in a special cemetery where Agnes Smedley was buried.

BIBLIOGRAPHY

Allan, Ted and Sidney Gordon. *The Scalpel, The Sword: The Story of Dr. Norman Bethune*. Boston: Little, Brown and Co., 1952.

Andrews, Roy Chapman. *Heart of Asia*. New York: Duell, Sloan and Pearce, 1951.

Backhouse, E. and J.O.P. Bland. *Annals and Memoirs of the Court of Peking*. London: William Heinemann, 1914.

Berridge, Virginia and Griffith Edward. *Opium and the People*. London: Allen Lane/St Martin's Press, 1981.

Bloodworth, Denis. *The Messiah and the Mandarins: The Paradox of Mao's China*. London: Weidenfeld and Nicholson, 1982.

Booth, Alan. *The Roads to Sata: A 2000 Mile Walk Through Japan*. New York and Tokyo: Weatherhill Inc., 1985.

Boulger, Demetrius Charles. *China, A Short History*. New York: Peter Fenelon Collier, 1898.

Cooke, George Wingrove. *China in 1857–58, from The Times*. London: G. Routledge & Co., 1859.

Crow, Carl. *China Takes Her Place*. New York: Harper & Brothers, 1944.

Endicott, Stephen. *James G. Endicott: Rebel Out of China*. Toronto: University of Toronto Press, 1980.

Ewen, Jean. *China Nurse 1932–1939*. Toronto: McClelland and Stewart Limited, 1981.

Fitzgerald, C.P. *Revolution in China*. New York: Frederick A. Praeger, 1952.

Fraser, John. *The Chinese, Portrait of a People*. New York: Summit Books, 1980.

Gentzler, J. Mason. *Changing China*. New York: Praeger Publishers, 1977.

Giles, Herbert A. *The Civilization of China*. London: Williams and Norgate, 1911.

Goodwin, Jason. *A Time For Tea*. New York: Alfred A. Knopf, 1991.

Goforth, Rosalind. *Goforth of China*. Toronto: McClelland and Stewart, 1937.

Greene, Felix. *China, The Country Americans Are Not Allowed to Know*. New York: Ballantine Books, 1962.

Hahn, Emily. *China Only Yesterday*. New York: Doubleday, 1963.

Hahn, Emily. *The Soong Sisters*. New York: Doubleday, Doran, and Co., 1941.

Harris, Florence Powell. *How Beautiful the Feet*. Hongkong: Luen Shing Printing Co., 1968.

Hart, E.I. *Virgil C. Hart, Missionary Statesman*. Toronto: McClelland, Goodchild and Stewart, 1917.

Harvey, G.E. *British Rule in Burma*. London: Faber and Faber, 1946.

Hearn, Lafcadio. *Japan, An Attempt at Interpretation*. New York: MacMillan, 1905.

Hersey, John. *The Call: An American Missionary in China*. New York: Alfred A. Knopf, 1985.

Hewlett, Sir Meyrick. *Forty Years in China*. London: MacMillan & Co. Ltd., 1943.

Hibbert, Christopher. *London, The Biography of a City*. London: Penguin Books, 1980.

Hughes, E.R. *The Invasion of China by the Western World*. New York: Barnes and Noble, 1968.

Isaacs, Harold. *The Tragedy of the Chinese Revolution*. London: Secker and Warburg, 1938.

Kawasaki, Ichiro. *Japan Unmasked*. Tokyo: Tuttle; New York: Prentice-Hall, 1969.

Landon, Margaret. *Anna and the King of Siam*, New York: John Day and Co., 1943.

Malraux, Andre. *Man's Fate*. New York: Modern Library, 1961 (1934).

Mao, Tse-tung. *Quotations from Chairman Mao Tse-tung*. Peking: Foreign Language Press, 1966.

Mao, Tse-tung. *Five Articles by Chairman Mao Tse-tung*. Peking: Foreign Language Press, 1968.

Massie, Robert K. *Dreadnought*. New York: Random House, 1991.

Maugham, Somerset. *On a Chinese Screen*. Oxford: University Press, 1922.

————. *The Gentleman in the Parlour: A Record of a Journey from Rangoon to Haiphong*. London: William Heinemann, 1930.

Morris, James. *Pax Britannica*. London: Faber and Faber, 1973-78.

Payne, Robert. *The Revolt of Asia*. London: Victor Gollancz Ltd., 1948.

Pollak, Oliver B. *Empires in Collision*. New York: Greenwood Press, 1979.

Putnam Weale, B.L. *Indiscreet Letters from Peking*. London: Hurst and Blackett, Limited, 1906.

Ronning, Chester. *A Memoir of China in Revolution*. New York: Parthenon, 1974.

Schram, Stuart. *Mao Tse-tung*. London: Penguin Books, 1966.

Schwartz, Harry. *China*. New York: New York Times, 1965.

Sheppard, Francis. *The Infernal Wen, London 1808–1870*. Los Angeles: University of California Press, 1971.

Sheridan, James E. *Chinese Warlord, The Career of Feng Yu-hsiang*. Stanford: Stanford University Press, 1966.

Simmons, Dawn Langley. *Golden Boats from Burma*. Philadelphia: Macrae Smith and Co., 1961.

60 Scenic Wonders in China. Beijing: English Language Services of Radio Beijing and New World Press, 1980.

Snow, Edgar. *Red Star over China*. London: Victor Gollancz Ltd., 1937.

Somerville-Large, Peter. *The Irish Country House*. London: Sinclair Stevenson, 1995.

Stilwell, Joseph W. *The Stilwell Papers (The American General's Experience in China)*. London: Macdonald & Co., 1949.

Stursberg, Peter. *The Golden Hope: Christians in China*. Toronto: The United Church Publishing House, 1987.

Sutton, Jean. *Lords of the East*, New York, Naval Institute Press, 2000.

Teng, S.Y. *The Taiping Rebellion and the Western Powers*. London: Oxford University Press, 1971.

Walmsley, Lewis C. *Bishop in Honan, Mission and Museum in the Life of William C. White*. Toronto: University of Toronto Press, 1974.

Walmsley, Lewis C. *West China Union University*. North Newton, Kansas: Mennonite Press, 1974.

Whipple, A.B.C. *The Clipper Ships*. Amsterdam: Time Life Books, 1981.

White, Theodore H. and Annalee Jacoby. *Thunder out of China*. New York: William Sloane Associates, 1946.

White, William C. *Chinese Jews*. Toronto: University of Toronto Press, 1966.

Williamson, Capt. A.R. *Eastern Traders*. Cambridge: Jardine Matheson and Co., 1975.

Wong, Jan. *Red China Blues*. Toronto: Doubleday Anchor Books, 1996.

Xue, Muqiao. *China's Socialist Economy*. Beijing: Foreign Language Press, 1981.

INDEX

DATE DUE
